The Vie

By
Albert D. Rylak

Without the kindness of friends like Lizette Scannell, Susan Ryan, Beth Sosidka, and "Al's Gals," this book could not have been written. Jon Sosidka, you were invaluable in teaching me the creative and technical process to get from the End to the Beginning. Without the love of my sons, their wives, and of my grandchildren I would still be in a dark unknown place. Thank you all. Especially, thank you Amelia for reasons that will be evident as you read on, to Benjamin who gave my Ginny a reason to struggle to live, and to Daniel, because Ginny always knew you would come along.......eventually.

Al Rylak
October 2, 2014

Contents

The End.

When I was 16 years old, 1961, I met my wife Virginia Ann Campbell for the first time while we were in high school and immediately fell in love. It was mutual. Actually, her father Willard S. Campbell had picked me out. He named me as his student PSSC Physics substitute teacher for a day. I brazenly walked down the hall and upon seeing Ginny, placed my arm around her and asked how my daughter was doing. How uncool was that! Our first real date was bowling on June 1, 1961 at the Hiohela Bowling Alley near Pennington with our mutual friends Bill and Judy. Bill had a car for this "double date" as it was called. Although Ginny was not a particularly good bowler, she beat me handily and both of our scores were under 100. That was an invitation to try again. And we did. She was quite tricky with that one. We were together for fifty years until she died at the age of 65 years of pancreatic cancer. I more than hate pancreatic cancer; I detest it. Who does not?

Ginny was a New Jersey girl through and through. Born in Trenton, she lived most of her early life in the Town of Pennington graduating from Central High School. Yup, a varsity cheerleader a marimba player, honor roll student, basketball player, fantastic swimmer and diver at Penn Brook Swimming Club where she was also a life guard and swimming instructor, and she did all the things you would expect a bright, confident, pert person to do. In those days women were not allowed to sweat or exert themselves to any extent. When she played basketball each team had six players on the court, three designated as defense and three as offense. After two dribbles a player had to pass the ball. I never could understand why. When Ginny got home from school and in the summers, she would play basketball the masculine way with her younger brother Will and his friends. She had a very good outside shot. Everyone loved Ginny.

My family was lower middle class. My father Frank, having an 8th grade education, was a chrome buffer at the General Motors Ternstedt Division in Trenton, NJ. My mother Lottie or Loretta, depending on her mood, was a homemaker with the better education, 11th grade. Ginny's mother and father were both college graduates and worked in education. Her mom, Gra, was the smartest person I ever met, having graduated from Wilson College in 1933 majoring in French and Latin. Both Gra and PT, Ginny's dad's pet name, adored me. My lovely wife said on many an occasion that they liked me more than even her! Ginny left New Jersey in 1968 for four years to attend Keuka College, in the wine country of upper New York State, and received her BS and teaching credentials in elementary education. During that time I was either a student at Rutgers College or Rutgers Law School. Since money, or lack thereof, was a real issue, we visited mostly by dormitory hallway telephone and letter except on her college vacations and breaks. Of course we saw each other every summer. Somehow and for unknown reasons, we simply stayed together as if it was meant to be, no matter the obstacle.

As was the custom then, we were married within a month after Ginny's college graduation (for her not to do so would make her an old maid), and she took a teaching job in Nutley, NJ while I finished my last year of law school and my research job with the City of East Orange Law Department. Everyone at the wedding said "it's about time" as they knew we were in love and would get married. I still remember our first car which we purchased shortly before our marriage for $1,800.00 with our down payment and an interest free loan from Ginny's parents. It was a 1968 yellow Opel Kadett L and we paid back the car loan in one year. We loved that car and thought we were pretty hot stuff. Ginny was the primary driver as I was busy taking the train into Newark. Our only other debts upon marrying were my college and law school loans. Although I worked painting houses to earn money, and received need based and academic based scholarships, Ginny's parents paid for her entire education. Likewise, these education loans were paid off quickly since neither of us wanted or liked debt. After our wedding, we took off for Long Beach Island, NJ. No plans had been made as we were dirt broke at this point. So, as we drove our Opel Kadett L to the Island with two big flowers taped on it, we came to the ocean and turned right. We spent our first and only honeymoon night at the Viking Motel in Ship Bottom. As I walked in to check the availability of a room "for my fiancée" and me, the front desk clerk looked at me quizzically. I swore that we had just been married and pointed toward the small yellow car with two large flowers on it. It was okay. Things were different in those days. We had a lovely night and then the next day drove home to be able to go to work. Ironically the Viking Motel was torn down for housing years later and Ginny had our sons and me get some bricks and other items as souvenirs. Still have them. Our first home was in the Town of Pennington, NJ and we house sat a home on Burd Street while the owners were in Europe for the summer. We then moved to Orange, NJ. While in Orange, I remember thinking we lived in the Taj Mahal in our fifth floor apartment. On Saturdays we would buy a steak for $1.25 as a special treat. All of our apartment furniture was purchased for $35.00 at a used furniture shop in Lambertville, NJ. We found an old television for free and it was our entertainment. We even got Katie, our first dog, a beagle-terrier mixed breed. We truly thought we had reached the American dream. Who could want more!? After my law school graduation and the bar examination in 1969, we took our one and only long vacation off to Vermont and Massachusetts during which time Neil Armstrong walked on the moon and Teddy Kennedy drove off a bridge in Chappaquiddick, killing Mary Jo Kopechne. There was no connection with any of the events to our trip.

Then we settled down in Blawenburg, NJ as I finished up working for a large Newark law firm and took on the job of clerking for a Federal Judge named Leonard I. Garth in Camden. Justice Samuel Alito later clerked for the same judge. I was not as smart or politically connected as he. During this time Ginny taught math to third and sixth graders in Hopewell Borough Elementary School to help support us. Where in Nutley Ginny was a little unsure of her teaching abilities, in Hopewell she blossomed into a confident young, fantastic, educator who was highly respected by everyone; especially the students. Since she taught math, she would be up nightly until almost 9:00pm at least four nights a week correcting papers and adding cogent and thoughtful comments for all her students. Her parent-teacher conferences were legendary for equal give and take between all parties. Ginny had absolutely no necessity to feed her ego and readily engaged all in discussions which would benefit the student who was the most important topic of discussion. She was a wonderful model teacher.

After I finished my clerkship and took a job in Clinton, NJ, we bought our first home and settled in the Town of Clinton for the rest of Ginny's life. I will never forget how Ginny swooned when she saw the home, yet I kept telling her to pretend it was just okay and needed a lot of work. She was unable to control her happiness as to the house. We paid $37,500.00 for our first home and after paying 20% of the purchase price as a down payment we borrowed the balance from the First National Bank of Central Jersey with an amortized 25 year loan at an interest rate of 7%. It seemed like such a large sum of money. Our aversion to debt continued and we paid that mortgage off in seven years. Because of the required down payment and income verification at that time, no one ever defaulted on their mortgage obligations. We were not going to be the exception. And yes, Ginny took care of all financial matters relating to wherever we lived. After all, she taught mathematics. Yes, we had our sons in that idyllic small town. Ginny was very active not only raising our sons, but also with volunteering for assorted positions, the major one being on the Town Parks and Recreation Commission. She was the "key lady". Anyone who wanted to use the Clinton Community Center had to go through her to get the key! Teacher Rylak's teaching career ended so as to engage a new career of motherhood. Of our three dogs, Freddie was her favorite and the two of them walked about the entire town as if they owned it. Life then in the Town of Clinton, Hunterdon County, NJ can never be replicated. I would never even try. We were the perfect family in the perfect house in the perfect town lacking for nothing. I mean that.

To Ginny, her family, husband, and sons came first. Always. She willingly dedicated herself to us all. Although no longer gainfully employed, she would have been able to run the entire Veteran's Administration while juggling three balls with one hand. Ginny tolerated my insane work week and never even once complained that my work was too consuming. On the contrary she would have a homemade cherry pie awaiting my return in the evening or night and we would always eat together. Many times we would slip in a quick late breakfast at the Towne Restaurant at 10:00am. She never complained once. Nor did I. Because of the nature of my law practice which at times created hard feelings and animosity with some people, we rarely went to parties and the like as some people made Ginny feel somewhat uncomfortable with their innuendo and snide glances toward me. I could care less what they said or did, but my wife a tad more sensitive. Ginny and I simply enjoyed being alone with each other. We did not need to be entertained and did not require the approbation of anyone. I guess you can say we were very comfortable in our own skin. We would talk about all things without reservation and nothing was off limits. All holiday occasions for our broader family were held at our home, with Ginny doing whatever was necessary to ensure that every one had a great time. For those of you that have prepared such a feast, I need not say any more. For the rest of you, think hours of preparation from creating the menu, shopping for the food, preparing the food, and then being the perfect hostess, always gracious in every way. I smile as I now recall seeing card tables set up for the kids, candles on the table with fine china, and sterling silver cutlery. Ah the aromas that emanated from the kitchen. We schleps always tried to help, but usually did more harm than good. Somehow all the food came out at the exact correct time. Clean up was reserved for me and those I could coral into helping. At least Ginny could linger over coffee. I think Ginny's greatest complaint about cooking was that the meal ended too quickly but always required so much time to prepare. Her second greatest complaint was selecting the menu. So many times she said "please, give me some food ideas here". Nonetheless, Ginny generally did not like to cook and viewed it as a chore. She certainly did enjoy her daily 3:00pm Guinness Draught while sitting on the screened-in back porch talking to her best friend Ginny about heaven knows what. Boy could they talk; and talk; and talk. Their beautiful friendship went back to elementary school days in Pennington and never ceased. They probably still talk to each other today somehow. That would not surprise me at all.

All of our sons' friends hung out at our home and Ginny made sure that there was sufficient food and drink for them all. The Rylak house was the center of all activity for any young person in the town or its environs. I am still amazed at how so many of our son's friends would talk to Ginny about their personal problems, their girlfriends or boyfriends, their philosophy of life, and many highly personal issues in their lives. Mrs. R was the go- to lady. And she relished that role. After all, she taught us all and modeled how to be caregivers and listeners. These traits were passed on to her sons by example which is the only way to teach important topics.

Ginny so often practiced random acts of kindness. When our friend and repairman, Carlton Bridge, told us he was he was an expert guitarist, he asked Ginny if she would like to buy his first CD for $10. Ginny gave him two twenty dollar bills. When Carlton asked, "Why?" Ginny replied that the extra money was for his next CDs. Carlton told me this story many times because it made such an impression on him. When the Food Pantry for the poor needed supplies, Ginny bought hundreds of dollars' worth of food and supplies for the group, most of which sat in our entry foyer until it was picked up.

In a very true sense, we grew up together and became the best of friends and did all the things that married couples of the 1960s did in attaining the American Dream. Our vacations, which were few, were at the Jersey Shore or as they say," Down the Shore". We loaded up Ginny's large Buick Estate Wagon station wagon and were off. There is no place in the world like Kinsey Cove, Harvey Cedars, NJ. When I was at Fort Jackson, SC in the National Guard, Ginny held the home fort. As a manner of expressing our love for each other, we would tell each other every day to Shut the Door or STD which was our loving way to say I adore you; je t'adore in French. It was funny as a teenager or later as an adult to ask out of the blue if the car door was shut or some other nonsensical door and smile. We knew the message and smiled. I have no idea how this tradition evolved. Such closeness you have never seen and may never see again. Never once did we argue but always simply talked and came up with the best solution for any issue. Our life together was one of earned privilege and we were blest with our two fine sons, David and Mark. I remember seeing each of them born. Ginny and I stressed education as the way to succeed in life and you could never expect less from an educator. Together we later took care of or arranged for the care throughout their lives of my younger brother Jack who suffered from many serious psychiatric and psychological issues, my mother Lottie who had Alzheimer's disease, and Gra who was just getting beautifully old. Ginny bore the brunt of this care giving, never once complaining. It was the right thing to do. Ginny Rylak never had a mean bone in her body. We looked forward to our retirement and time with our grandchildren. On my 66th birthday, August 29, 2010, I retired from the practice of law to gaze upon a sign Ginny prepared saying "41 and done". Although the thrill of retirement wore off quickly, Ginny continued doing what she loved best, loving and taking care of her family. In late April 2011 Ginny had difficulty sleeping as she had very excruciating pain just above her stomach which would not go away. She was initially treated for GERD with a medication called Nexium.

And then May 16, 2011 arrived and Dr. Bae told us that Ginny had pancreatic cancer, stage 4. He had an alarmed look in his eyes. Ginny said out loud, "I'm dead". I knew it too. There was no hope of long-term survival. When we arrived home from the Hunterdon Medical

Center, our son David had already driven up to New Jersey from Virginia and was waiting for us. As a physician, he knew from the symptoms described earlier on the telephone by Ginny exactly what was going on. We all cried. We told Mark. Somehow we managed to get through the next nine months until Ginny died on February 12, 2012, not once wanting that result or losing our love. She fought as hard as she was able against insurmountable odds to prolong her life. She was able to meet our new grandchild Benjamin. I still hate a God if one exists for doing this to my sweet and lovely wife. To further humiliate her to 60 pounds of weight was the ultimate insult. As she was dying she asked me to please not let her go away. I could not stop the inevitable. Never once did she say "why me" but on the contrary answered such a question from others with "why not me". The indignity of cancer consumed her and my family and now I am alone for the first time in my life. The look in my children's eyes as we watched her die and her continued gasping for air will remain with me always. My anger and sadness were overwhelming. I walked the streets at or near our home whenever Ginny did not need me, almost like a zombie and totally unaware of my surroundings. I focused inward so as to keep myself going on. Ginny told me that only by pushing the thought of what was going on inside her out of her mind completely could she exist. She was an amazingly strong woman. She taught me so much about living as she died.

Throughout this death period, I kept a log of how my sweet wife was doing so as to keep family and friends apprised. In my heart I knew pen had to be placed to paper to show others what really happened in our lives. I am still amazed at how little we knew about cancer generally and pancreatic cancer in particular. Calls and visits eventually became an emotional burden and we kept to ourselves as much as possible. The following diary helped Ginny and me cope with her cancer. The blur from May 16th until May 25, 2011 is just that. We reacted normally as much as possible but were stunned and still lacking in acceptance. Disbelief is an understatement. A large portion of this portion of my book is so very sad but it is all true. In order to present truthfully the battle with cancer and in particular pancreatic cancer, it was necessary to present in detail the events that unfolded. At times I sound like a repeating broken record, but in dancing with the devil, there is no simplicity or easy way to present what occurred. I now show others these events and feelings with the hope that they understand this portion of one of the realities of life. Intentionally, the spelling and grammar are left as originally written. These writings reflect our emotions at that time.

First Day of Chemotherapy
5/25/11

Dear Friends.

This is the summary of what happened with Ginny very early today at the Hunterdon Regional Cancer Center in Flemington, NJ. Prior to going into the Cancer Center Ginny had to have a port installed to allow ease of access to her veins. A port is a device that they use to draw blood, administer drugs, and also administer the chemotherapy. It is a permanent device inserted under the skin and into a vein. We arrived at Hunterdon Medical Center, the Radiology Department, to have this procedure done. Everyone was quite pleasant but it was not completed until about 11:30 AM. It took about an hour to get the port installed but there were a lot of things to do pre-surgery and post-surgery.

We then walked over to the Cancer Center arriving at about noon or a little before. A sense of fear grips people entering the Cancer Center and there are many nervous laughs. Although at times I suspect there is a sense of hope, the patients and their families are extremely vulnerable and it is important to be very nice to everyone. Each one fights a different battle but in the same arena. We did not get home until after 5 PM. Basically there were tons of explanations, pre-chemotherapy drugs given through the port (about 45 minutes) and then the chemotherapy (3 hours) followed by post chemotherapy drugs(45 minutes). It is a very tiring process and very complicated. Ginny handled everything very well but there still was the possibility of side effects later today. We are prepared for the side effects with other drugs! Also, Ginny is wearing a fanny pack which has a pump in it as chemotherapy continues to be pumped into her until our next appointment tomorrow. And, we are back at the hospital tomorrow, Thursday, and Friday. Thursday is at 1:00PM and may last to about 5:00 PM again (with the fanny pack and pump again) and Friday is short with a side visit to the Radiology Department to make sure the port incision is healing properly; they take the pump off at that point until another week. To be candid with you, we are both exhausted but Ginny is doing better than I which is unusual since she had to undergo the treatment. We have no choice here in view of the horrible diagnosis. So, the battle begins. I hate to paraphrase a quote of Ted Kennedy, the Hero of Chappaquiddick, but in a speech he gave to the Democratic National Convention on August 27, 2009 he said it right: "The work begins, the Hope rises, and the Dream lives on." As an aside, the people at the Hunterdon Regional Cancer Center are compassionate, caring, and will always have our gratitude no matter what the result. Ginny is on a very aggressive chemotherapy regime which only last week was published in the New England Journal of Medicine. I seem to be unable to really believe what is going on with my lady. We can use all the help you can give. Keep the prayers coming.

Second Day of Chemotherapy
May 26, 2011

Ginny had chemotherapy today from about 1:00PM until 4:15PM. We got home a little after 4:40PM. She handled it like a trooper and we hope that the bad consequences that can occur tonight do not happen. Last night was fantastic and Ginny had none of the bad stuff happen. We will see. All of the effects of chemotherapy are cumulative so there will be some/many bad days in the future for sure. Ginny is now wearing the pump and is getting chemotherapy while I type; just like yesterday. I read these notes to her and we e-mail them to family and friends. Tomorrow we will be at the Cancer Center about 3:45 PM and the pump will be disconnected and removed until a week from next Wednesday. Yes, Ginny can then take a much needed bath. Then on Tuesday, the Radiologists will check her port to make sure the surgery is healing properly. It will be too late to do that tomorrow. Ironically, Ginny's speech slurred at times while on chemotherapy. The slur is gone now but was definitely there. Chemotherapy kills cancer cells, but also lots of white and red blood cells, depending on the type of drug used. So, they check the white and red cells quite a bit as there are serious consequences to killing the good cells which I do not understand. Next Wednesday is just a blood test and the following Wednesday starts the second round of chemotherapy. After six rounds, the Doctors will check out how the chemotherapy is working vis-a-vis the cancer cells. They will do CT scans and other tests to see if the tumors as well as some of the cancer cells in the liver, spleen, and adrenal gland are shrinking. The Doctors will also want to make sure that the cancer has not spread to the lungs or the brain. So clearly the battle goes on with so many variables. Thank you for your support and prayers. Ginny is just too nice a person to have all this happen to her but it is what it is. She is looking forward to the hair loss and wearing a nice feminine hat. Hair loss is a minimal consequence. Since the port is now installed, today was an easier day except checking on Ginny's mother Gra, as the dear 99 year old had fallen out of her bed somehow during the past evening. A huge lump and black and blue coloration surrounds the right side of her head, but she is okay. I refused to tell her of her daughter's circumstance and condition. Later she would die never knowing that her daughter had predeceased her. So, all is somewhat good with the world today.

Third day of Chemotherapy
May 27, 2011

Well, last night was good. Ginny slept very well with no symptoms of nastiness again, all the while the pump was putting chemotherapy into her system. It is so hard to believe that the chemotherapy is poison and the poison was being injected into her body as she slept. I could hear the pump pumping every few minutes as I lay beside her in bed. Today was uneventful except the pump finished early and so we got to the Cancer Center early and had it removed. So, as of this afternoon there is no pump and Ginny is off of Chemotherapy until the week after next. Her appetite is not great but we are working on that. We left the Cancer Center and went to Radiology to have the port inspected. All is well with that too. A bath is in order now but the port area cannot get wet until another week passes. It is strange how I hope that means Ginny will be with us at least another week. I hope Ginny goes to the beauty shop tomorrow to have her hair washed as it is difficult to do in our house without wetting the port. She is relieved to have the pump off and all the lines removed for now. As an aside, Ginny was given a shot before she left to try to build up her white and red blood cells; this is normal. Chemotherapy does not discriminate between cancer cells and good cells, and health issues arise if the white cells go down too low; those cells fight infection etc. Next week, on Wednesday a blood test is given to see what is going on-that is all. The following Wednesday chemotherapy starts all over again; round two. So there you have it. Ginny finds it difficult to eat as she does not have a good appetite. Yet, she has a plan the Hunterdon Regional Cancer Center would like her to try in an effort to get food into her system by eating a large number of very small meals. Also, she is always interfering as I try to do house and other work which I do not like as she is so tired. She is simply unable to stop caring for people. I will work on changing that. She has to learn to let people take care of her. So that is all I can say for now. Thank you for your support and concern. I will not be on line re this too much in the future as there will essentially be a repetition of the regime. I will however give good or bad news as it appears. Ginny really is amazingly strong to have so few side effects from the chemotherapy right now. Hug someone you love a little tighter tonight. You never can tell what is on the horizon.

First weekend off chemotherapy
Memorial Day weekend 2011

I have to say that Ginny's first weekend after heavy doses of chemotherapy was difficult at best. Saturday, Sunday, and a portion of Memorial Day Monday led to no drinking or eating to speak of at all. Ginny just sat around unable to do anything. We called the Oncologist on Sunday due to her circumstances and he stressed that Ginny had to drink. That eating was secondary and unimportant. It was unable to be done. On Memorial Day we tried the bath routine and it was difficult; still no food or liquid of any kind. We went to the Hunterdon Medical Center Emergency Department about noon and were there until about 4 PM; as Ginny said a hell of a way to celebrate such a special day. Ginny was pumped full of a saline solution, two bags worth and given other medication to help her with the pain and nausea feeling and to bring her blood levels closer to normal-they were way out of kilter. The nurses and doctors in the ED were wonderful and Ginny was treated as if she were their only patient! Candidly, to say things were terrible is an understatement; it was horrible to see this vibrant matriarch of the Rylak in such dire straits.

After we got home to Clinton, Ginny was feeling so much better and was able to drink and even eat some strawberry shortcake! She was able to take care of her "girlie needs" like plucking her eyebrows etc. Today, Tuesday, Ginny goes back to the Hospital to get another bag of saline solution as they hope that her blood levels are better and to keep her hydrated. She also has a hair appointment at Artiste this morning to get her hair washed and cut which will make a great difference I am told. Then, the Virginia part of the Rylak family arrives today as will the Bedminster part of the Rylak family (Ang has to work but we will see her for a while anyway!). Ginny has promised to take it real easy and just enjoy us all taking care of her; Amelia already has some DVDs for she and Grandma to watch! It is difficult for someone such as Ginny, who has given us all care for so long, to learn to accept being given care. We will teach her this; we will demand this.

So happy belated Memorial Day to all.

Virginia doing better
Mon, May 30, 2011 11:09 PM

Ginny is doing much better. I guess previously she got caught in the cycle of dehydration which has now been broken. She is drinking ginger ale, taking her meds a little early, and eating some hard food. We are both tired after an afternoon at the ED, but happy and just resting. The resting will continue for the next few days and we will enjoy seeing you all when possible. You too Amelia.

Love and hugs,

ADR

Ginny in hospital
6/2/11

Ginny went into the hospital again yesterday late afternoon. Since the chemotherapy ended the Oncologists have been unable to stop the nausea and pain in her stomach. She has not really eaten or consumed liquids to any degree. It is believed that this is largely due to the massive dose of chemotherapy that was received. Clearly that regimen will have to be altered no matter what the consequence. Ginny's quality of life has suffered greatly since and we have been at the hospital, ED, or Cancer Center almost every day since the first round of chemotherapy ended and even before. With a little luck, the new nausea medication will be successful as they now know what she is able to tolerate; or not.

Ginny's spirits are wonderful and the family and friends, as expected, have circled around her to get her through this difficult time. There are many good days ahead but it is just true that pancreatic cancer, or any cancer, is a difficult thing to fight. So there is no misunderstanding, the battle continues, but we and the Oncologists are much more attuned to Ginny's quality of life during this battle. As an aside, 50 years ago today, June 2, 1961, Ginny and I had our first date and she beat me at bowling! Let us pray that she is out of the hospital today. If not, let us hope that she feels better nonetheless. I did not expect to be typing these reports so often, but such is life; I hope for a decrease in the number of reports soon!

I am getting very tired as things progress and feel a sense of abject helplessness and anger. I wish I could stop these ridiculous feelings of just wanting to grab her about the shoulders and making her eat and drink. But alas and alack, she cannot do more than she is doing.

Ginny as of 6/9/11

Well I have to tell you, Ginny has lost a lot of weight and feels yuck, mostly due to the effect of Chemotherapy vis-a-vis her lower intestinal tract. No one advised us she would have at least 5 straight days of horrible diarrhea (this is quite unusual I am told) to top off the 5 straight days of nausea. Nonetheless, they are trying to prolong Ginny's life and we will do what is logical to help Ginny in this regard. Anyhow, she has further chemotherapy scheduled this coming Monday but may not be strong enough for it and it will have to be put off for a little while. We will see. Her Oncologists are now having Ginny given three shots per day of Octreotide as the other remedies for the lower intestinal tract issues did not seem to work. So far she has had three shots and there is progress. We are optimistic, or perhaps the right word would be hopeful, that the issue will clear up soon and she will start to gain back some of the lost weight. We have spent much time at the Hunterdon Medical Center, the Emergency Department, and the Hunterdon Cancer Center as those places are our second homes.

The emotional issues of care at the Cancer Center are present at all times. It is difficult to smile and be nice all the time; particularly for me. Ginny gets away with it because that is the way she is. I have become quite protective and will not let anyone see or talk to her unless she is able to handle it. I am confident that once Ginny gets some food in her system, things will improve for her. It is hard to believe, but sometimes you just do not want to eat-chemotherapy causes that. We are trying to break that vicious cycle. At least as of today she is able to drink lots of fluids and I am optimistic or hopeful that she will return to eating food soon; she has no choice. My goal for Ginny today is to have her not have to leave the house for any medical reason, to drink lots of fluids, to eat some real bland food if possible, to sit down and rest, and most importantly, to have the lower intestinal tract issue resolved!!

All is under control on the home front for now. Thank you all for your kindness and prayers. I think Ginny and I both got a little down yesterday, but today brings some hope for which we are thankful. What type of hope? I have no idea what that means. I just want my old Ginny back.

Chemotherapy can have horrible results
6/10/11

Well, although we were at first very optimistic about the three shot a day regimen to get rid of the lower intestinal issue resulting from Ginny's chemotherapy, so far it has not been much help. Things are certainly better, but it has not fixed the problem. In my line of work I fix things; not necessarily here. I hope that today there will be a different result so Ginny can finally gain some strength. I seriously doubt if they will do another round of chemo on Monday as planned as Ginny is simply not strong enough for that; nonetheless we will be at the Hunterdon Cancer Center to discuss this with the Oncologists. The last two days Ginny has really tried to eat solid food and has done a good job at that. This is the first time in weeks that this is happening. Eating food alone may help things along. I am so very proud of her. I think she is doing it to try to please me.

Dear friends from all over have provided such a wonderful help; you know who you are. Thank you. Ginny's spirit has not been destroyed by this disease and its treatment. She continues to do all the "girlie things" she can, albeit at a slower pace. Ginny still makes up Gra's weekly TV list so Gra can know on what channel she can watch her favorite TV shows. We will never tell Gra about her illness as it just does not seem right. Yesterday we were able to leave the house for a short ride in the car and stopped at a shop in Clinton at Ginny's insistence to get a little stuffed animal to send to a friend's little daughter who just had heart surgery. You see, no matter what is going on, Ginny is still Ginny and she will not change.

It is clear that the first round of chemotherapy was just far too strong for Ginny and that it will have to be changed, no matter the consequence. At times I get extremely frustrated and I am sure Ginny does too. I do not want my frustration to turn to anger but at times it almost does. Our highly organized pill, shot and patch regimen is followed every day and Internet Skypes with our dear little granddaughter Amelia are preciously important to Ginny. So my friends, today brings a new day and renewed hope that at least the lower intestinal functioning will get better with the three shots and that Ginny will begin to gain strength so as to be able to physically continue the fight against her disease or at least have a good quality of life, no matter how long that is. Try saying that about someone you love. I will continue to be very protective of Ginny based upon her condition and I know you will be very understanding of that. Thank you again for all your prayers and kindnesses.

Nearing the end of the results of the first round of chemotherapy:

My dear sweet Ginny is now ending the results of her first round of her chemotherapy. After the massive doses of chemotherapy received, there had to be consequences and there were. For the first 4-5 days after chemotherapy your body enjoys nausea, exhaustion, and pain. Ginny handled this as well as anyone could. It was difficult to even think of food or drink. Hence, Ginny was in the Cancer Center or the Hunterdon Medical Center almost every day for saline drips and pain medication. She fought like a champion although she had lost weight. We had great family support during this time. The next three days the chemotherapy demon decided to try a different approach and although a normal result, Ginny has suffered from exceptional diarrhea with accompanying indignity and pain.

Thank God for our family and friends. The handling of Ginny's medication regimen is perfect now but was quite confusing without exceptional organization. Ginny is able to take liquids and I suspect her body will allow her to get back to eating and drinking in a more normal way until chemotherapy starts again next Monday the 13th. As I have continually said, chemotherapy is essentially the injection of poison into your body, as much as you can take, to try to destroy the cancer cells; unfortunately, it also destroys other cells as well. Your body responds to all of this in the above described ways.

I am hoping that today, Sunday, is a good day for Ginny to relax, eat and drink, and to just be herself. Even yesterday she was trying to get her Clinton Community Center materials in perfect order for others to handle. She is in charge of the scheduling of the use of that wonderful facility. Every day I admire Ginny more than ever for her indomitable spirit, grit, beauty, strength, and love. She does not know how to be mean and continues the struggle for now as best as she is able. I made a wonderful choice fifty years ago. I have never felt closer to Ginny than now nor been more proud of her. So keep the prayers coming and thank you all for your cards and many other ways in which you help. If at times I seem down, do not tell me that as I have absolutely no control over it.

15 June 2011 Report

Today I will relate a little about what happened at the Hunterdon Cancer Center last Monday and what may happen today. Ginny's blood tests (red and white) were good except for her potassium levels. We have dealt with that since Monday and will continue to deal with it the rest of the week. When they weighed Ginny she was 101 pounds which frankly was good considering the lower intestinal thing she had for 10 days. When she started this cancer fight she had weighed in at 115 pounds; her normal weight is about 117 pounds. The past 4 days or so Ginny has been eating quite well and I am so pleased. The Oncologist said that the extreme diarrhea was due to a reaction to one of the drugs of the chemotherapy, CTP-11. It happens and will be taken out of the next regimen. The genetic test was fine and a chemotherapy drug called Oxaliplatin will be used instead of the CTP-11. Although Ginny was too weak to have chemotherapy Monday, they did give her 4 hours of saline drips and a potassium drip. It is so very strange and sad to sit in the room with all these people hooked up to drips of one sort or another, all in some sort of distress. We returned home in the afternoon of last Monday and Ginny continued eating and drinking in a wonderful way. I wish I could stop talking about that issue. Our dear friend Paula, who has four young children, has religiously come over at 8:00AM, 2:00PM, and 8:00PM to give Ginny her the requisite shots to try to stop the diarrhea and we hope that they will soon no longer be needed since the lower intestinal tract seems to have improved considerably as of last night (Ginny is sleeping right now so I am uninformed re today so far). Paula has brought her children over at different times and they have given Ginny great joy. We had the old Ginny back this week. She is gaining strength and eating well and just being her old perfect self. She is using a drink called Simone for extra electrolytes and other good things.

Today, 6/15/11 we arrive at the Cancer Center at 8:45PM to meet with Dr. Bednar to see if Ginny can have chemotherapy today or if it should be put off until next Monday. He and Ginny will make that decision. My only concern is whether to put off the chemotherapy until Monday will allow the cancer cells to further replicate to an extent that Ginny's life expectancy will be further shortened; we will ask the Doctor about this. I want to have her with me as long as possible. Of course, we want to know as well if Ginny is physically able to handle chemotherapy at this time. In short, an informed medical judgment will have to be given so Ginny can decide. So, we will either be home early today or late, depending on how things go. Interestingly enough is the fact that Ginny has unilaterally reduced her use of some of the drugs that she has been taking to feel better. We will see if that continues once chemotherapy starts up again, whenever that will be. Ginny continues to want to fight for a longer life and hopes for a miracle. Me too. On the other hand, I know full well that we are just counting the days. Everyone at the Cancer Center seems to have hope, no matter what type of cancer they have; except those with pancreatic cancer. I am so very happy for others as they fight their battle and survive, yet it is impossible to not be jealous and envious of them. Luck is a relative term. So how should I feel? You tell me.

Second round of chemotherapy:

Well today Ginny and I go to the Cancer Center presumably to have Ginny start her second round of chemotherapy. I cannot conceive of that happening based on her medical condition now, but leave this decision up to the Oncologist whom we trust. Ginny still has the lower intestinal issue, albeit to a much lesser extent, but does not really have her strength back. At least now she is eating and we are both so pleased with that fact.

We have to again thank Paula and her family for the daily 8:00AM, 2:00PM, and 8:00PM visits to our home by Paula to give Ginny the shots that are trying to fix that lower intestinal issue. Hopefully those shots will be able to cease soon and Paula can get back to taking care of her husband and four children. The bottom line is that Ginny's quality of life for at least 8-9 days was terrible but the last three days have been so much better. Mark and Ang have been able to stop over, food in hand, to have a couple of really good visits. On one visit in particular Mark was power washing the cement around the pool and the basketball court to clean it all up, and he wrote the name MOM on the cement with the power washer. Ginny liked that a lot. David, Lena, and Amelia have been here via Skype and the telephone all of which is wonderful. Also, many friends have called, sent letters or dropped off food which has been appreciated. Mark's friend Jeb was on the telephone as soon as he heard of Ginny's diagnosis. I want to point out one person that brought such wonderful tears to Ginny's and my eyes. Dana Matthews Mulligan is one of David's high school friends and sent the sweetest and nicest Facebook note essentially validating all that Ginny had done in raising our sons and how Ginny treated their friends. She mentioned all the love, soda, food, use of our shore house, the pool here in Clinton, and so many other things, ending by saying that she tried to emulate "Mrs. R" in the manner in which she raised her own children and treated their friends. What a wonderful thing to say. We will see what follows.

I got up at 2:30AM today to get a lot of things done before we go to the Cancer Center at 8:00 AM. It takes Ginny a long time to get her energy up and get ready to go to Flemington. Also, I want to try to get a good long run in to help my head stay on straight! Today is an important day. I do not think the Doctors will completely stop chemotherapy forever, although that thought has crossed my mind and scares me. Such a decision would mean that Ginny would go into Hospice Care or something similar; it would mean the battle had ended. They may modify the current regimen or try a different regimen of chemotherapy. The only issue is that the current regimen is Ginny's best chance to have the longest survival possibility. On the other hand, if her quality of life is to be as horrible as the past week, perhaps we might consider a change. I use the term "we", but in reality, this decision is totally up to Ginny as it should be.

Again, as always, thank you all for reading this summary. I want you to be kept up to date on things. You may share this with whomever you wish. There is no doubt that Ginny got the worst deal in the world with her diagnosis, but there also is no doubt that she is handling this with the class and dignity that is part of her essence. No matter how long this takes to resolve itself, Ginny will be Ginny and we can ask for no more. And yes, I continue to be so very angry.

Just before restart of Chemotherapy

Ginny did not have chemotherapy on Wednesday through Friday as she and the Oncologist felt it was best to give her more time to recover from the lower intestinal tract issue and to be able to eat and drink more and gain more strength. He also felt the additional delay would not adversely impact Ginny's efforts to feel better and prolong her life so it will start on Monday, June 20, 2011. This was a wise decision.

I have to say that Ginny has done just what the Doctor ordered and eaten and drank up a storm. She has gained back a lot of her strength and even gone shopping with me to get smaller clothes to replace her "large" stuff when she weighed 115 pounds. Some of her hair has fallen out but that may cease with the new and different chemotherapy treatment.

Ginny's indomitable spirit to fight continues and I admire her gumption tremendously. Just the other day she was on the telephone with at least ten of her friends! Our sons call daily. One person even mentioned that the entire Town of Clinton was rooting for Ginny in this battle and I know that is true for Ginny is well-known and respected here in the Clinton, New Jersey area. Friends have dropped off food and offered to help in many ways. She receives cards and well-wishes daily. I am a little less protective of Ginny right now as she knows when she gets tired and is able to tell this to people when appropriate. I expect today and tomorrow (Saturday and Sunday) to be good/great days as well. I know too that Ginny will continue to gain strength and be ready for chemotherapy on Monday, Tuesday, and Wednesday. Then I expect there will be a number of difficult days with the nausea and inability to eat or drink much. It apparently is a cycle which you must go through with chemotherapy. We have been promised that the lower intestinal tract issue will not occur to the vast prior extent with the change of one of the medications. That better be true. Ironically, when I see Ginny now it is as if there is nothing wrong with her at all. She is my old Ginny. Yet, deep inside I know that she is extremely ill and hoping for a miracle to prolong her life; me as well. So to all you fathers out there, have a great Father's Day. Let us see what Monday to Wednesday brings. Gosh. Another holiday has gone by and I do not really care.

Second round of chemotherapy almost over.
June 21, 2011

Well folks, Ginny spent another day getting chemotherapy. Yesterday went very well and ditto with today. She looked absolutely beautiful sitting there as the ugly chemicals were being delivered into her body to kill cancer cells. I am not kidding. She looked radiant. In a sense she was telling the cancer to go to hell by her example. There are a number of patients getting the chemo and many had nice conversations with Ginny. As per yesterday, they have this pack on her that continues the chemotherapy until tomorrow at 11 AM when she will be disconnected from the pack and it will done for a while; over a week. They did not use the chemo drug CPT-11 or whatever it is called so we are optimistic that the lower intestinal challenges will not return to the same extent. Ginny cannot take that drug easily if at all. We will see. Ginny's weight did drop a tad below 98 pounds but that is to be expected considering what she went through for the 10-12 days of diarrhea. And, she started this at 115 pounds. Ginny continues to eat and drink considerably and soon some weight may be put on once her intestines recover which should be soon. Why do I keep caring about this weight thing? The Doctors are not at all concerned at this time about the weight loss. Unfortunately, the nasty effects of chemotherapy will reappear for a while in a day or two, so we have got to get through that period which hopefully will last 3-4 days. Assuming things go as planned, after a few days Ginny will be back to her old self and eat and drink as is appropriate. For those of us lucky enough to have avoided chemotherapy, pat yourself on the back. It is not enjoyable to put poison into your body and hope it does a good job of helping you. Then you have to recover from the chemotherapy. Quite a task. And yet, it is not a cure we seek but only the prolongation of a good quality of life. How I wish it were a cure.

So keep your good thoughts coming and your prayers are nice too. On the other hand, I do not really care about prayer at all. Ginny is fighting this illness with all of her strength. The loss of weight and some hair are okay. The love and help of good friends are priceless. And, the Doctors have assured us that this second round of chemotherapy will be much better in terms of the effects on Ginny. So this is all that I have to say at this time. No one should judge me.

26 June 2011 and Ginny

The first three days after chemotherapy, Round Two, have gone well. This past Thursday, Friday and Saturday were as good as they could be. Ginny felt tired as you might expect but was able to consume large quantities of liquid and by Saturday (yesterday), a good amount of food. Periodically she would need time to just rest as the poison in her body tried to kill the cancer cells; that process can be and was exhausting. David and Mark and Ang visited so all was very good with the world. Lena and Amelia stayed in Virginia as Ginny could not really enjoy Amelia as much as she would want in her current state...so Lena had Amelia on Skype each night which was wonderful. Ginny, in a real sense, had her entire family with her for the three days. How horrible it must be for my sons to know that their mother is going to die. I hate it.

Ginny has lost weight, but her recovery from some of that weight loss and tiredness hopefully will take place this coming week which is a rest period from the chemotherapy. Ginny is trying so hard to deal with this burden and I admire her so; she is quite the fighter. Late last night there was one complication from the chemotherapy and that related to the lower intestinal tract on three occasions. Imodium has been taken as prescribed and we pray that the horrible effects exhibited for ten to eleven days after the last chemotherapy do not occur again as that was debilitating, demeaning, and caused so much weight loss and weakness. This makes us nervous as you might imagine. So when Ginny awakens this morning and throughout the day today (Sunday) we will see what happens. That is the least concern we have. We hope those shots taken to cure the issue after the last round of chemotherapy will not be necessary. If Ginny can get through today and tomorrow as far as the lower intestinal tract, we will know that her recovery period will blossom and Ginny will have a wonderful quality of life and be in the recovery mode until the third chemotherapy session on July 5th when the cycle starts over anew. If she is unable to get through the "difficulty", you can bet I will be on the telephone to the Oncologist "on call" to get additional help.

Time for my run and my continued trepidation as to how Ginny will feel when she awakens and throughout the day.

Optimism rules today.

Sunday (6/26/11) was a day of uneasiness as Ginny just did not feel right; okay, but not right. Monday was full of fear as the lower intestinal bug came back resulting in calls to the Cancer Center. Nothing much occurred after 11 AM but you can imagine that we were so fearful after the first chemotherapy debacle. All was handled well through medication, and although Ginny drank as much liquid as a race horse, getting food down seemed difficult but was accomplished a little at times. Today as Ginny sleeps I just know that we are going to have a great week prior to the next chemotherapy. Having passed the difficult stages with a little difficulty, I feel for no medical reason that Ginny is poised now to recover and have good quality days. I know she will be tired at times, but that is okay. Food, drink, and great weather will be of immense help. Also, a visit from a special little girl named Amelia for a couple of days will bring sunshine to Clinton. I do not believe that I am just being overly optimistic here, but realistic based on our prior chemotherapy experience. And I guess a little hope as well.

So let us all pray that Ginny has that good/normal/healing week to which she is entitled and which she needs. Anyone of us could have been placed in Ginny's situation; she did not ask for this. It is not pleasant and requires tremendous strength, physically and emotionally, to go through the chemotherapy and feelings that present.

Let us all keep praying for a miracle as we need one here. I hope another report from me isn't needed for a week.

I jumped the gun
Tue, Jun 28, 2011 4:25 PM

Sorry guys, but I jumped the gun today. I will try to stop that type of action in the future. We just returned from the Cancer Center. Ginny has a low grade fever, possibly due to a bladder infection. Also, her stomach hurts a bit, possibly due to the intestinal issues of an earlier date. Bottom line is that Ginny is going to sit and rest today. I doubt if she will eat much if at all, but at least she will be comfortable. She has lost a little more weight but is not dehydrated. My poor sweet wife.

All for now.

Me

Third Chemotherapy
6/28/2011

The third chemotherapy round started today. The second round was much better than the first, but Ginny only had a few good days for some reason. At least the lower intestinal issues were minor. Anyway, the day started poorly as Ginny felt quite tired and just could not get going. We discussed this with Dr. Bednar and asked if the chemotherapy could be put off until next Monday. He felt Ginny was strong enough to proceed and did not want to hold it off-particularly since the second round of chemotherapy had been delayed. He wanted a consistent pattern of attack on the tumor and on the cancer cells that had spread. So, we went ahead. All was just fine and Ginny seemed to get her strength back and handled it quite well as I had hoped. The chemotherapy was finished about 2 PM or so. Ginny was able to maintain her weight this time as she is eating more often; in short she did not lose any weight!!! Nonetheless, she has lost a lot of weight over all, particularly with that horrible first chemotherapy round; she picked a heck of a way to hit her ideal BMI (Body Mass Index)! (A sick joke-sorry). The past two weeks Ginny is able to eat more and has a bite almost every hour-she is unable to eat large meals so this seems to work. The Doctor thought that this was a good thing. Her red and white blood cells are fine now. The bottom line to all of this? Chemotherapy continues tomorrow and Friday at 10:15am.

It is interesting to note that Ginny's hands have become very sensitive to ice cubes and cold things. Also, she is losing some skin on her fingers. All of this is normal. Ginny still speaks daily to her sons David and Mark and very often sees Amelia on Skype. She reads the newspaper daily and has time to send thank you notes to many of the wonderful people whom have shown acts of kindness in so many different ways. We proceed as best we are able. Sometimes our emotions and the reality of what is going on get the best of us, but we are doing the best we are able with great support. I hope that none of you ever have to go through this. We continue to hope for a much needed miracle so those of you with higher connections, please try to use them!!

End of Final day of Third Round:

Today we arrived at the Cancer Center and Ginny was disconnected from her portable chemotherapy pump. The pump pushed the chemotherapy into her system from the time she left the Cancer Center yesterday until 10:15 AM today when it was removed. We will not be back there again until Wednesday of next week and that is just for a blood test to check Ginny's red and white blood cell counts; so far they have been great. Then the following Wednesday we will be back again for Round Four. Ginny handled everything quite well and has been fantastic mentally and eats and drinks so much better than previously. I am not suggesting that Ginny will gain lots of weight as she has always been unable to do that, but we at least want to try to keep what she has! Once the effects of the chemotherapy kick in a day or so, eating will become a real burden but so far Ginny has been able to hydrate herself well. As I have said before, Round Two was better than Round One and hopefully that trend will continue.

So you understand how all this works, I think I have a cryptic understanding. You start with the premise that pancreatic cancer at Stage IV cannot be cured and will kill you. What we are trying to do is prolong Ginny's life as much as possible provided it has a good quality. Sorry to be so blunt, but that is exactly what we are talking about unless there is a miracle; and again, we still hope for that. The Doctors start out with a chemotherapy regimen and use it until the patient can no longer tolerate it or the regimen stops killing cancer cells and shrinking the tumors on the pancreas and other organs. At that point they change to a different regimen of chemotherapy. They have a number of models in their bag of tricks and they will use them all at different times with the intent being to kill cancer cells and reduce the size of the tumors. Remission may or may not occur for short periods and one may or may not go off chemotherapy for a while. There is also a point where the Doctors run out of their bag of tricks with reference to chemotherapy. Then they can do no more. At that point other decisions have to be made. Hope cannot ever be lost and no matter how horrible all this is to the victim. Mental attitude has a significant degree of importance in terms of having the will to continue the dance. We can only live one day at a time because the broad picture is overwhelming and will drive you insane. We try to not look into the future.

So, at the next round of chemotherapy, they will do some blood tests to see what things called "markers" show with reference to the tumor. Depending on the results of those "marker" blood tests, they make keep or alter the chemotherapy that Ginny is getting. So that is where we are now. Longevity is important but quality of life is the trump card in many ways. At least that sounds good on paper.

Thank you for your continued support.

Thank you
Fri, Jul 15, 2011 03:46 PM

Well, we are at the Cancer Center again. Diarrhea came on big time yesterday, last night, and this morning. So, Virginia is getting a potassium drip and some sodium chloride right now. Her spirits are good and she is going to get on the BRAT diet with lots of good bland food such as white rice, bananas, toast, and applesauce. Some of the food I have been giving her may have exacerbated the diarrhea concept. My fault entirely.

On a positive note, the first good thing has happened since May 16th. Ginny's tumor marker dropped from 7900 at its peak to a current 1800. The Doctor said it had dropped way down, "big time". This may mean that the tumor on the pancreas is shrinking and ditto with the one on the liver etc. Dr. Bednar seemed quite pleased. We keep trying, but this does not mean that Ginny can be cured. It is what it is and may help with our goals of good quality of life and some more time!!! So, this sounds good even though the chemotherapy effects are horrible!! Perhaps all of this effort will not be in vain if we get some benefit.

Love and hugs,
Albert D.

On Jul 14, 2011, at 9:05 PM, Dave Rylak wrote:

Sorry about the diarrhea and the hamstring. I hope that they get better. Amelia really is getting into bandages. She went to bed with ACE wraps on both legs. Odd child. Get some rest. I'll call tomorrow before work. Love, David.

Wed, Jul13, 2011 at 8:44PM

Dear People, to wit, my family-

As always, thank you so much for the Amelia show. She is such a dear.

Ginny is really feeling better now. It may be because she is taking the medication and that is helping with the effects of the chemotherapy. I know seeing her family whether in person or on Skype is quite helpful too. Thank you.

I am a little anxious about getting the tumor marker results perhaps on Friday or Monday. I understand Stage IV, but we could use a little good news soon. So far it has all been yuck. I am not optimistic for anything different, but I have to keep hoping about something. Will keep you posted.

Have a pleasant tomorrow.

Love,

Albert D.

The Insanity of the Donut Hole
Tue, Jul 19, 2011

Well people, Ginny starts Round Four of chemotherapy tomorrow at 9 AM. She has had a relatively good week and in particular, the last few days. We will keep trying to deal with this disease and prognosis as best we are able; it is very hard as you might imagine. I wanted to tell you about the Donut Hole a/k/a Coverage Gap in Medicare. Ginny went on Medicare on February 1, 2011. You are able to enroll in Medicare the first day of the month you turn 65 and Ginny turned 65 on February 22, 2011. We took out a Horizon Blue Cross Blue Shield Medicare Blue Access with RX Enhanced medical plan which substitutes for Medicare;

has the same benefits and much more I was told. It has been a good plan as of yesterday and we had relatively minor co-pays for drugs and a $35.00 specialist co-pay every time we arrived at the Cancer Center or the Hospital. These costs add up quickly. How do people who earn an average salary pay for all this? In prep for chemotherapy we affix to Ginny's arm the afternoon before the start of chemotherapy what is called a Sancuso Patch. It is kept on for 6 days to alleviate the nausea that accompanies chemo; it gives Ginny medication for that period of time and so far, thank God, nausea has not been a problem. I called the pharmacy to reorder the Sancuso Patches (they come in four separate boxes, one to a box) so we would be ready for the Fifth Round of Chemotherapy and as we had used up the other patches. The pharmacist advised me that the cost of a single Sancuso Patch had gone up from $136.00 to $614.80. Seemed interesting, so I called the insurance company and they explained the situation to me. Apparently Medicare has a coverage gap so get a better policy than we obtained to try to cover this gap! The cost of all drugs get good co-pays up to $2,840.00 in total cost of the drugs used. I have no idea how that number was derived. Some idiot bureaucrat must have thought that one up. Thereafter, for the next $4,550.00, we will pay 50% of the total cost of the drugs used. Prior to Obama care, the rate to reach $4,550.00 only included what we actually paid--start by adding in only the $614.80. Since Obama Care, they add in the actual total cost of the drug, $1,228.35, not just the $614.80 we will pay. (Thank you President Obama). After total drug costs exceed the $4,550.00, catastrophic coverage applies and we only pay 5% of the cost of all drugs thereafter. So essentially, we are on the hook for half of $4,550.00 or $2,275.00. Now there is a catch. The $4,550,00 number is an annual number and the time period goes from 1/1/11 until 12/31/11; it then picks up again so that for the calendar year 2012, a new Donut Hole is created for which we must pay. Of course, if we can use generic drugs, the cost factors are minimized---except the Sancuso Patch does NOT come in generic form. Even if it did, I would not want it as Ginny does not need nausea on top of all the other issues the chemotherapy brings. Now is not the time to experiment. So there you have it. A nice way to start your afternoon.

Mark stopped over yesterday and David will be here tomorrow. That is very nice for us. We hope that none of you ever has to go through this demeaning and devastating process. Another great time we have is Skyping Amelia and Lena. Calls, letters, food, etc. from Ang and so many others also help. Sometimes our emotions get the best of us, but we continue hoping for a miracle to help us along. And so tomorrow starts the process again for the fourth time. Wish Ginny health and wish us both well. Ginny made a very prophetic comment as follows: "Many say, Why me?" Ginny says, "Why not me?" She continues being Ginny and writes thank-you notes when she is able. And so it is; and so it goes.

Fourth Round of Chemotherapy done.
Sunday 7/24/11

Well, the fourth round of chemotherapy is done. Ginny had chemotherapy from Wednesday 7/20/11 through the AM of Friday 7/22/11. She handled the chemotherapy well and there were no real changes until days later. David was here during the chemotherapy and Mark and Ang will be here today. Lena has been wonderful with the Skype so we see her and Amelia all the time. Saturday Ginny felt like abject garbage until the end of the morning; she was so exhausted. Then she felt much better in the afternoon. Today, Sunday, is not great but better than yesterday. Ginny is eating much better and our dear neighbors and friends have sent lovely cards, and brought over flowers, chocolates, a turkey dinner with all the trimmings, pasta, desserts, and other great dishes.

So far the lower intestinal issues have not appeared so Ginny will perhaps be stronger until they do come again. To avoid these a bit the Doctors gave Ginny a shot on July
15th that supposedly will help and will be given every month. We will see, but it takes about two weeks for that shot to work at its fullest. So today is a day of continued rest and some fun time with family. The oppressive heat has been observed but minimized due to two very good air-conditioners. Otherwise, we would have gone to a hotel!

In early August they will do another CT scan to see the status of the cancer. They want to know if it is spreading or regressing and want to see the impact on the tumor, which was initially 6cm in length, all based on the chemotherapy currently given. Based on that CT scan, they will either continue the current regime, modify the chemotherapy regime, or stop the chemotherapy. And, we have no real control over this. Ginny's spirit remains strong. We know if the chemotherapy had not been done things would have been totally different now. Ginny would be dead. Sometimes we lose control of our emotions and that is called being human. Our only real hope here would be to have a remission for a while. We would take that in a heartbeat.

That is all I have to say about this for now.

Fifth Round of Chemotherapy starts tomorrow:

Well friends, the Fifth Round of chemotherapy starts tomorrow. Do not know how many more they will allow, but we hope all goes well. We meet with the Doctor at 8 AM and then the chemotherapy starts, lasting until Friday AM. We will discuss things such as CT scans, further blood work and tests, and anything else the Doctor thinks is appropriate. Wish Ginny well. The results after the Fourth Round were relatively good. The lower intestinal issues did not eventuate although there was lots of tiredness. Ginny has eaten better than ever yet we do not think there will be much weight gain. All we can do is the best we are able and that is what we are doing. As Ginny said, "I am still here". The bottom line is that the fight goes on in an effort to prolong Ginny's life and to make her life's quality as good as possible. We have met some wonderful people during this travail and have tried to live as normal an existence as possible. Today Ginny and I went up to Walmart to get some things and that was good. Our family members keep in touch in one way or another on a daily basis and that is great. So many wonderful people have brought over food of all sorts, from Italian to American, entrees and desserts, libation of all sorts. Thank you to all of you. Ginny still religiously sends out her "thank you" notes and in many other ways keeps the house going.

So, thank you all for being whom you are and pray that you never have to go through this process. Many times I feel like we are a yoyo on a string and that our emotions are getting seasick. I will report back when I have some news, whatever it may be.

Some new and interesting information today
Thursday 8/4/11

Well, we received some new information today which is hopeful. As you know, last time they monitored Ginny's tumor markers, I told you that the markers dropped from 7900 to 1800. That 7900 number might have been 6900. I get confused at the Cancer Center sometimes. It is an overwhelming experience to be there.

Anyway, Ginny just finished her second day of Round Five of chemotherapy with one more day to go. Actually, she again wears a pump which gives her chemotherapy until it is disconnected at the Cancer Center tomorrow at 10 AM. When we arrived at the Cancer Center, Ginny was up at the main desk and I was collecting things. Dr. Bednar said in a happy voice that Ginny's tumor markers had dropped to 900 from I think 6900. About 15 minutes later after I got Ginny settled for chemotherapy and was walking to get a cup of coffee, Dr. Bednar saw me and gave me the thumbs up and said, "did you hear that Ginny's tumor markers came down to 900?". He seemed extremely pleased and amazed. I said I assume that is a good thing. His comment to me was, "you bet". This is so typical of the good doctor who looks like the twenty year old television character, Doogie Howser, M.D., but has the tenacity and fighting instinct of Muhammad Ali. This may be all smoke and mirrors as the CT scan is scheduled for next Wednesday at 9 AM. That will be quite telling about the cancer and the growth or lack thereof of the tumors. They are also going to do a chest x-ray. The bottom line is that we choose to use this as good news and it is. With stage 4 pancreatic cancer, you have no idea what "good news" means in terms of longevity and quality of life, but it sure beats having the numbers go up. I like happy Doctors and Dr. Bednar seemed so pleased!

As an aside, there is something called neuropathy which gets worse after every round of chemotherapy when you take certain unknown drugs. Essentially, Ginny's fingertips tingle and feel like ice cubes when she touches something cold. Usually it lasts only a couple of days. Sometimes it affects the throat which it did today. Ginny went to the water fountain to gulp some water with a pain pill that she takes. It was cold water coming from the fountain and when I returned to see her, it was clear that her throat felt as if it has seized or frozen in some way; poor dear had a very strange look on her face.

All of this is perfectly normal with the type of chemotherapy we are told, but is scary nonetheless.

So now it is 1:15PM and we are home. I hope Ginny is able to just relax and read and heal. I have much to do right now as to the house. As an aside, Ginny brought one of the nurses who is expecting in a couple of months a gift for the new baby, a little girl due in October I think. That is Ginny being Ginny. So that is it.

Wed, Aug 10, 2011 09:12PM

Well, Ginny and I had a great couple of days. I know Ginny's stomach was acting badly, but seeing our sons and Amelia made life worthwhile. Her stomach is pretty good now. We love our daughters-in-love but know that Ang has to work and Lena needs to stay close to home because the baby is due soon. So, it was all good. Seeing Mark and Amelia bond was wonderful. Amelia likes Uncle Mark. Mark took care of Amelia while we were at Walmart and they were like best friends! It was like that each time Mark was here. Amelia really loves Mark, is comfortable with him, and that is good- having the electric cars in the cellar helped too! Someday Mark will be a great father. David and I did our gun stuff and I really enjoyed that. He is a superb father and should write a book on how to handle the job! Swimming in the pool was fantastic and Amelia must have been in the pool at least 4 times a day. She still will not get her head wet!! Seeing Amelia be herself was wonderful and we even went to get hot chocolate in the early AM, read books and did all sorts of fun things! Ginny gets sad at times since she cannot do a tenth of what she wants to do with Amelia. I admit to being a little down at times as I was stressed over Ginny's CT scan coming up this AM. Also, as a member of the human race, I sometimes get a feeling of sadness because of Ginny's condition which is difficult to handle. It usually passes. When David and Amelia left, Ginny was very emotional. What do you expect? It saddens Ginny to not know if she will see Amelia again or meet our newly expected grand-baby. She does not think that sweet Amelia will even remember her which is probably true since she is just three years old. I am trying to change that. Living without much of a future is a very difficult thing. Hence, we need a miracle and dang it, it has to come. I know realistically that it will not.

So, I guess we say that after Round 5 of chemotherapy finished last Friday, Ginny was okay for a while but her stomach really caused some issues in the nature of cramps and tiredness. We all made the best of a difficult situation and hope for good CT scan results when we see the Doctor on Friday AM. Unfortunately, the control over that does not rest in our hands. Things sure have changed since the diagnosis was made on May 16, 2011. All of our lives have been turned upside down with just a few words from a Doctor. Pancreatic cancer is the first thing I think of when I awake and the last thing I think of at night; sleep is not exactly kind to me. It also intrudes into my awake time as well. Somehow we have had the strength to continue the fight. Ginny suffers not only from the pancreatic cancer and emotional torment of her condition, but also from the actual chemotherapy which is essentially putting poison into her body almost to the point of killing her, hoping that she has a couple of good days, and then doing it again two weeks later. She has the hard job. It would be so much easier if we had hope of a cure, but that is not the case. I just deal with the sadness and anxiety of it all. My Doctor has given me some Valium to help me along. So, we had a great couple of days which were necessary. Thank you all for either being here, or just listening or allowing our sons to visit sans guilt. Amelia, do not change one bit. You are about to be the big sister soon and will set a wonderful example for your new brother. So, there is nothing further that I care to add to this note.

August 12, 2011 meeting with Dr. Bednar

We just returned from a meeting with Dr. Bednar. Ginny's blood work is fine and she was given the monthly shot to continue to stop the lower intestinal issues. As to the pancreatic cancer, there is some good news. Start with the premise that the cancer cannot be cured. Then we deal with how the cancer is responding to chemotherapy after actually seeing things with the CT scan. The CT scan verified what the drop in tumor markers has shown. The tumor at the tip of the pancreas has decreased in size from 6 cm to 5 cm. Some cystic components along the gastric wall, the largest which was 3.2 cm, are now 2.5 cm. Lesions in the spleen have also decreased in size, the largest having dropped from 2 cm to 0.9 cm. They really could not read the node on the left adrenal gland. The liver is markedly improved. The largest lesions on the right lobe have decreased in size from 5cm to 2.8 cm. Some spots on the liver are gone essentially. The impression in the CT scan report is that the tumor on the pancreatic tail, gastric wall, and splenic hilum slightly decreased in size with the cystic and hypodense components decreased in size. The hypodense metastatic lesions throughout the liver (the pancreatic cancer growing in the liver) have markedly decreased in size and number. The masses in the spleen have decreased in size although there is an enhancement in the pattern of the spleen (that I think is not the best news).

What all this techno-jargon means I think is that there is good news and that the cancer looks better; in other words, better for Ginny and worse for the cancer. This will possibly result in a decrease in symptoms as well. Dr. Bednar said that there is no question but that Ginny has bought time and extended her life expectancy. Baring an auto accident, Ginny will see the birth of our new grandson. Dr. Bednar said that if things keep going this way she will be at his/her first birthday party and who knows what else. He was realistic but optimistic. Yes, Ginny's weight is now down to 90 pounds but we are working on that with a drug called Creon to assist food being absorbed into her system. I was hoping that the Doctor would say that all was cured or apologize for a misdiagnosis and that Ginny was fine, but that of course could not happen. He called what is going on a partial response to the chemotherapy and will schedule another CT scan in three months. So, we just keep hoping for a miracle and like what is going on to date. Things can change at any time, but we just keep plodding along, keeping as much good news as possible in our hearts. Only in this way can you keep your sanity.

Next Wednesday Round Six of chemotherapy takes place and we hope that between now and then Ginny has "good days" to enjoy.

Sixth Round of Chemo
8/17/11

The sixth round of chemotherapy starts today at 9:15 AM and continues for three days. Yesterday was the third month since we learned of Ginny's illness. In a sense, a milestone has been reached. Without treatment she had perhaps two months to live. Ginny will handle the chemotherapy well if all goes to pattern, but she will start feeling weak on Saturday, may have some lower intestinal issues, and will have cramps for some time in the future. The good news is that the last three days have been good. Actually Sunday and Tuesday were superb. So, there is something good happening. We have to hope that the chemotherapy continues to battle the cancer and that the tumors continue to shrink. It is not the cancer in the pancreas that eventually takes your life, but the cancer that has spread to the liver. We are hoping that when the CT scan said that the liver tumors had "markedly improved" that that process continues. We have no control over this but are at the mercy of the Doctors and the chemotherapy. So, keep hoping that we get lucky and that Ginny's genetics and will to live take over and control the situation. Ginny has been eating well and taking the drug called Creon which may help her intestines absorb her food in a better fashion. Would like to see Ginny put on a pound, but all I can say is that she has done all that she can do to achieve this goal. If it works, great. If not, we are at peace. Ginny does look and act so much better. She is fighting with all the energy she has. We even went on a shopping trip to get some cards and a gift or two for some very nice people at the Hunterdon Regional cancer Center. Again, this disease has not changed Ginny one bit. The thank you notes continue and we have contact with our friends as she is able.

So I hope that you all have a great day and continue to recognize what really is important in life. I'll be back to you later.

Just a little supplement to today's email re: Sixth Chemotherapy

Just thought I would take the time to give you a little update on today and some additional information. This is particularly important as so many people are getting cancer nowadays. Ginny takes two major cancer fighting drugs: Fluorouracil (known as 5-FU) and Oxaliplatin. Oxaliplatin is given while at the hospital and then 5-FU is given by pump attached to Ginny when she leaves the hospital and goes all evening and all night until the pump is disconnected the next day at the hospital. Then the cycle is repeated for Thursday as well with the pump being disconnected on Friday AM. While at the hospital Ginny is also given Levoleucovorin to decrease the damage to healthy cells and to assist the cancer fighting drugs. All this time and for an additional four days Ginny is wearing a Sancuso patch to help halt nausea. At the end of chemotherapy on Friday Ginny is usually given Neulasta to boost her white blood count and hopefully protect against chemotherapy related infection. So that is what medication she is currently taking. This can be changed at a later date when it or any part of it is no longer effective. It is amazing how new words enter into your vocabulary at a time like this.

Today Ginny had a reaction to the Oxaliplatin. Nothing is easy it seems. A drug is working to kill cancer cells and then an allergic reaction occurs. Simply put, Ginny's forehead, hands and couple of other spots became quite red. To counter this chemotherapy was stopped immediately and Ginny was given saline and Benadryl intravenously via the port that had been installed for chemotherapy.   After about a half an hour the redness disappeared and eventually they continued with the chemotherapy. This apparently happens at times and may or may not happen again. Hence, after arriving at the Cancer Center about 9 AM, we did not get home until 4 PM. A long and tiring day.

On a good note, Ginny has gained a pound and is a whopping 91 pounds now. When you are so slight, this is a big deal so all were very happy about that. She continues to eat well and feel well.

I have nothing more to say except God Bless America and our newly expected grandbaby.

Meeting with Dr. Bednar on August 24, 2011, or
From the ridiculous to the sublime.

Well, Ginny and I met with Dr. Bednar today at 3:30PM. Ginny has lost weight. Now I must stop focusing on the weight as the Doctor has indicated that her cancer is better nonetheless. So, no more reports on weight. The pancreatic cancer makes you lose weight as does the chemotherapy. Ginny is doing an amazing job of eating and will try to eat even more. Also, the drugs Ginny takes for pain and other issues can have certain side effects. We are trying to improve Ginny's quality of life. So, we are cutting back on two of the drugs she takes and adding a drug to help with her energy/mood/fatigue situation.

The major problem has been that Ginny has no energy, particularly in the AM. To even take a bath and come downstairs is difficult. That is caused by the pancreatic cancer, the chemotherapy, and the medication she is taking. We do not want to stop the chemotherapy yet. So, the Doctor suggested that to try to help with the fatigue, that Ginny decrease some of the medication she takes and she will do so as she does not need the same dosage as early on due to the decrease in the size of the tumors. Also, the addition of certain mood medication will be helpful. I can only tell you that this is going to be tried as we all want Ginny to have a good quality of life. Unless she directs otherwise, Ginny will be on some form of chemo or other treatment for the rest of her life. The Doctor has things in his bag of ideas that Ginny may choose to use in the future. We will see.

I have no more to add now. I just want Ginny as happy as she can be at this time. To learn that you have pancreatic cancer means usually that it has advanced to stage 4. Who would not be depressed with this knowledge? We just keep trying to do the right thing for her quality of life. Longevity is not as important as quality of life and that is what we must focus on. So, we now embark on trying to deal with a real difficult side effect of Ginny's current condition. Sadness is expected. Long term hope is not expected. Nonetheless, there is hope and we will grab it happily.

Supplement-the sublime: Today has been wonderful for Ginny. It is almost as if nothing is wrong. Why? It is such a strange situation. Energy galore. I feel better. God bless America.

Seventh Chemotherapy Round

Well friends, the seventh round of chemotherapy started today. Ginny handled it very well as expected; she even had a private room for the activity! There was a little allergic reaction again to the Oxaliplatin in the form of rashes, but that was cured with intravenous Benadryl. How difficult it must be to be a doctor nurse trying to treat people with cancer.

Then when we got home the good news followed re the birth of our new grandson. Nothing can go wrong today!!!!! Ginny currently wears the pump which is putting the chemotherapy into her body all night and we will appear again at the Hunterdon Cancer Center to repeat the process all to be disconnected on Friday.

As horrible as the first five days after chemotherapy were last week, the last 4-5 days were very good. When I wrote on 8/24/11, I was a little too down I think and I apologize for that; sometimes emotions are hard to control when someone you love is in dire straits, but you must go on. Ginny will undoubtedly be without energy after chemo ends on Friday until next Thursday, a week from tomorrow; that is five very difficult days. We will live with it. In this last good period, Ginny had high energy levels, ate quite a bit of food, went out shopping on a couple of occasions, and was almost her old self. We had good talks and nice times on our various porches.

The patients at any Cancer Center are special people. You must be extra kind to them as they are fighting very serious battles. You develop a collegiality with them as everyone is afraid, fearful, in pain of one kind or another, and recognizes their own mortality sometimes sooner than they wish. All of that is hard to get used to. Nonetheless, we know so many people there either from prior encounters or new friendships forged at the Cancer Center. Ginny always ignores the question of "why me"? She simply says "why not me"? There is sadness, but no anger in her heart. We should all be that way. A smile and a few kind words go a long way in the process of emotional healing. And I do find it amazing how many people I know receiving care and treatment at the Cancer Center. Too many.

So grandson, whomever you are, welcome.

Update after Seventh Chemotherapy Round
Tue, 9/6/11 11:20pm

As you know Ginny underwent her seventh chemotherapy round last Wednesday, Thursday, and Friday. As always, she handled the extensive sessions very well. Then came Friday afternoon and things got bad with cramps and exhaustion. Usually these things come about on Saturday. To keep the white blood cells in good shape, they gave Ginny Neulasta which is a pretty potent shot that can cause bone pain. So, discouragingly, Saturday, Sunday and Monday were not good. Actually, Monday was horrible. Nice way to spend Labor Day. Lena had had enough labor delivering our new grandson Benjamin David Rylak on August 31, 2011. Emotions were particularly low for both of us. We decided to try a new technique to try to ease the pain and tiredness and it is called Traditional Reiki & Integrated Energy Therapy. Ginny had a one hour session in the early afternoon and we felt that the results were non-existent; although we were glad we tried it. Well, this morning, Tuesday September 6, 2011, Ginny felt very good. She had her energy back and did not have the horrible stomach cramps. Whether the Reiki led to this or it just happened, I do not know. Bottom line? After some really bad times post-chemotherapy, Ginny feels really good about two days earlier than usual. She was able to get all the things done that she could not do for three days. You see, part of the emotional issue with chemotherapy is that you are essentially helpless to do even basic stuff; this creates an arena for depression and sadness in which to grow and of course that can impact you in a very bad way. We do not know what tomorrow will bring, but we will be at the Cancer Center at 9:30AM for blood work only. Hopefully all that will be satisfactory to the doctors. I do not know if they will check the tumor markers but it is what it is.

As an aside, we are having another battle with the insurance company. Sit down for this one. Ginny gets a pump on Wednesdays, Thursdays and part of Fridays so that the chemotherapy can poison her all night. The provider of the chemotherapy infusing pump is from Philadelphia, Pennsylvania and all the supplies for the pump originate there as well. The pump is installed through the port at the Hunterdon Medical Center, Hunterdon Regional cancer Center--Flemington (Raritan Township), New Jersey. Our insurance company says that because of the origination of the pump in Pennsylvania, the pump is deemed to be "out of network" and they will only pay a small percentage of the cost of it and the supplies it uses, after we pay our "out of network deductible". We are having a dispute about this as you might imagine. The insurance representative was taken aback when I suggested that this made no sense and that an appeal would have to be taken. When I likened it to bandages and other medical supplies made in another state or country, she was offended. I told her this country manufactures nothing anymore and that I assume she checked each item a hospital provides, bandages and rectal jelly included, before paying a hospital bill. She was further disheartened when I suggested if they would rather Ginny spend 2.5 days in the hospital for the procedure, that could be arranged although it would not be cost effective. So, that battle will rage on for a while as I have time on my hands to deal with it as I see fit. My Ginny is good today and so long as I look only at today, life is good. I hope it continues. I tell her nothing about these insurance issues. God Bless America.

Round Eight of Chemotherapy deferred until Monday the 19th Wednesday the 21st
Wed, Sep 14, 2011 04:09PM

Dear People, to wit, family:

The last two weeks had some high moments but most of the moments were on the downward slope. Day three of the Seventh Round of Chemotherapy ended on Friday, 9/2/11. Most of the days thereafter were difficult except for about 2.5 of them. My notes reflect too many "not a good day" notations. The problems encountered are lack of strength, and fatigue coupled with pain in the area of the stomach and back. Reiki did not seem to help too much. When Ginny Whyte and my brother Frank visited, they were the only two good full days but there were some good half days. The causes of this can be varied. Of course it has to do with the cancer, but also the chemotherapy. It is ironic that in the time period after the Seventh Round, Ginny had 4-5 consecutive good days. It is discouraging to deviate from that quality of life. Anyway, when we got to the Cancer Center today it was agreed to defer the chemotherapy until Monday the 19th. Reason? Well, Ginny had a sore throat and a very low grade fever. She also felt weak and the pain in the stomach area and the back was palpable. I am confident that Ginny will feel better after the added five days of recovery and that there will be no adverse impact on the fight to kill cancer cells. They can on that day continue pumping poison into her body. Actually, they took blood for checking the tumor markers and our hope is that the downward progression from 6,900 to 1,800 to 900 will continue. When I hear about that I will advise. So, an extra prayer would be a good thing for those of the religious persuasion. Calls from the boys have been great and watching our new Benjamin on Skype is wonderful; he just lies there looking like a dear little baby boy. Also, Amelia has been a source of great entertainment on Skype with her guitar and singing. No one said this battle would be easy and it is not. No need to panic yet. This is just a minor setback on the road to something better. More to follow.

A little more good news and a little yuck news-9/16/11

Well, it has been a rough few days for Ginny. What with chemotherapy deferred on Wednesday until Monday, Ginny has not felt well. She has had a sore throat of sorts and also has had stomach and back pains. We had taken a ride to Flemington today and I convinced Ginny to go to the Cancer Center. They checked her out and feel that the stomach issues are related to her intestines and not the pancreatic cancer necessarily. So, they are giving her stuff to help with the digestive process. It is sad that she did not have a few more good days and candidly irritates me somewhat. Anyway, we try to now get the bowels working properly with medication. On a nice note, Ginny's tumor markers dropped to 700 which is a 22% reduction from the 900 level of some weeks ago. So, the chemotherapy is still killing cancer cells. Beats going up 22%. So, we have two more full days until chemotherapy starts again. Let us hope that they are good days.

And yes, I do have a damn headache. It is difficult to continue writing about these terrible issues. Such is life!

Retry on 8th Round of Chemotherapy today
Mon, Sep 19, 2011 10:21AM

Well, today we will retry the 8th Round of Chemotherapy. We have many questions for the Doctor and hopefully he can help us deal with Ginny's pain and uncomfortable feeling. Since my e-mail to you on Friday, things have not been particularly good. The pain continues as does the uncomfortable feeling; she even had a low grade fever again. It is a shame as Ginny needs some good time to make all of this effort worthwhile. So, we will see what is in store for us. Thank God for the calls from David and Mark as they enervate Ginny very much. We are trying to get things together so Ginny can take a trip to meet Benjamin and see Amelia, perhaps September 28, 29, and 30. Just do not know yet how Ginny will feel as we have not taken any long trips since the diagnosis on May 16, 2011. If we can pull this trip off I think it would really help Ginny's spirits. On the other hand, I have learned that you cannot predict how one will feel when dealing with pancreatic cancer. You simply take what you are given and hope. It is also very hard to take one day at a time. Candidly, that works only in theory, not reality. Anyway, I will let you know what goes on soon.

Well, this is a special day. It has been four months and four days since Ginny and I went out for dinner. We shared a very nice meal at the Cracker Barrel in Clinton. So this is a good thing. I am happy/sad about this as you might imagine. We have been out a few times to shop for gifts or clothing, but nothing like dinner.

We spoke to the Oncologist Monday AM and Ginny did not feel very well at all at that time. He changed the pain portion of her medication a tad and that has made all the difference. Ginny hugged the doctor and thanked him for helping her be around for the birth of her grandson. She slept well last night and handled the chemotherapy well not only on Monday but also today, Tuesday 5/20/11. The infusion pump is still giving her chemotherapy at this time and will do so until tomorrow at about 10:15 AM, the scheduled appointment time to disconnect the pump. Then there is the recovery time to try to get over what has been done to her. So, essentially we have had two good days. Nastiness is coming, possibly on Wednesday afternoon or Thursday, but we expect that. I have a Hunterdon Medical Center Board of Trustees meeting at 4 PM Wednesday and a Court appearance at noon on Thursday so Ginny will be disconnected from her primary caregiver for a couple of hours over the next couple of days. Thank God for cell phones!!

It is still our hope to get down to Staunton, VA on Wednesday afternoon to meet Benjamin and see Amelia, but we cannot determine that until that day. Wish us well.

9/28/11

Time for a change. Well, this has been a very bad post chemotherapy time from an emotional point of view as well from a pain management point of view. Since chemo ended on May 21, 2011, Ginny has not felt good at all except when she speaks to or Skypes the kids and grandchildren. She did have another CT scan yesterday to see if there was a blockage in a duct from the pancreas or a nerve issue, but that test showed no problems in those regards. This morning and yesterday evening were really bad from a pain point of view so we got in to see the Doctor again. Dr. Bednar announced that the CT scan, even though given earlier than usual because of Ginny's pain, showed that the tumor on the pancreas is a little smaller yet then previously and there is greater improvement on the liver tumors. Some more liver tumors are gone and others continue to shrink. In short, the cancer is still losing the chemo battle right now; for how long we do not know. The pain meds have been changed to give Ginny a quality of life better than she has now. We will see if the stronger medications work as they were just started an hour ago. We will also go and see a pain specialist in the near future, Dr. Susan Bell. It is felt that there is a nerve called the celiac plexus and that the pain Ginny feels originates from there. It is not due to the chemotherapy or the cancer per se, but because things have resettled in that area. An MRI is scheduled for Friday at 10:15 AM and we will see what is going on at that time. As you might imagine, this has been a difficult time for us. We were supposed to go and meet Benjamin and see Amelia today, but that had to be put on hold. Candidly, Ginny could not have driven a tenth of the distance. So, we work on a new visit sometime after October 11th. Now you know it all to date.

Again, those of the religious persuasion, keep the prayers coming. Kind thoughts from the rest of you are appreciated too. A special thanks for those people that brought wonderful meals to our house the past week. You know who you are! Appreciate the important things in life.

Ninth chemotherapy session tomorrow.
Sunday, October 2, 2011

Tomorrow Ginny starts the ninth chemotherapy session. Since my last note to everyone, things have been good once the effects of the prescription change kicked in. I do feel Ginny was taking way too little medication previously by choice. Controlling the pain is the most important thing right now. With one exception all has been quite good. Ginny is sleeping better and feels less anxious due to the absence of the bad pain. Nonetheless, pain is still part of the equation. The MRI scheduled for Friday did not occur as we did not get the preauthorization until that evening. Apparently insurance companies have two days to review and decide if the MRI expense is warranted and took the full two days. Since the approval was obtained after 5PM Friday, we could not schedule an MRI until we call on Monday, tomorrow October 3, 2011. Usually Ginny has no problem with the chemotherapy and I am expecting at least Monday and Tuesday and part of Wednesday to be good days. She cannot have the MRI during chemotherapy as she wears the infusion pump which cannot go through the machine. Yesterday Ginny's brother Will visited and Mark was able to come as well. So all of that was good. Jack and Donna brought the finest meal ever over to us and even brought breakfast today, Sunday. Amazing people. Carol, Jennifer, Nancy, as well.

Well, we hope the MRI brings good results if we get it scheduled this coming week. Hopefully it will show why the pain continues in the celiac plexus area. We have no control over this. If it shows nothing I do not know what to do. If it shows something perhaps it can be dealt with properly. I am very anxious to have Ginny speak to the pain specialist, Dr. Susan Bell next week. Perhaps that will help. As an aside, I took my office building off the real estate market earlier in the week. I was tired of dealing with ground-feeders and it is the one thing that I am able to control. So, I controlled it my way. Ginny has suggested that I work on the restoration of the 1780 building and I am giving that some thought. Ginny is right. It may help me emotionally. No more to add today. We just keep trying to deal with a very difficult situation. If we can keep our sanity we will be okay today. Tomorrow is a different story and different day.

Radiation to begin soon.

Ginny handled the chemotherapy well as always. The neuropathy did enter into the equation so that is under control as well. Dr. Bednar increased the pain medication and that has helped. Yesterday after chemotherapy was finished, Ginny went to get her MRI. It was a tiring day as you might imagine. There were a few minor complications and Ginny removed her pain patches so as to avoid burning. You see, pancreatic cancer is spelled "pain" and we have to deal with that. Today was a pretty good day and we got a call from a nurse that the cancer Doctor wanted to see Ginny at 2:45PM. Well, as you can imagine, this was a little disconcerting. So, we appeared as requested. Turns out our fears were unjustified and that they are working on the pain issue. This is what the issue seems to be: Ginny's liver looked good. That is due to the killing of cancer cells by her current chemotherapy which includes 5 FU. The MRI showed that the pancreas and the tumor or one of them were pressing on the nerves near Ginny's stomach. Hence the pain from the outset, even before May 16, 2011 when the diagnosis of pancreatic cancer was made was made. The CT scan did not show this but the MRI made it quite evident. Dr. Bednar indicated that they could do a nerve block but did not want to do that at this time. So, they have chosen to radiate (kill) a portion of the tumor on the pancreas so that there is less pressure on the nerves near the stomach from the pancreas or the tumor. That area will definitely shrink. Because the 5 FU is so strong, they will change the chemotherapy treatment to Gemzar which is a weaker form of therapy. It works well with radiation apparently. Radiation will last from 5-10 days and Ginny may go bald from this Gemzar chemotherapy which will be given in the middle of the radiation for just one hour, one day. Eventually they hope to go back to the 5 FU which has worked so well. The radiation oncologist is Doctor Oren Cahlon and we see him at 2 PM tomorrow. So, that is all that I have to say about this.

Meeting with Dr. Cahlon
Fri, Oct 07, 2011 10:48 PM

We had a nice meeting with Dr. Cahlon today. He seems very competent and is extremely compassionate. Monday is busy as Ginny has her blood checked at the Cancer Center at 9:30AM. Then we see Dr. Bauman who is a pain specialist at the Hunterdon Medical Center at 10:30 AM. Then on Tuesday at 11:00 AM Ginny has her MRI and is scanned for an hour to make a map of her insides. Then Dr. Cahlon meets with a physicist to plan the actual radiation. The Doctor seemed confident that the odds are that he can stop the pain considerably. In 60-70% of the cases there is relief. What about the other 40-30%? The radiation will be for about three weeks and maybe more and lasts an hour. We will see. They like to go with it Monday to Friday. On Wednesday they do the radiation and also chemo for about an hour-expect hair loss. In short, we are going to try to have a pain free result but will be very, very busy for at least the next month. The good effects of the radiation take 2-3 weeks to be achieved. Biggest drawback? Nausea. I think they should give us a parking place at the Cancer Center!!!! Anyway, the thought is that the radiation will decrease the size of the tumor on the pancreas and the ensuing pressure on a nerve near the pancreas. We hope to try to go to Virginia mid-next week, see Amelia and meet Ben. Hope all comes together for that. See, with cancer, even simple things are complicated. So hug the one you are with and be happy that life at times is uncomplicated and that you have what you have. It can be taken away in a flash.

Pain Go Away
Tue, Oct 11, 2011 01:32PM

Well good morning to you all. Today we go to the Hunterdon Cancer Center and the radiation department will do the mapping of Ginny in preparation for the radiation efforts which will begin soon. Hope it works in the end. Last night's pain was pretty severe and is clearly related to a number of things, including Ginny's bowels. You must be so sick of hearing about bowels. Anyway, we had a wonderful meeting yesterday with the pain doctor, Susan Bauman, MD. I even called her this morning since Ginny had pain issues that concerned me and she called back quickly with suggestions. So the team expands. Although the pancreatic cancer is very important to deal with, the pain concept has taken on equal importance.

The radiation oncologist and the pain specialist will have a very important role in the future as quality of life needs to take precedence over longevity.

I did get additional information from the oncologist, Dr. Bednar. He indicated that next Monday he wanted Ginny to do the usual chemotherapy for the three days with the infusion pump (oh happy days) as it is unclear when the radiation oncologist would have the plan of attack put together. Then the following week during radiation there would be a shift to the Gemzar chemotherapy on a limited basis, one hour once a week I think. I was wrong about the hair loss and there will only be a thinning of the hair-much as is the situation today. To combat nausea the old reliable Sancuso patch may be used in conjunction with other medication. Dr. Bednar seemed to feel that not only would the radiation have a beneficial effect in alleviating the pain, but would also help in improving Ginny's overall fight against the cancer as cancer cells do get zapped.

So my friends, as we travel this road seeking to avoid perdition, we must hope that in a couple of weeks this battle against pain will be won. Pain is an amorphous concept, but nonetheless is very real, especially in Ginny's form of cancer. We have much on our plate to deal with right now, and how I wish it were just a nice fillet mignon, asparagus, and mashed potatoes!

Montezuma's Revenge
Tue, Oct 18, 2011 12:15 AM

A lot has happened since my last e-mail/note to you all. We were able to take the trip to Staunton to hug and love Amelia and of course do likewise with dear little Benjamin for the first time. We are so lucky to have these two beautiful grandchildren. The trip down South was okay but Ginny did have some lower intestinal issues and we did make a number of rest room stops. All Ginny wanted to do was hug her grandchildren. That is not asking too much. The meeting of Ben and everyone was just perfect. Friday turned out to be the day Montezuma's Revenge kicked in but David and Lena were very understanding as was

Amelia. Ben just was Ben! We had a great day overall. I can truthfully say I ate too much! We left Saturday and Ginny was fine. Sunday had a few more issues as if the cancer gods (lower case on purpose) had to have a little more "fun" with Ginny. Nancy brought over a meal Sunday which would knock your socks off together with some homemade apple pie. We went to see Dr. Bauman today, October 17, 2011, and she made some suggestions to help with the pain. That is her specialty. There is a delicate balance in chemotherapy as they try to kill you and help you at the same time. Then we saw Dr. Bednar and Ginny had about 1.5 hours of chemotherapy-Gemzar (Abbreviated Round Ten). It apparently is not as effective as her 5 FU mixture in fighting the cancer, but it is good with the radiation which will be started tomorrow. 5 FU is a three day regime, 24 hours a day as opposed to 1.5 hours. After a short trip to the pharmacy to get extra pain and other medication, we got home. It was a very tiring and full day. I then did a little restoration work (with the help of my son Mark) at the office and Ginny rested as one of the side effects of Gemzar is/are flu-like symptoms. The Gemzar will be every Monday AM just before radiation. Tomorrow the radiation battle begins and Dr. Cahlon is in charge of all of that. Due to the lower intestinal issues Ginny has lost even more weight but she is doing what she can. No more can be expected. So that is where we are today. We want to be optimistic and try to do another trip to Staunton if the radiation helps to deaden the pain through shrinking the main pancreatic tumor.

A couple of days ago my mother passed away at the age of 89 years from Alzheimer's disease. It adds stress to this entire situation but my priorities must be with my wife and they are. To a certain person, you know who you are- thanks for the lovely dinner which appeared at our door. Most people tell Ginny she looks great. As she says, BS. Ever since the diagnosis she has had more compliments on her appearance than in her entire life!!!! Ginny can tell you her view on that! I could say much more but I am tired and mentally drained right now. Hug someone you care about today.

First week of radiation almost done
Thu, Oct 20, 2011 09:18PM

Good day every one. I thought that I would bring you up to date on the radiation experience. Ginny has completed her third radiation session. The actual radiation is about 10-15 minutes in total time. The prep work and the drive down to and from the hospital of course makes it take much longer. The effects of radiation are cumulative so each time there is a radiation, the tiredness etc. gets worse and worse. So far no nausea.

Right now Ginny is sitting in her chair with her eyes shut, just resting as best she is able. She is quite the fighter. It is interesting to note that at first Dr. Cahlon was going to do three basic attacks on the pancreatic tumor-attack it one third each time. That has changed. Now Dr. Cahlon is having the radiation move all over the tumor in very small increments in the hope that it will be more effective. Instead of one-third at a time with three passes at the tumor, there will be maybe fifty passes at the tumor in very small increments. It will take quite a while to see if this is working to relieve Ginny's pain. Also, an MRI will be taken about two to three weeks after the radiation is ended. At that time a decision will be made whether further radiation is appropriate. Ginny and I are very tired. Ginny has to go through the "treatment" and has the worry, stress, and knowledge that there is no cure. As a caregiver, I worry of course, but want to make sure I do all I am able for Ginny. We are two tired people, both physically and emotionally. Cancer treatment is difficult at best. Cancer treatment knowing there is no possibility of cure is even worse. However, we do not give up.

My mother will be interred on November 5th and I choose not to be there based on all the things happening now. Such is life. We deal with it. For those with miracles in their bags, feel free to let one fly out toward Clinton, NJ!

Second radiation week-10/25/11
Tue, Oct 25, 2011 02:14PM

The second week of radiation began yesterday. Actually, we again need a permanent parking space at the Cancer Center!! We started by seeing the pain Doctor, Susan Bauman. She is really sweet and caring. We like her a lot. Ginny's pain has diminished what with an increase in the pain medication. I do not care about the increase in medication but only the lessening of the pain. Afterward Ginny had a little over an hour of the Gemzar chemotherapy followed by the radiation at 2:30 PM. Without getting too specific, Ginny did put on a pound which is good. Also, some minor sores are developing where her beautiful bony frame hits certain clothing, but ointment and a bandage works well with dealing that.

Overall yesterday was a very nice day and really nice for us, albeit tiring. I did run off to Court in Raritan Borough for a little bit of time. Yes, I am practicing a little law on the side. Today seems to be good so far so keep your fingers crossed. The weekend was difficult and worse. Ginny was lethargic and pretty much smacked from the radiation which is to be expected. Actually I was surprised with how well she felt yesterday. Even had a lovely woman come to our house to cut her hair and have some womanly chit chat. Sunday, but for a nice visit from Ang and Mark, Ginny spent most of her time in her living room chair just resting with her eyes closed. Saturday was similar. I was able to get the entire house pretty clean considering I did it. Received some lovely cards and e-mails from friends which were quite sweet. It gets difficult to keep "up" for any long period of time. We keep trying. So, another eleven daily radiation treatments to go with chemo once a week on Mondays. Thereafter, back to perdition-the 5 FU cocktail every two weeks for three days. Enjoy the lovely fall weather we are having. It is quite pleasant. I am trying to be cautiously optimistic today and will see what happens. Ginny and I are usually quite private people so it gets a little lonely at times; but that is okay. We are off at about 1 PM today to attend to our hospital routine and pick up some more drugs.

What a day 10/26/11
Wed, Oct 26, 2011 10:37 PM

The saga continues.

Today was really a bad day. Ginny awoke totally exhausted and in pain. She even had some doubts if all the things being done to her were worthwhile. Emotions were running quite high as were the tears. This happens in cancer situations. I called Doctor Bauman, the pain doctor, and like the angel she is, she called back quickly and had a nice talk with Ginny. The pain medications were increased a tad and she gave some ideas about how to deal with the situation. That was a good thing. I took Ginny to the Hunterdon Medical Center a little early, 12:30 PM, as I had to drop the Subaru off for a recall repair, so I dropped the car off and jogged from the dealership back to the Hunterdon Medical Center to attend to Ginny. Ginny's blood was drawn and her platelet count was 17, or as they say, low. I was advised that the chemotherapy Gemzar causes this and is a platelet eater. Dr. Bednar said that he wanted Ginny to get some platelets tomorrow. Then we went off to the radiation department to have that process taken care of properly and we waited a little. Low and behold Doctor Bauman had contacted a Social Worker to discuss things with Ginny. Her name is Nancy Robins. Ginny and she had a very nice talk (I was out getting the car back from the Subaru Dealership) and Ginny and Nancy will continue those discussions next week. Ginny really needs to talk to someone who has had experience with her condition to help her emotionally. I guess we have got to learn to reach out to friends or professionals for help at times which is very difficult for us to do.

After the radiation, Doctor Cahlon spoke to us and told us that what Ginny was experiencing was typical. The pancreas gets angry when you attack it with radiation and chemotherapy and was probably swollen and in general, was just pissed off. After the radiation ends on November 8th and the pancreas has a chance to heal a bit, the odds are that Ginny should feel much better. We will see as no one ever knows for sure. Thereafter we went to the Admitting Office of the hospital where they technically admitted Ginny and we went up to the blood lab to have Ginny typed and whatever. That took a while and by about 4:45 PM we got home. Tomorrow we must go back to the Cancer Center at 2:30PM for more radiation but also have to be there no later than 8:30AM where they will do further testing on the platelets and eventually give Ginny more platelets. The entire process will probably take all day again. Friday it is back to the Cancer Center for more radiation and blood work re the platelets. The team approach to cancer care is not only great but necessary. Clearly we were both a tad overwhelmed today. It is nice just to sit but the normal chores around the house seem to be in need of completion all the time. Unfortunately my eosinophilic esophagitis or EE has come back with a vengeance and my stomach is in quite a bit of distress. So, in a sense, Ginny and I are both experiencing issues right now in the stomach area! As I noticed presumably healthy people walking and jogging by our house when we got home, I envied them for their health. We really need a war on pancreatic and all cancers although it will not help our current situation. No one should have to go through this. Ever.

Well, that is all that I have to say about this topic for now. Actually, I have a lot more to say, but it is not printable in this forum. God bless America.

Catch 22 Again
Sat, Oct 29, 2011 03:09 PM

Catch 22 again. Nothing seems to go as planned in this cancer battle. Every time something seems to be going well, it turns around and goes bad. Tired of this to tell the truth. Anyway, Ginny did not have radiation on Thursday as her platelet count was just too low. So, Ginny was admitted to the hospital on Thursday to have one unit of platelets infused into her. Got there about 8:15 AM and did not leave until about 2 PM. The actual infusion took 45 minutes but all the prep and typing and crossing (no idea what that means) took a while. Then they give you stuff such as Benadryl to help in some way.

The Hunterdon Medical Center served Ginny a great lunch and the nurses in this Magnet Nurse Hospital are superb. They all were so happy, professional, and caring. That is good! The platelets are yellow/brown, more yellow than brown, and an IV gets them into you. Anyway, when we left 3 West to go to the Cancer Center, I was told that Dr. Cahlon did not want to do a radiation today (Thursday 10/27/11) because Ginny's platelet count was 17 before the infusion which was too low. Ginny felt pretty good the entire day and night Thursday. On Friday (10/28/11) we arrived at the Cancer Center and they did do the radiation but the platelet count had only climbed to 37. So, Ginny is to rest this weekend and on Monday, there will be NO Gemzar chemotherapy apparently. We will meet with Dr. Bednar to come up with a plan as it is clear that Ginny is not accepting the Gemzar as well as hoped. Since platelets are in the bones, the Gemzar is screwing them up-the platelets that is. If you think of the Atari game called Pac Man, which is what is happening to Ginny's platelets. We do not know if Ginny will have more radiation on Monday. So, of the sixteen radiation sessions, Ginny has only had eight of them. Perhaps they will adjust the amount of Gemzar. Perhaps they will give Ginny more platelets. We do not know. This morning Ginny awoke feeling quite crappy as is usually the case. Mornings are particularly bad for her. A good portion of the underside of her lower left arm is particularly black and blue, probably due to the platelet situation. So, we will try to get through this weekend as best as possible and await Ginny's fate on Monday at 1 PM. Enough said.

By the way, thank you to all the kind people who continue to send cards and letters, gifts, and food. You are all very sweet and your thoughts are appreciated.

Fate
Tue, Nov 01, 2011 03:32 PM

Another victim of fate. There is clearly a conspiracy to take this side of the Rylak family down but we will keep fighting. Saturday afternoon was a good afternoon and Sunday was fantastic. Ginny and I even did a little shopping for some gifts for Amelia and Benjamin at The Cracker Barrel. Of course, that did not last as on Monday AM things took a turn for the worse. Ginny just felt like garbage. That is the beauty of pancreatic cancer. It usually wins. Anyway, we arrived at the Cancer Center to find that Ginny's doctor had been called away on an emergency so we were seen by a Nurse Practitioner named Pat. She was very nice but had no idea that chemo was to be canceled and a "plan" put in place to deal with Ginny's low platelet count due to Gemzar. That means to me either to give Ginny platelets or to reduce the amount of Gemzar which loves to eat platelets. Another doctor relayed the message that the chemotherapy would be held off until next Monday and no more. I do not fault him as he was not present when I had discussions last week re the "plan". That plan was not a "plan". Anyway, I spoke up a little but let it pass. We then went over to radiation and were told that Ginny would have the radiation as her platelet count was not under 10. I know that Gemzar helps the radiation kill the tumor so I decided to press the issue. The radiation nurse agreed with me and was quite vocal about essentially not holding up the radiation treatment. So, after a bit it was decided to give Ginny another blood test today (Tuesday 11/1/11) and if the platelets were too low, to at least consider putting Ginny in the hospital to give her additional platelets as per last Thursday. The oncologist understood the issue once it was put correctly to him. Then they could then continue radiation. So I felt better and Ginny was off for the radiation. Unfortunately I could not let this go completely as we are dealing with my lady here, so I pressed a little further and thanked the radiation nurse profusely for fighting for Ginny on this issue. After radiation we arrived home and were a tad down. There were some tears at times. A knock at the door was heard and my faith in humanity was again restored. A wonderful neighbor arrived with a turkey dinner and turkey soup. Ginny and I both gave her a big hug. Although Ginny was only able to eat the soup, it was a hearty soup and she felt better for a while. Then she was emotionally drained again due to the radiation I am sure. This AM Ginny was really tired which is a typical cumulative consequence of the radiation treatment. She has spent most of the morning in her chair and just now is taking her shower/bath etc. to get ready for another trip to the Cancer Center in two hours. They will draw blood and determine the platelet count. If the platelet number is 10 or lower there will be no radiation. Then I hope we discuss what to do to increase those platelets. If the platelets have gone up, then maybe I can get them to not only give radiation but Gemzar when medically appropriate in a day or so. At least Ginny's lower intestinal tract is functioning today which can be quite problematic. Ginny is so very anxious to speak to her best friend Ginny but as of 10 minutes ago, simply did not have the energy to do so. So, off we go into the wild blue yonder with a great sense of uncertainty as to what is going to happen next; or not happen next. The diagnosis breeds certainty in end result but these daily issues make a bad situation worse. And that is all I have to say about this today.

A twist
Sat, Nov 5, 2011 05:42 PM

Well, here it is Saturday November 5th, 2011 and we have a twist. Previously I described our lovely Tuesday at the Hunterdon Regional Cancer Center. Wednesday did come about and Ginny was in the hospital most of the day having a platelet transfusion. Think about what this dear woman is going through. She seemed quite good and I was pleased as was she. No chemotherapy. No radiation. Good times. Thursday came and Ginny felt quite good until the afternoon. Radiation number ten took place but there were intermittent tears and a serious question as to whether all this was to be continued. The down feeling and stomach pain continued into Friday when the eleventh radiation took place. Five more to go!! On Friday evening Ginny felt great and the stomach pain seemed to have gone away. In short, we assumed that the chemotherapy and radiation were working and the road to remission and

Valhalla were approaching. Wrong!!!

So today is Saturday and Ginny woke up feeling wonderfully. She needs good days. All was well today until about 9 AM. Then the twist occurred. Vomit. So, on two occasions, the second being at noon, the God/Goddess of Radiation decided to interpose his/her will. Not since the diagnosis on May16th has this occurred so we have a twist. Dr. Cahlon had told us that this might happen as the effects of radiation accumulate. Also, the tumor which is being radiated is right near the stomach and causes the pain and also gets some of the residual radiation. So, the question is whether Ginny can do the final five radiation sessions next week and remain in one piece. Other than "chucking up" her guts once in a while, Ginny feels pretty good but of course, she refuses to put food in her body at this time. A new medication has been added to supplement the Sancuso patch (to avoid nausea) and that is called Compazine which does the same thing but a different way. My brother Frank and his wife Julie came east from California for my mother's interment today and will stop over; we will see if Ginny is up for it. I am glad that I did not attend the interment as I am needed here right now and my mother would understand. Let us hope that the stomach pain stays away, that the nausea and vomit end, and that Ginny has a good couple of half days until Monday when they give her Gemzar chemotherapy again as well as radiation, all assuming her platelet count is acceptable. That is it for now. The beat goes on.

Al is peaking out. We need change.
Wed, Nov 09, 2011 04:20PM

Saturday 10/29/11 turned out to be okay. Ginny spent most of the time exhausted and Frank and Julie and Mark and Ang did stop over and we had a good time. The stomach effects eventually subsided at bedtime. Sunday was a really great day. So as to avoid consistency, Monday was a day of exhaustion and badness. Ginny had her Gemzar chemotherapy and radiation. They must have given Ginny some steroids then as she had the most fantastic day ever on Tuesday. We even went out to look at the great weather and shop for a few items. Ginny had gained six pounds from her lowest weight which was good. Radiation was no problem at all. It was as if Ginny was just Ginny sans the cancer.

We sold the office the office yesterday so I was not around too much in the AM as I was at the closing, but when I would call, Ginny said she was just fine. The boys Skyped and Ben and Amelia just made us both smile. And then today came, Wednesday, 11/9/11. Ginny feels like crap and understandably so. The pain medications clog up your system and the ensuing constipation exacerbates the pain. That is why God invented prune juice and the chemical companies invented Miralax. It seems as if Ginny's pain cycle is directly related to her stomach/intestines. So we wait and prepare for radiation at 2:30 PM feeling poorly and somewhat teary and if you are me, angry, that my sweet Ginny has to go through all of this for no good reason. To top it off, the telephone rang and it was the Hunterdon Medical Center. I feared it had something to do with Ginny's Mom, Gra, so when they asked for Ginny I gave her the telephone. The call had nothing to do with dear old Gra (aged 99 years) but was a bill collector from HMC dunning my wife. When I realized this Ginny gave me the telephone and I "chatted" with the woman on the other end of the line. She explained that Ginny had not paid a $125 bill on November 2nd for a procedure; and on one other time as well. She wanted me to pay those two bills by credit card now. She was very nice mostly, but I told her that as my wife had pancreatic cancer she did not need to be dunned by bill collectors; that we always pay our bills; that I had never gotten a bill on these; and that as a member of the Board of Trustees of the entire

Hunterdon Healthcare System I always pay my bills. I also indicated that I do not give my credit card information to persons randomly calling me on the telephone. I asked what the bill was for-she did not know. Candidly, I was testy and irritated, telling her to never call my wife again re bills and to note that on her file, i.e., that all calls were to be directed to me. As I said above, Al is peaking out. They will send me a bill for the money owed and I will pay it; not my problem that someone forgot to collect moneys allegedly due at the time of platelet service or whatever it was.

Ginny still feels terrible, so the pancreatic cancer gods win another battle. The frustration of all of this can be overwhelming and I think you can see that the ups and downs of your emotions make it even more difficult. So we hope that nature takes her course and that Ginny feels better before the radiation today. Thereafter Ginny has two more radiations, one on Thursday and one on Friday. Then radiation is done. Chemotherapy of the Gemzar variety will be given on Monday afternoon, November 14th, the same day the Maid Brigade arrives to clean the house. I do not do cleaning very well but it has gotten done in my way. Then I think Ginny has a couple of weeks off until Thanksgiving so her pancreas and stomach can relax and feel happy. Then some form of chemotherapy will take place and Dr. Bednar will do at CT scan or MRI to see if the radiation has diminished the size of the tumor on the pancreas and hence alleviated pain, and also if the Pancreatic cancer on the liver, spleen, and adrenals, is still in an improved state or has gotten worse. At that time we will see Doctor Cahlon again to determine if radiation is really to be done.

So there you have it for today. Al is peaking out and change is needed in the entire billing and payment process for health care. But that is for another day. And I would not mess with me today!

Sunday 11/13/11

Since my last e-mail to you a couple of wonderful people have brought over some delicious meals which have been very good for Ginny and for me. People are not afraid to look me in the eyes when they talk about Ginny and what we are going through; that is a good change. I guess our true friends accept the fact that when you are diagnosed with pancreatic cancer, your chances of living a year are less than 75%. Your chances of hitting the 5 year mark are about 5%. So, it is a horrifying and deadly disease. Reality is reality. We just have to deal with it.

The radiation sessions on Thursday and Friday went well. No real problem. Sixteen radiations are done and now it will take a couple of weeks for the stomach area and the pancreas to try to heal up a bit. We can then see if the main tumor on the pancreas has diminished in size and hence the pain level has diminished as well. Effects of the radiation can last for weeks. After we returned home on Friday Ginny felt pretty good. Then of course Mr. Vomit decided to make an appearance. A very nice and happy day had unexpected yet expected consequences. Drat. We got through that until Saturday when on three occasions he appeared again. The concept of consuming food was difficult for Ginny and the overwhelming sense of tiredness/fatigue appeared. This is normal stuff and Ginny spent most of her time in her chair letting the medication work. Later we did go out to The Cracker Barrel to get a few things. Then today appeared and Ginny had a very bad morning. It was hurtful, sore, frustrating, and tiring. Teary as well. Somewhere along the line I heard a phrase that Ginny might not want to go through all this pain any more. It passed fortunately. Early afternoon Ginny felt so much better that she even was on the telephone with our boys and her best friend, Ginny. As I type this e-mail she is reading the paper and has eaten a bit. A therapist who is part of the Team at the Hunterdon cancer Center called to talk to Ginny at one point but I/we advised her that a talk was not necessary. All Ginny needed to do was feel well enough to chat with people that know and love her. She did that today and apparently was right.

I cannot help but wonder how people dealt with this disease prior to the advent of pain medication. Even though it is terrible today, it must have been so much worse a couple of hundred years ago; unbearable. Anyway, tomorrow the Maid Brigade arrives to clean to house in a fashion better than I am able and we leave for Gemzar chemotherapy at 12:30 PM. After a blood test re the red and white cells and platelets, Ginny will meet with Dr. Bednar to see how things are going. Assuming all is well, chemotherapy will ensue; perhaps there will be a surprise. Remember that Gemzar chemotherapy is only an hour unlike the three day 5 FU version.

Perhaps this will be the last chemotherapy until after Thanksgiving so as to give Ginny a rest from all that has been happening since 5/16/11. We hope to try to get down to Virginia for Thanksgiving if possible as Amelia and Benjamin really need to see us!! As to me and my feelings and thoughts ask me no questions and I will tell you no lies.

Albert D.

Sixth month anniversary.
Wednesday November 16, 2011 06:08 PM

Most anniversaries are pleasant and nice. We celebrate them happily. On May 16, 2011 Ginny was diagnosed with stage four pancreatic cancer. Today is November 16, 2011. I celebrate nothing.

The Maid Brigade came Monday at about 8:30 AM and spent almost three hours doing a very nice job in cleaning everything quite nicely about the house. They are a tad expensive, but certainly things needed to be done and they are now done.

We arrived at the Hunterdon cancer Center on Monday and Ginny was given her usual blood tests etc. prior to chemotherapy starting about 1:30PM. During chemotherapy our dear friend Nancy Mathews visited Ginny at the infusion room and spent about an hour with her. I left for most of the time but could see that Ginny was feeling well and was having nice "woman to woman talk" with Nancy. Nancy has been through this before and it was helpful for Ginny to chat and brag about her two grandchildren. Eventually we left for home after 3:30PM. The rest of the day was nice and all seemed well. Then the Devil came to Town on Tuesday, 11/15/11. It was a bad day for Ginny and me as well. The fatigue was horrific and the pain demonstrable. Ginny had a totally crappy day; could not even chat with our sons for more than a few minutes. I had an unexpected invitation to brunch and went with a friend; feel guilty about leaving Ginny alone but it was a very nice gesture on his part. Most of my friends are afraid to call as I understand that they know the conversation will be sad and unpleasant. Somehow we got through Tuesday and here we are today, Wednesday. It has been worse than yesterday. Today is mostly pain. With pain comes a desire to NOT eat and just sit; sadness sets in. We had enough of this and went to the Hunterdon Cancer Center this morning and all they could recommend was more pain medicine, which I expected. Even Dr. Bauman, our pain doctor, was kind enough to call and reinforce the added "breakthrough" pain medication concept. So we will try that. I suspect that the pancreas is really irate right now and will try to punish Ginny as best as it is able because of the prior radiation the past few weeks and the Gemzar chemotherapy delivered on Monday. The Devil indeed has come to Town and will leave when he is ready.

So! It is anniversary time here at the Rylak household. Send us no cards or good wishes. Since I do not have anything nice to say about this anniversary and since some of my comments might offend sensitive ears I will end this note now.

Thanksgiving
Tue, Nov 22, 2011 08:40 PM

Well, since my last e-note Ginny has had perhaps two good days. On one of them we even went out to shop for a couple of things for Amelia. Not knowing what the realistic time Ginny has left she wants Amelia to be spoiled and will do so. The good days are marked by little or no pain and minimal fatigue. We still think the results of the radiation are evident today and hence although concerned, are not overly concerned. When I spoke with the radiation people they said the fatigue can last a month or so. Anyway, we must focus on the good days and not the bad days. We must hope that the main tumor on the pancreas has had its butt kicked very hard. We will know in a few weeks when they do the CT scan or whatever test is appropriate.

Thanksgiving will be here in two days. We all have a lot to be thankful for. Although I did not celebrate the 6 month anniversary of this thing we fight, I do celebrate Thanksgiving. Ginny agrees. For one thing, Ginny is still here. For another, Ang, Mark, and the two of us will be in Staunton to have a great time together as a family with Amelia and Benjamin. Oh yes, David and Lena too as well as Jordis the dog and Minnie the cat and the two fish named Cat and Bluto will be there as well. I intend to eat and drink well and hope that Ginny gets some of the dinner down in her belly.

With a little luck Ginny and I will leave for Staunton tomorrow; Mark and Ang on Thursday. We will stay at the Hampton Inn as it is nice for Ginny to be able to have the time and space she requires, particularly in the morning.

We will be packed later today and what with the medications Ginny requires I hope we are not stopped by the police for any purpose. The medications are numerous and expensive. There ought to be a program that helps people with catastrophic illness fund their medical expenses. We are fortunate to be able to handle this cost but what of the millions of people whom are in a different position? This old conservative Republican sees the need to modify our healthcare system at least in these types of cases.

So have a very happy Thanksgiving. Ginny and I are blessed to have great family and friends, only a few of which have received these notes. Your friendship and concern are much appreciated. Feel free to toast the main lady of this family at your Thanksgiving dinner and let us hope that there are other major events to follow. I must admit the difficulty in maintaining an upbeat attitude at times. Nonetheless, there are forces far stronger than I that control this situation and I keep hoping that there is "hope" and not just "wish".

Wonderful Thanksgiving
Sun, Nov 27, 2011 03:14PM

Well, our trip to Staunton, VA was quite nice. We left Wednesday, November 23, 2011, and made the trip South sans any real problems, arriving about 3PM. Although Ginny felt a little yucky at the outset of the trip, we only made two rest stops and all was fine. Arriving at the Fairless/

Rylak house was a joy and Amelia seemed so very happy to see us (the adults too). Benjamin was just beautiful. Jordis is the most outstanding dog I have ever seen and even she was happy to see us! We were treated to a very nice dinner of grilled chicken and grilled green beans and Ginny ate quite a large amount of all of it! I was surprised at her ability to consume! We had a good night at the Hampton Inn at Waynesboro/ Stewart's Draft near the hospital where David works as an ER doctor. We were tired, filled, and happy to be in Virginia. Only one emotional moment of sadness when we thought if this was our last Thanksgiving as the family is currently constituted; we were able to push through that however. And yes, Amelia did have a good time swimming in the hotel pool and being with her Grandma in the hotel room. So Wednesday was a good day.

Thanksgiving arrived and so did Mark and Ang. We had the entire family together for the first time since Mark's and Ang's wedding a couple of years ago. It was clear that Lena and David had really gone to a lot of trouble for Thanksgiving Day and the entire time we were visiting. Although Ginny had some stomach pain, most of the day was just wonderful. We met Lena's friend Jackie and she made a delicious pumpkin soup. The table was filled with delicious food and yes, Ginny again ate wonderfully. At her 86 pounds, that is a good thing. The main course and all the desserts were just outstanding. So we had another good day. And yes, at assorted times on Thanksgiving and each day we were in Staunton we all participated in, or watched, the following: tractor driving, croquette, chain sawing, bocce ball; shotgun shooting, rifle shooting, a visit to Staunton to "pick", playing basketball, skeet shooting, and in general, just doing or watching fun things. Mark and Ang had never driven a tractor before and never shot a gun before either. It amazes me that they are really such rednecks now!

On Friday Ginny was quite tired in the AM. Fatigue probably due to all the activity and the radiation as well. So Ginny spent the AM at the hotel resting. The afternoon and evening were quite good and Amelia and Ginny really bonded again so nicely. Benjamin and I got to know each other quite well with our numerous long walks all the time we were there. Amelia made a point to take us all to her huge basement to show us all her stuff and danced beneath her lighted disco ball, let us push her on her swing, kicked and threw balls and in general took charge of her territory. She enjoyed showing everyone her basement, with its playrooms, bedroom, worm farm, cardboard boat, etc. She also enjoyed showing Ang and Mark her upstairs bedroom.

We left Saturday for Clinton about 12:30PM. On our way from the hotel to Niswander Road, the cancer (Note the lower case "c" from now on so as to diminish its importance from this point forward) or radiation appeared again as Victor Vomit, and we settled on the side of the road for a bit. Nonetheless we got through this and were able to get to see our children, our daughters-in-love (not a misspelling) and grandchildren again and had a very nice rest of the morning. The spirited bocce ball contest between David and Mark was a highlight for us all. I really enjoyed long walks with Benjamin. Amelia sat in her Grandma's arms for a considerable time which was beautiful. More food was consumed and the chili on Saturday was just as good as all the meals we were given.

Then we left with tears of happiness and sadness and now here we are in Clinton. We had such a good time with so many memories. David and Lena really did go out of their way to insure that everyone had a great time and we thank them so much. We all knew that it was our last Thanksgiving together. Usually Ginny and I were the ones who cooked the Thanksgiving dinner, did the entertaining, etc. We did not have to lift a finger. We are two very lucky people even in the current circumstances.

Tomorrow, Monday, November 28, 2011, another round of chemotherapy (number 14 I think) begins after blood work at 1:30PM and reality once again enters the picture. At least Ginny had a few good days!

At least we were like it was meant to be. A special thank you to David, Lena, Mark, Ang, Amelia and Benjamin. What a great family!!!!

Emotional roller coaster ride.
Tue, Nov 29, 2011 10:00 PM

The roller coaster ride never ends when dealing with cancer. The harder you try to be emotionally strong, the more difficult it becomes. It is as if there is a very bad aura out there trying to do nasty things to you. And so it goes.

After our arrival in Clinton on Saturday evening, Ginny and I felt so great to have had such a nice time with the family in Staunton. Sunday arrived and Ginny felt "okay" and was cheered up when Mark and Ang stopped over to show us their pieces of smooth "river glass", literally found alongside a river. We ended up having a very nice dinner together and felt pretty good. Also, Ginny's best friend since childhood called Ginny and they had a great conversation. Lovely angels called as well Saturday and Sunday and cooked meals were given to us. You know, I never knew how important it was to give prepared food to ill persons and their families. We are able to buy food of course, but there is something so special about a meal that has been prepared with TLC--and I am unable to do that still!

On Monday Ginny felt pretty poorly and of course we had to go to the

Hunterdon cancer Center to have poison pumped into her body. Nancy was so gracious to come and stay with Ginny during most of the chemotherapy and Ginny was able to show her pictures of our time in Staunton. Ginny seemed to perk up quite a bit. I was really unable to be much help to Ginny on Monday for unknown reasons. Fell asleep in my chair after dinner and slept until bed time. Then I overslept until 5 AM. Bottom line I guess I was a little exhausted.

And then today (Tuesday 11/29/11) arrived. I did not know what to expect. Our Staunton and Bedminster family had a half cord of wood delivered in the morning which was stacked neatly on our porch for the fireplace. I had neglected to mention in my prior note that David had a fire burning every day we were in Staunton and it really warmed Ginny's somewhat demure body. Ginny felt wonderful all day today. The old Ginny was/is back and seemed to have energy and less pain. Sweet. Warmth is a good thing. Also, Mark arrived and helped me clean the house and change the bedding. We are so very lucky people!

So, this cancer thing really affects you in inconsistent and unpredictable ways. I remember when a dear friend had melanoma on her leg. Ginny was devastated for her friend's condition and so upset that tears flowed. After biopsy and other tests of her friend, Ginny cried again when she found out that the melanoma was localized and had not metastasized to other areas. And so life goes on. The end result of this stage 4 pancreatic cancer is known. Let us hope that Ginny's genes (her Mom is 99 years old) and Doctor Bednar and the entire team working with us help in the fight to let her remain with us as long as long can be!

Some good times but a sad happening as well.
Sat, Dec 03, 2011 05:01PM

The past Wednesday and Thursday (11/30/11-12/1/11) were what we expected. Bad days. The chemotherapy had to have its effect and there it was in all of its pristine beauty. Even called the pain doctor, Doctor Susan Bauman, on one occasion as that is the issue. Nonetheless I got the porch tree and wreaths up to have some Christmas spirit about the house. And yes, the fires continue unabated.

Friday started out pretty good and was a great day overall. Natasha Nausea reared her ugly head on two occasions but her effect was minimal. We got out of the house and stopped at T.J. Max and the Cracker Barrel, getting some Christmas gifts. Saw Nancy and Carol which was pleasant for the two of us. The Town of Clinton Christmas Parade also took place and we sat inside the warm house and watched a good portion of it go by. We also had some wonderful chicken soup from a dear friend. So, we had a nice Friday.
Only one problem Friday was that we saw in the Hunterdon County Democrat that Dorothy died. Who was Dorothy? Dorothy was a sweet and wonderful lady with a great smile and the bluest eyes you ever saw. We met her at the cancer Center as she had been diagnosed with stage IV pancreatic cancer in January 2011. It brings reality to the forefront once again. We were devastated. I called her husband Russell to express our condolences and he was just wonderful saying that he had thought of Ginny and was praying that her fate differ. I thanked him.

So, today is Saturday and Ginny awoke with a lot of pain in her stomach area. How can this happen? Don't ask don't tell. We are hopeful that Ginny feels better later and that we are able to get out of the house and shop, look around, and in general have a good day. We also have a little more Christmas decorating to do. We have decided not to send Christmas cards and will limit our gifting for now. That is a big change as we love to give cards and gifts to family and friends.

Ginny's schedule for the rest of the year will be chemotherapy on Monday, 12/5/11, and Monday, 12/12/11. She will see Dr. Oren Cahlon the radiation oncologist on Thursday, 12/15/11, and have an MRI on Monday, 12/19/11. We hope to leave for Virginia after the MRI on the 19th if possible and spend time with an early celebration of Christmas with David, Lena, Amelia, and Benjamin. We should be back on the 22nd and thereafter have another Christmas with Mark and Ang. That is it for cancer stuff for 2011--except the all important part of getting the results of the MRI. That will really be important as we will know if the radiation helped reduce the size of the tumor and if the cancer has spread. This plan is subject to change at any time as you know. All depends on how Ginny feels.

So there you have it. I am done talking about cancer for a while. I hope.

Update again
Tue, Dec 06, 2011 04:25 PM

Well this is getting silly. Nothing remains constant and when you are as anal as I, change is not appreciated or welcomed. Anyway, I wanted to bring you up to date as to the goings on here in Clinton relating to cancer and certain changes in our schedule that have occurred.

Saturday continued as I had predicted and was a crappy day for Ginny. Think pain. Sunday likewise was a day that the cancer God had his way with my little lady. We got through it as best we were able. The fire was burning all the time with the wood that David, Lena, Mark, Ang, Amelia, and Ben had given to Ginny as an early Christmas present.

Ginny won Monday, December 5, 2011 and even today so far things have been pretty damn good. So there cancer!!! I hate you.

So many friends have been so helpful and sweet. At the Hunterdon cancer Center yesterday Ginny had another round of chemotherapy with that Gemzar stuff. Nancy was sweet to sit with her for a while as well. Ginny was able to have "girl talk". Other persons at the infusion room stopped by and said hello as well. There is a certain collegiality in the infusion room as everyone knows to be extra kind as people are fighting very difficult battles. And they were. No one messes with cancer patients in the infusion room. People have been absolute Angels in dropping off meals and breads and the like. Even some people I do not even know. It is for that reason that Ginny's weight has gone up to 89.2 pounds. That is a 7 pound increase!!! Does it matter? Beats me but it is a fact and the amount of the Gemzar chemotherapy is determined by weight. Many e-mails have come in from people that missed seeing Ginny at the Christmas Parade here in Clinton last Friday.

The only problem yesterday was that Ginny's white blood count was quite low. So, a change in schedule was required. We will be at the cancer Center today at 3:45 PM for a special Neupogen shot, and likewise Wednesday at 2:30 PM, and Thursday at 2:30 PM for a similar experience. So, these three days were unexpected but necessary to get the levels up to where they belong. And Carol, that pea soup and quiche you made today will fill Ginny's belly tonight unless cancer chooses to cause problems.

Ginny next has the chemotherapy on Monday, December 12, 2011, and that is it for 2011 until she has the MRI. And yes, the MRI has been changed from December 15, 2011 and pushed to December 27, 2011 at 10:15 AM. That was Ginny's doing as she is not particularly excited about getting the results prior to Christmas. All of this necessitated changing the appointment with Dr. Cahlon, the radiation oncologist to December 30, 2011. In short, on that date we will know much more about the progression of Ginny's cancer or lack thereof and the effects of the radiation on the main tumor. And yes, the January 4, 2012 chemotherapy will continue, we will chat with Dr. Bednar, and start the New Year out with a big bang. Oh happy days.

We are definitely going to try to take that trip previously mentioned in another note to Staunton, VA. Amelia and Benjamin really need to see us. We will leave the 18th or 19th of December and spend a few days there. I am optimistic that Ginny will be able to make the trip and of course I will not go without her.

And so ends another note as to what cancer has caused this family to endure. I will continue to be polite so will end this note now knowing what the rest of this week will bring if consistency is the hobgoblin of little minds. And yes, although cancer may be very powerful, it has a very little mind if any at all.

Science trumps; always.

Mon, Dec 12, 2011 10:55 PM

Chemo was canceled today because Ginny's platelet count was too low. As mentioned previously, Gemzar causes this to happen. Science wins again. I am disappointed as I want as much as anyone to have Ginny be able to kill cancer cells. So, she will make up the chemotherapy after Christmas on December 28, 2011. The MRI is still scheduled for the 27th. Also, the first chemotherapy in 2012 is still scheduled for January 4th as well.

Anyway, Tuesday and Wednesday were both very bad days this week. Science wins again. Thursday was okay and the afternoon was better. Along came Friday and Saturday which were bad. Science wins again. Sunday was quite good and we did some shopping. Today okay. Our sons are in contact every day which is great, but at times Ginny had to end the conversation early as she was so tired. Such is the fight and the nature of our circumstances. The boys are very understanding. Ginny gets very teary eyed.

Why do I say "science wins again"? Well, I guess it is because in science and mathematics, there are fixed answers to problems. $1+1=2$. You either know the answer or not. In the Social sciences and liberal arts, the ability to BS an answer exists and there are not necessarily "correct" answers. Look at the political candidates' debate to see what I mean. So with cancer, the doctors, as scientists, know what the answers are. After today I was a little down. Dr. Bednar did not sugar coat anything and said to me upon questioning that there really were no new treatments present to help Ginny through this time. He is going to look at some more research, but I am not optimistic; nor is he. I cannot help but think that his goal is to try to keep my Ginny alive in the hope that new treatments (not cures) may come about. He stressed that the MRI will really show us where we are and what the next steps will be. We have known this all along. At that time we will see what the next stage of treatment will be. That can range from further chemotherapy, radiation, to Hospice to whatever. He said that pancreatic cancer treatment is really difficult. So what else is new?! Dr. Bednar was just being honest which is necessary and appropriate. So, the MRI results will answer many questions; more than we want to know perhaps.

So today, things were not particularly great. Science is entering into the equation more than I like. I cannot change it. Thank you to all the people who have been so supportive with kind words, ideas, food, concern, understanding, and even prayers. We are going to have a very nice Christmas no matter what. The cooked meals given to us this week were off the charts wonderful.

I did go to the Fireman's Banquet at Beaver Brook Country Club yesterday for a short time; I have represented them for 39 years. It just was not fun to be there without Ginny although everyone was as gracious as they could be. My dear friend Tony had invited me to his house for a Prosecutor's party, but I could not emotionally go there. In short, even though Ginny is trying to kick me out of the house at times, I did not wish to go. After all, it has been over fifty years since our first date and I have to have my priorities in order!! And I do.

So, today I am a little down and I apologize for that. On the other hand, we have some Christmas presents to wrap; dear sweet Amelia is in a play tonight in Virginia; a chicken pot pie is in the oven; and a fire roars in the fireplace. Not bad. Keep the prayers coming if you are of the religious persuasion. If not, kind thoughts are equally appreciated.

May the SHA not be with you.

Sat, Dec 17, 2011 03:40PM

Today is our first of two Christmas Eves this year until next week. We hope to leave for Virginia tomorrow and to celebrate Christmas a week early with our Virginia portion of the family; the following week with Mark and Ang. Time will tell. Sadly to say the odds are very good that this will not happen again so it is quite special. Ginny also changed her mind about gifts and wanted to make sure we gave some; so we got them!!

Tuesday, December 13, 2011, was an okay day. We went shopping and had a very nice time. What with the fire in the fireplace in the evening, all was very nice. We awoke with trepidation, but Wednesday turned out to be even better. So we shopped again and had a great time. I made sure Ginny did not notice the people staring at her as she was fast approaching 60 pounds. To you that stared at my lovely wife, how cruel. We then stopped at the Spinning Wheel Diner for a small meal-this was a big deal as we have only been out for a meal perhaps three times at most in the last 7 months. So many people dropped off food and cookies this week as well that at least I put on weight! Ginny did pretty well too, particularly with soup and cookies. Thank you all so very much.

Thursday, December 15, 2011 was an extra special day for us. Ginny felt quite weak but we had our dear friends Larry and Ginny up from the shore for a few hours. It was wonderful as we have been best friends forever. So the day started out poorly for some unknown cancer reason, and got better. We had wonderful talks and good food! It was sad saying goodbye as we both felt badly not knowing whether Ginny would be able to ever see them again. The odds were that this was the last time Ginny would see them. And it was.

Friday arrived on schedule and as most of you know, it was the seven month anniversary of Ginny's diagnosis. Overall I would call it a fair day with frustration as to what could have been. We were able to wrap a large number of the gifts we had purchased and that was fun but very tiring for Ginny. You see, the weakness caused by the radiation or the cancer continues unabated most of the time. Of course the boys have been great as have their wives, our daughters-in-love, Lena and Ang. Amelia is quite understanding and Benjamin did cooperate on Skype and withheld his tears!

So here we are with Saturday, December 17, 2011. Not a great start to the day but I have a feeling things will get better. Ginny is currently resting in her favorite chair and is allowing the pain medication to do its thing. Today will be okay. Have the car to pack, a few more gifts to wrap and a big fire to build in the evening. So optimism is high.

I wanted to talk about feelings or emotions for a minute. There are at least three major feelings one can get in dealing with Ginny's cancer. An enormous sense of sadness permeates the day; helplessness is evident as well, particularly when you are used to solving problems; lastly, a constant sense of anger which is non-dischargeable. I call this the "SHA". For seven months it has existed and will not end soon. Different cancers have different responses. The first type of cancer is the one that is or may be curable with treatment. One is alarmed and fearful, but the SHA can be minimized because there is hope. The second type of cancer involves one that cannot be cured, but with treatment can be managed for a long time. The SHA in that type of cancer is evident, and with a hard fight and some luck, can be mastered. The final type of cancer is the type we are dealing with, and that is the one that cannot be cured and may be managed but perhaps only for a very short time. There is no way to deal with the SHA in this situation. SHA is dominant and controls the situation for every hour you are awake. You simply try to live moment by moment. I have overly simplified this of course, but in large part I am right. May the SHA not be with you.

Back from Christmas in Staunton
Thu, Dec 22, 2011 02:45 PM

Well, we are back from a wonderful first Christmas of 2011 in Staunton;
our second Christmas of 2011 will be with Mark and Ang on or about the
25th of December. We had a good trip down on Sunday and the day
was quite nice too. David and Lena's house was perfectly decorated and
the Christmas tree looked wonderful. We had such great food every day.
I even gained a pound or two. It seemed that the mornings were bad for
Ginny, at least on Monday and Wednesday. But, after a few hours she
was much better. Ginny watched as David and I shot guns including a 10
gauge shotgun.   David and I even cut down a tall but skinny tree with the
chain saw. The weather was perfect.

What can I say about Amelia and Benjamin? Amelia was a dear and so
gentle with Ginny; she knows that Ginny is ill and likes to sit next to her
and cuddle up to her. When we exchanged gifts on Monday, Amelia was
in her glory; not just getting gifts, but distributing them to everyone. Such
fun. Benjamin has no idea as to what Christmas is of course, but he was
just a dear as well. Although Ginny was afraid to hold him and walk, she
did cradle Benjamin in her arms as Grandmas are want to do. And yes,
he looks just like me! Benjamin likes to be held and has started smiling at
us. David and Lena are such great parents and you can tell that they
adore their children so much. If nothing else, their parents (Fairless/Rylak)
must have left a fine impression raising them as they carried it over to their
children.

Leaving was quite difficult for obvious reasons. We know what the future
brings. The cancer battle will continue after Christmas Day this year and
ominous news will undoubtedly be forthcoming at the end of the year; I

hope I am wrong. Somehow we will get through all this in an appropriate way. Candidly, it still brings tears to our eyes to think of all of the future issues. Ginny has good times of course, but there are so many painful bad times. She keeps fighting as best as she is able. I perceive that she weakens a tad every week, but her spirit is indomitable. This will be our last Christmas in Virginia. So there you have it for now. Have a great day.

Schizophrenia
Mon, Dec 26, 2011 02:39 PM

Today I have happy things to report. Only one bad day since my last e-mail and that was on Saturday when we sadly had to cancel a visit from the Kearns Family. Friday was a very nice and optimistic day and Sunday, Christmas, was the best entire day that Ginny has had in months and months. We had Mark and Ang here, exchanged gifts, and had Ang and Mark put together a wonderful turkey dinner with all the fixings which they brought to our home. Mark and Ang really went out of their way to make memorable what would be Ginny's last Christmas ever. We had our old Ginny back for the entire day and she did not want to go to sleep Sunday evening. I have never seen Ginny eat so much; ever in 50 years. Cannot ask for more than that. We will see what today brings.

Believe it or not, we had Santa arrive at our house Friday night in a large fire truck dropping off a delicious coconut pound cake. Actually, there were four fire trucks outside the house with lights flashing and siren's blaring! Quite fantastic. There is nothing like small town America!!!

We are such lucky people to have the family and friends we are blessed with. They are the true gifts of this holiday. But for the kind acts of so many, I cannot say where we would be. So many people have just dropped off food and gifts, expecting nothing in return. Sometimes we do not even know the source of the cookies or other such item---they just appear. A nice e-mail comes unsolicited as do letters and cards. Our boys call daily. There truly is a Santa Claus Amelia and Ben; always remember that. We have to say thank you to all of you. For fear of missing a name, we just say thank you and look forward to 2012 with happiness to get to it, but with much trepidation as you might imagine.

Tomorrow, Tuesday, Ginny has an MRI scheduled at 10:15 AM. The makeup chemotherapy is on Wednesday at 10:30 AM. Friday we see Dr. Cahlon to discuss the size of the tumor on Ginny's pancreas and what the radiation did or did not do to it. Perhaps he will also tell us more about what the MRI showed. Finally, on Wednesday, January 4, 2012 we see Dr. Bednar, Ginny's oncologist, at 9:30AM, and Dr. Bednar will continue the chemotherapy and tell us more about her prognosis and expected treatment; or the next course of action if treatment is not in the cards.

I have given up trying to understand cancer. At least the pancreatic variety. Why one feels good or fair one day and horrible the next is an enigma followed by a conundrum. It just does not make any sense. It is for this reason that one must always be extra nice to those engaged in this type of battle for they are fighting or subject to demons few of us are able to understand.

For me, every holiday or event is a mixed blessing. It is so strange to be filled with so much happiness and sadness at the same time. These feelings come to the forefront mostly when I am out running the streets of Clinton at 5 AM or earlier. I think I now understand schizophrenia. Have a great day.

Sometimes no news is better than news.
Fri, Dec 30, 2011 05:26PM

Just returned from seeing Dr. Cahlon, December 30, 2012. The reality of Ginny's disease is finally sinking in. Not very pleasant. Sometimes reality is more than unpleasant.

Overall, Monday continued to be a good day. Jordan and Meg and the kids stopped over for a short visit and it was quite nice. Ginny had the MRI on Tuesday, December 27, 2011, and the day was a bad day for her. On Wednesday we drove to the Hunterdon cancer Center and Ginny got her Gemzar chemotherapy. It turned out to be a very great day and we did not want it to end. Thursday and so far today, Friday, have been terrible. Yesterday Ginny spent most of the day sitting in her chair with her eyes closed, hoping that the pain medication would keep the pain away. It did not work very effectively.

Our discussion with Dr. Cahlon was not very good at all. He is a very kind and compassionate man, and asked Ginny how she felt. She told him in no uncertain terms that the hoped for pain relief from the radiation did not occur. Dr. Cahlon indicated that the tumor on the pancreas was a little bit smaller and would continue to shrink in the weeks ahead. He said it was less active and less angry. I guess that is good news.

I asked Dr. Cahlon about the liver tumors/lesions and he indicated that there were a few small new spots on the liver. This did not surprise him as the radiation treatment had shifted to the pancreas only and the tumor located on it. Gemzar is much less effective with tumors on the liver. Essentially what he said was that the liver tumors would be treated by Dr. Bednar systemically and not with radiation. He was quite candid and was not sure Ginny could handle the old 5 FU treatment that had made the liver "markedly improved". That decision would be made by Dr. Bednar. It is a tad disconcerting when your doctor tells you that you have fought an incredibly hard fight and that you have given it your best shot. That essentially you are now going to die.

So, the bottom line is after a teary time, Ginny will have to make some very important decisions when meeting with Dr. Bednar on Wednesday January 4, 2012. If Dr. Bednar does not think that he can reduce the size of the liver tumors and other tumors with chemotherapy or that Ginny cannot handle the treatment, chemotherapy will probably end. Ginny will have to weigh the benefit or lack of benefit of any chemotherapy against the side effects. Clearly some very important decisions will soon be made. The worst case scenario will be that chemotherapy stops and Hospice is then put into the equation. Hospice tries to put you in as much comfort as possible for the rest of your life which is wonderful, but also signifies a totally different approach to the illness; comfort instead of fight.

So, that is all I have to say about this. Our spirits are not exactly at their peak right now as you might imagine. Happy New Year. Safe travels.

It gets harder and harder to deal with this mess.
Wed, Jan 04, 2012 07:49 PM

Since my last e-mail to you things are between static and a little better. I feel better but of course I am not going through what Ginny is going through. Saturday, December 31, 2011, was New Year's Eve. Ginny had a pretty good day and we even went for a ride. She has begun taking Vitamin B-12 as her feet and finger tips are very numb and this may help. A dear sweet angel brought us a dinner that was so good I cannot describe it. Thank you. Victor Vomit made an entry into our lives in the late evening, but it is what it is.

New Year's Day and January 2, 2012 were bad days with respect to pain and tiredness. Ginny could hardly move and spent most of her day in her chair just trying to feel good. It is a sad thing. As an aside, I called my cardiologist as my blood pressure was so very high and I had a very terrible headache for days. You see, this cancer thing affects not just the patient but others. Thank God for the calls from the boys.

On Monday, January 2, 2012 Ginny had a bad morning and a "little" better afternoon. In short, there were three consecutive bad days. The calls from the boys were lifelines. Thank God for yesterday, Tuesday. All day was a great day; I stress great. We went shopping and Mark stopped over. Why such a change? Beats the crap out of me. Makes no sense at all.

So today, January 4, 2012 is here. Ginny had chemotherapy at 9:30 AM. Not a good day today either. This is getting a little discouraging as you might imagine. In a week Ginny had two good days. Her mood is down and that is understandable. We did have a nice talk with Dr. Bednar. He had a slightly different take on the radiation and MRI and Ginny's status than Dr. Cahlon. He said the main tumor had gotten smaller and would get even smaller yet in the next few weeks. Apparently the effects of the radiation will continue to help Ginny. The tumors on the liver that were now evident were pretty much the old tumors that had been systemically dealt with the 5 FU. He stressed that even though the tumors had grown, Ginny's tumor markers were still 733 which is so much better than when she came to him when the tumor markers were about 9,000 (or 8,000, I forget what he said). He seemed optimistic that the current Gemzar would hold the tumors in abeyance a while longer and wanted to add Tarceva to the mixture to try to help kill cancer. In other words, perhaps the end is not as close as one might think.

Now Tarceva is a pill you take daily and is used to fight cancer in conjunction with Gemzar, but is not a form of chemotherapy. You can Google it to see how it tries to work. The cost of a one month supply of Tarceva is $1,649.70. Actually, the cost of the drug for one month is $4,294.00, and the co-pay is $1,649.70 a month!! Hard to believe, isn't it? Almost a joke. Such is life. I wonder if that donut hole stuff I wrote about previously will kick in at some point. Also, Dr. Bednar wants to have Ginny take a pill to boost her energy such as Ritalin, a drug used mostly for children with ADD. It is clear that there seems to be a pill for anything in the cancer treatment area; except a cure for pancreatic cancer. Lastly, Dr. Bednar might suggest a pancreatic nerve block of some kind in the future to help kill the pain.

As an aside, this is pancreatic cancer Month. Not much has been done to deal with the disease in the last 40-50 years. Let us hope that something new comes on the horizon--or should I have said dream that something new comes on the horizon as I do not use the word "hope" any more, but rather "wish". Right now Ginny is just sitting in her chair feeling like yuck. She is trying to get comfortable in a dark room and has taken medication to try to move that process along. I am off to the Hospital to deal with an effort to help with the cost of the Tarceva. There are programs for the very poor, but what about the middle and lower middle class folks? How do they emotionally survive? I have nothing further to say about cancer treatment as it might raise my blood pressure.

As an aside, the dear Dr. Bednar brought us a picture of his Christmas card which shows his family on my old office's front porch with the red front door given prominence. That was a nice thing to do. He is a kind man.

Collateral damage
Sat, Jan 07, 2012 02:40 PM

Today is a beautiful warm winter day, Saturday, January 7, 2012. Although Wednesday January 4, 2012 was a bad day, we were wrongfully optimistic that Thursday would be better. Thursday was just horrible. It was also a day of collateral damage which I will explain below, Jennifer stopped in for a second and was able to see the pain Ginny was suffering. Sad. Yesterday on the other hand was so wonderful. Ginny was her old self and had very little if any pain. We were out in the car, saw Lois in Clinton Town and chatted for a while. We even had a "dinner" at the Spinning Wheel Diner. Ginny cannot really eat a lot of food, but she is able to enjoy what she eats! So today has come, and the pain is back, but not in a horrible way. Ginny is able to be comfortable and is currently resting in her favorite chair, just having taken some of her pain pills. Today may yet be an okay day. We are both optimistic about that.

Now as to "collateral damage". I write this mainly for my sons as I do not want this cancer crap to harm them any more than it has already. On Thursday I had taken my usual 6 mile run and about three miles into it felt pain in the center of my chest and had shortness of breath. Just could not get enough air inside. I continued the run and when I got home took a nice shower and then decided to go to the ER at the Hunterdon Medical Center as I just could not get enough air inside of me and the pain persisted. Ginny was feeling badly as I mentioned and I was able to reach Nancy to check on her; later to put on her pain patches; Fentanyl. Thank you Nancy. I spent seven hours at the hospital as they tried to determine if I had a heart attack; I did not and actually, the nuclear stress test ran out of paper at the highest level as the Doctor tried to get my heart rate up and make the machine beat me-it did not. The point of this is that the cancer SHA (Sadness, Helplessness and Anger) I had previously mentioned had reared its ugly head and this time produced physical manifestations high blood pressure; anxiety; stress; depression; lack of sleep; and much more. This response is so evident with care-givers, friends, and family. It is collateral damage of the worse kind. The first thing I think about when I awaken is Ginny's condition as is the last thing at night if Morpheus is kind to me. The SHA exists the rest of the day. Ginny feels terrible about this but it is the result of cancer, and not anything that she did or could do or change. When your first date was June 2, 1961, and you have essentially been together since then, it is expected in its worst manifestation. Yet, this collateral damage effects everyone in the cancer battle and other battles too, be your family, friend, or caregiver. All of us will be there at some point and in some way and we will all have to deal with the collateral damage. I have nothing further to say on this issue as my notes are about Ginny primarily and not me. The roller coaster ride continues. Have a nice day and take care of yourself, particularly take care of yourself if this collateral damage is effecting you as if you do not, it will win.

Rule 17
Thu, Jan 12, 2012 11:15 PM

The time since my last note of Saturday, January 7, 2012 has been interesting. We learned that Rule 17 is that Ginny is not allowed two good days in a row even though day two started out okay for two hours. Sunday was a tiring and painful day but Monday good until Victor Vomit greeted us at 5:30PM. So it goes. Tuesday and Wednesday were terrible. By terrible I mean that Ginny had pain and fatigue in such dimension that she could only sit in a chair had hope the pain patches and medications would work to make her comfortable. This gets very depressing for both of us. It can be very hard to watch this and experience this as well.

Wednesday I decided that I had had enough and went to the Pain Center at the hospital and met with the Nurse Practitioner Colleen. Eleanor was so helpful in arranging this. Ginny had been cutting her conversations with David and Mark short because of her pain and even with her best friend, now in Florida. These were bad signs. The Nurse Practitioner was a lovely professional who was more than understanding and agreed to meet with our oncologist today to assist us in presenting issues to be discussed. I vented all of my concerns and the fact that Ginny seemed averse to taking some of the medication Dr. Bednar had recommended. Ginny's main concern was whether the medication would make things worse which she could not tolerate.

So today, Thursday, January 12, 2012 arrived and Ginny seemed so much better. Who wuddah thunk! We attended the meeting with Dr. Bednar and the Nurse Practitioner anyway. All of our questions were answered and Ginny will take the medicine suggested. She will take the Ritalin to give her energy, starting out very slowly. She has to get strength. She will take the Tarceva (co-pay of $1,649.50 per month) every day starting next Monday or perhaps sooner. That will help the Gemzar work a little better--not necessarily prolong Ginny's life, but make it better by killing cancer cells in the liver. It could help the pain. We really did not discuss the nerve block for the pancreas as I think that it is really a last resort concept. We have some time for that hopefully. After our discussion at the cancer Center I wheeled Ginny to up to the second floor of the Hunterdon Medical Center and have a surprise Reiki session. She was feisty in the AM and very relaxed after the Reiki. Her day has been just wonderful today. Great talks with our sons and even a Skype with

Amelia and Ben. Amelia has advised that she would be taking ballet lessons and performed for us beautifully even though she has not yet had a lesson.

So tomorrow will come and we will see if Rule 17 pertains again. At least we have the Ritalin to pep my lady up and we have the telephone number of the pain center if a call has to be placed. Apparently pancreatic cancer is known to work in the aforementioned ways and we will continue to deal with it for the duration. I suppose that at some point the anger will turn to acceptance but not yet. Or, perhaps the SHA I referred to in prior notes will become the SHAA with the final A being "acceptance". Don't hold your breath. On the flip side, a wonderful woman fighting breast cancer who has five young children and a very supportive husband and family is recovering nicely from surgery. We are so pleased for her. Way to go MB!!!

Eight months and counting
Mon, Jan 16, 2012 07:03 PM

Well people, it has been 8 months since Ginny was diagnosed with stage 4 pancreatic cancer. This is a bittersweet day. I am so happy to have her with me still even though the survival rate is so miniscule. I am not happy that she has received this burden. Most of you know that I am beyond angry over this and until the other day had already experienced collateral damage from the disease and its effects on Ginny. It is not fun being in the Emergency Department for 7 hours although they were wonderful to me. Ginny has had many more bad days than good days and you have seen that in the 30 or so notes I have sent. Rule 17 was mostly in effect last Friday but not totally. Saturday was okay and Ginny's brother Will and his wife Jen came to visit which helped. Sunday seemed better and we saw Jen and Will again for a brief time. Now Monday is here and it is not going well. Thank you to the dear friends who have helped us with their kind food contributions. As to the wonderful friend who suggested that I try to focus on the wonderful legacy that Ginny and I have for ourselves, our family, and Amelia and Ben, and not the bitterness of my feelings due to what is going on, I say thank you a million. I am working on it; working on how to best write the rest of the story. There is some peace in that. No more today.

Things are tough
Mon, Jan 23, 2012 03:42 PM

Well friends, things are tough here at the Rylak household. Since my last e-mail to you of Monday, January 16, 2012, another week has passed. In that week Ginny has really not had any good days but perhaps a couple of okay days or portions of days. She has spent most of her time sitting in her chair trying to deal with her pain. On the 17th, we had a representative of Hospice here. Anne Boyle, RN is in charge of the program In Hunterdon County and was sweet enough to come over to our house to explain everything to us. Hospice is not giving up but stressing the palliative care Ginny requires. When we saw Dr. Bednar on Wednesday the 18th for chemotherapy, he agreed that Ginny was in no condition to have chemotherapy and needed some time off. He also said that Ginny really should not be on Hospice at this time; that she was still fighting the cancer well. This surprised us. At his suggestion, we are going to see an anesthesiologist tomorrow, a Doctor Peter Nyitray. It is a meeting to see if he thinks he might be of some help to relieve the pain. Today he and Dr. Bednar are chatting and I assume there will be a discussion of a "block" at what is called the celiac plexus and in particular at the location where the pancreatic plexus sits. The concept is to anesthetize the pancreatic nerve and hence alleviate the pain. Who knows?

Sorry for the run-on paragraph above. Sometimes I do not feel very eloquent. It is hard to be sanguine at these times. I think Ginny and I were ready for Hospice but for the comments of Dr. Bednar. A very wise person told us to find a physician you trusted and do what he/she says. We are doing just that and trying to avoid the naysayers who suggest we try alternative remedies, cures, institutions, and doctors. Ginny's cancer cannot be cured. She has already lived longer than expected. No matter how much carrot juice or celery juice she drinks, the result will not be changed. I hate saying that, but it is what it is. Miracles may happen but not here. Candidly, I still feel at times that all of this is a bad dream and I will awaken and then smile.

A further thank you to all the wonderful people that have brought us meals and treats, that have sent cards and letters, and of course to our lovely family for keeping in touch so very often. If I have been abrasive or short at times it is only because I am trying to protect Ginny, knowing how she feels at any given moment. And do you know what? We are so very lucky people. Some friends about a mile from here just lost their 21 year old son. How terrible they must feel. Yup, we are very lucky in so many ways and that is how we will define our battle with this disease.

That's it for now.

Hospice
Sat, Jan 28, 2012 10:12 AM

We were unable to see Dr. Kyitray on Tuesday January 24, 2012 as he came down with the flu. No problem. On Wednesday we went to the cancer Center and saw Dr. Bednar. It was clear that Ginny was in terrible pain, sad, and extremely weak. Ginny was admitted to the hospital. I felt relieved at that as the care giving was getting to be not just physically but emotionally exhausting. All the Doctors and Nurses at the Hunterdon Medical Center were just wonderful; the food is delicious. Although they could not end the pain they did help ease it at times with a cornucopia of drugs. Ginny's weakness did not diminish but perhaps was ameliorated. We did speak to Dr. Kyitray and he was kind enough to discuss the surgical options to relieve the pain; celiac plexus block or pain pump. We spoke to all the disciplines.

We mulled over various concepts. It is interesting that there are noticeable differences of opinion between the oncologist, the palliative care people, the Hospice people, and the interventional pain people (read "surgeon types") with reference to treating pain. I tried to get to the hospital by 6 AM every day and stayed until they kicked me out. It was very difficult to see Ginny in her hospital bed trying to sort out what to do while in so much pain. For a period of time all seemed well. Then things were just horrible. As I was exhausted I reached out to family and friends for some help and everyone was very helpful. Thank you all. Thursday and Friday came and Ginny was still in the hospital. The IV fluids were poured into her as she was somewhat dehydrated.

We made our decision yesterday, Friday, January 27, 2012. Ginny arrived home about 6:30PM and Tony helped me get her up the porch stairs to her favorite living room chair. Thank you Tony. You are a wonderful friend and such a caring person. The Hospice nurse (Barbara) arrived about 7:30 PM and we chatted with her and Ginny was given a physical. Ginny was so tired that we got her upstairs and into bed by about 8:30 PM and she fell fast asleep. Candidly, the nurse showed me how to give Ginny a stronger form of medication in the nature of morphine which helped to alleviate the pain. In other words, "we got by with a little help from our friends". Ginny is still asleep now at 4 AM. I like that. It is impossible to sleep in the hospital what with all the goings on and the general chatter. Chemotherapy is over.

Thereafter the Hospice nurse (Barbara) and I went over more things with me until a little after 10 PM. Candidly, the end of those conversations with her are a blur. My brain and my body are exhausted; all started dosing down. Yes, Hospice is the right course for Ginny. We feel that it is her best chance to have a pain free period in her life. You can get off Hospice and go back to treating the cancer but I do not expect that to happen. I simply want her pain to dissipate and her to get more energy. The latter may not be possible, but the former will occur. About 10 AM today, Saturday, the on-call Hospice nurse will be here with an aid named Dawn to help Ginny bathe etc. A nurse is on call 24/7 and will come to the house whenever we ask. Yes, this is the right decision for Ginny.

Better yet, our sons will be here today and so will the lovely and sweet Amelia. I cannot wait. Ginny is afraid that she may be too exhausted and she is right. So what. I am off for my daily run. Have a great day. And yes, to the extent that this note is disjointed, just know that I am operating on very little sleep and there seems to be a lump of denseness between my ears. I hope we made the right decision.

Hospice
Sat, Jan 28, 2012 01:05PM

I forgot to mention that I will be reaching out to some of you close by for some help. I hope this is okay as it will help me keep my sanity and benefit Ginny. The type of help I may need is to just be with Ginny from time to time while I attend to other things. It tires her out to chat a lot, at least now, but I think it would be nice to have you just sit with her in the living room from time to time. You can chat, read a book, do stretching exercises, and watch TV or whatever. Ginny may rebuff the idea at first but I am able to be persistent when I wish. It does not have to be for a long time, perhaps an hour or two every once in a while. That way I will not have to rush to get groceries, do the laundry, and do a lot of other things. Please always feel free to say no as I know how busy you are. My team approach to Hospice will involve friends and of course the aids etc. provided by Hospice. I am considering hiring a beautiful well-built blond young Norwegian woman to help on a full time basis down the road who has skills in massage, Reiki, posing and smiling as well (sorry, a little locker room humor which is necessary for my sanity). And again, thank so many of you for the dinners and sweet treats and flowers. We have some wonderful friends, many of whom I do not include in these notes.

Al

Our precious Amelia
Tue, Jan 31, 2012 11:04 AM

I know now that Hospice was the best decision for Ginny that we ever made. Months ago it was appropriate but we could not face making the call. The Hospice people have been at the house so many times checking Ginny and checking me. From the moment they arrived Ginny's care and peace were at the forefront and continue to be there. Ginny's pain has decreased measurably and I guess that is in large part from the medication that she is on and the fact that she knows so many people care for her.

Thank you Hospice. As an aside, when Hospice came in Sunday, Amelia told them that Grandma was sick and they had to make her better. So sweet.

Yesterday, January 30, 2012, the hospital bed arrived. This made a great difference. Getting Ginny up and down the stairs to her bed the last couple of days was so difficult for her and for me. It exhausted her; I was afraid she would fall. She is now in our downstairs den in an over-sized twin bed. The bathroom is 15 feet away and the room can be closed off with pocket doors. She is safe and as comfortable as she is able to be.

Most of Ginny's time is spent sleeping. That means there is no pain. She eats even less than usual and consumes just a tad of water. Baring a large change, it is clear that the disease process has taken over. I cannot change that. She is largely pain free, comfortable, and except for being quite teary when she thinks of what is happening, is doing so much better. That is all we can hope for. The outpouring of love and help from our friends is truly amazing. So many of you have called and visited in accordance with our new open door policy. I should have asked for help months ago.

David and Mark have been and are incredible sons. They have done so much here to assure that Ginny has everything she needs. They have helped with the house and with me. They even did everything to get the hospital bed made and keep the room dark at night and comfortable for Ginny. I have two wonderful sons. They have called every day since Ginny's diagnosis on May 16, 2011. The last couple of days they have done everything possible to help us here. Ginny raised them correctly.

I must tell you about Amelia. From the moment Amelia arrived at the house, she has specially cared for her Grandma. When she came in the first time Ginny was able to sit in a chair and Amelia just went up to her, sat with her, and cuddled. She was so gentle with Ginny. You see, Ginny was at first concerned that having Amelia here might be too much for her. Wrong!!! The entire weekend and now, Amelia has been so perfect for her. One of Ginny's greatest concerns was that Amelia would never remember her. Benjamin is just too small, but Amelia was her concern. Amelia has proven her wrong.

I must tell you about what happened after the hospital bed arrived and we got Ginny into the bed. Mark had placed a Schwinn bicycle bell on a railing attached to the bed so Ginny could ask for help when needed by ringing the bell. A great idea. In a little while, Amelia got into bed with Grandma, and lay beside her; Ginny had been sleeping. Ginny awoke and the two spoke for hours. Amelia rang the bell and wanted some strawberries! Got those and Ginny had one too. Then the bell rang again. Cookies this time for Amelia! Ginny ate a portion too. The bell was used many times until bedtime. Ginny really enjoyed that so much. When Ginny would doze off Amelia stayed with her and cuddled. To be candid, this was the most precious moment I have ever seen in my life. I get teary thinking about it. This little girl who loves her Grandma knew something was wrong, that Grandma was sick, and showed how we all should treat the ill. I will forever remember this. On another occasion, my friend Victor came to bring some food over for my sons and me, and looked from afar at Ginny and nodded "hello". Amelia blurted out, "Come over and say "hello" to my grandma". Victor did and he has told me how tentative he was until Amelia's comment and how precious the entire moment became. Ginny feels of course that she will miss Amelia, and that is true in a sense. On the other hand, I know Amelia will always remember her Grandma and I think Ginny knows that too.

Whether this special moment was the result of providence or whatever, it does not matter. It has helped to take the anger part of the SHA away for me. It gives me a sense that no matter how horrible this pancreatic cancer may be, in the end we are writing the rest of the story. It will take Ginny away, but it will not win the war. We have already won. The cancer has lost! The Rylak family survives. We have been mourning for over eight months and that is okay. Sadness will exist, but Ginny will forever be remembered for the wonderful person she is.

And yes, for the first time since May 16th I slept more than 3.5 hours.

Saturday, February 4, 2012
Sat, Feb 04, 2012 02:32 PM

Hospice continues to amaze me with all they are doing for Ginny. What a wonderful organization. Since my last note to you Ginny has weakened; swallowing is difficult; she seems confused at times. Amelia continues to assure her of her love and is just like a little caregiver should be. Her mere presence is all it takes to make Ginny smile.

Two days ago about 6 AM Ginny got out of her hospital bed. She had to go to the bathroom. I arrived from my run and she was standing in the living room, somewhat confused. Thank God she did not fall and hurt herself. It scared me. Last night, because of bowel issues, she had to get up four times between 2 AM and 5 AM. If I had not been asleep near her bed, she would have gotten out of bed again. Getting Ginny out of bed is exhausting for her and the same for me. The worry of Ginny trying to do things while I sleep had to stop. The pain medication causes these bowel issues which are the primary problem right now. So I contacted Anita's Angels out of Flemington and will have a live-in caregiver here 24/7 starting at 1PM today. I cannot worry about Ginny as I have been the last couple of days and yes, it is worth every penny. I feel badly about this, but reality suggests I can do no more. So, I will dispense the medications but the full time caregiver will do much of the rest that is required. He will stay by Ginny all the time and my night fears of her getting out of bed and falling will be alleviated. Hospice will still come every day and do all they have been doing. In a sense I feel as if I have failed Ginny in not personally giving her the proper care but there is no other choice. Eight and a half months is all I could physically handle on my own; mentally too. Crap.

Anyway, David and Amelia will leave tomorrow and I know Mark and Ang will be visiting Ginny soon. Of course Ginny really loves her children and their visits always make her happy. We will of course miss the boys, but Amelia is the one we will miss the most. She has been such a blessing and has filled a void that needed filling. The purity and simplicity of a three year old is amazing. My fondest memory will be of Amelia in Ginny's bed ringing the bicycle bell and at times simply sleeping in her Grandma's lap. On a walk she looked me right in the eyes and asked, "Grandpa, what is dying"? Out of the mouths of babes.... Amelia at the age of three has done her part to help her family.

So the inevitable approaches and Ginny is resting now. Her pain is minimal at worse and I am happy for that. The medications really have worked.

Since I have committed us to use Anita's Angels, I will not have to contact all the people that have offered to sit with Ginny. I still may use you but the urgency has dissipated.

Mon, Feb 06, 2012 03:34PM

Things are better for Ginny and for me since hiring Anita's Angels to help take care of Ginny. There was quite a bit of confusion at first as the person to come at 2 PM a couple of days ago could not make it. So they got a fill-in named Cynthia who came 9:30 PM on Friday and will leave today, Monday, to be replaced by the original person. I am still concerned that although Cynthia sleeps at night on the mattress near Ginny's hospital bed (I can hear her snore) that Ginny might try to get out of the bed, but so far she has gotten Ginny when she tried to exit the bed. Cynthia is a very nice lady from Ghana who is quite caring and loving. She caresses Ginny and speaks to her in dulcet tones. I like her a lot and will be sorry to see her go.

Ginny really spends most of her time just sleeping although she awakened last night at about 1 AM. Cynthia called me to help her with Ginny and all went well; it was a bowel issue again. I am not sure if Ginny knows exactly what is going on but she sure knew her sons (David and Mark), Angela, Amelia, Jen, Paula, and Dana who visited. Lena of course is in Staunton with Ben but when I mentioned their names Ginny lit up. This sleep may be caused by the increased pain medication or by the disease process. Very little food and water is being consumed by Ginny although she was able to eat a little cheese cake and mashed potatoes a friend brought over last night. David and Mark have returned home for a bit as it should be. Of course their departure was a sad moment for them, Ginny, and me, but Ginny is at peace, pain free, and resting comfortably. That is what we all want.

Candidly, I do not want this to be a death watch and I know Ginny feels the same way; hence I am glad the boys have gone to their homes. So I am trying to do everything I am able to put a less sad spin on what is going on. I know this disease will take the life of my lovely wife. I cannot change that. But Ginny and I will not lose our senses of humor in the process. This early AM I thought that the end was near. I told Ginny how much I loved her and then as I clutched her hand said "do not hang on for me". She said, "Stop that. I have to go to the bathroom". I laughed. She smiled. Then we got her onto the commode and she did what she was supposed to do---and felt much better. She does lapse into the sleep mode again for long periods of time and at times talks about things in the past as if they are current. The great thing is that she is not in pain. She may live another hour or another month. No one knows. We have had a wonderful life together and our entire family has benefited from her presence. I am sad however that Amelia and Benjamin with not be able to benefit as much as they would have because of her absence. I also have to add that one of Ginny's greatest fears was that Amelia would not remember her. After this weekend, the cuddling next to Grandma, ringing the Schwinn bicycle bell and the pictures I took, she will most certainly remember her Grandma. I sense that Ginny knows that too.

Speaking of sleep, I recall watching the Super Bowl last night and seeing a two point safety. That is it. Then when I awoke, the game was over!! Good. I hate the Giants anyway. My sleep cycle, even with a little help from my friends, is a little out of sorts. It will get better as it cannot get any worse. Also, a counselor from Hospice is coming here to speak to me today. It will be nice. Remember the next time you meet a caregiver of a very ill person to treat them gently as they are going through some difficult things.

So there it is for now my friends. Acceptance is a good thing. Acceptance sans bitterness is better. We continue to write the end of this story in a way of love and caring. No one or nothing will ever really take Ginny away from us.

Hospice continues.
Wed, Feb 08, 2012 05:55PM

We have had some good days and some bad days this week; the former predominate. I have not screwed up the medication yet and with some exceptions, Ginny is doing as well as she is able. Today we switched over to morphine. I agreed with the decision and I know Ginny would want that too. She is essentially pain free. The Fentanyl patch has been raise to 400 mcg and for break-through pain I will use the morphine. Also some Ativan every 4 hours. That is it.

Our permanent person from Anita's Angels arrived a couple of days ago and he is just great. He is from Ghana and his name is name is Kwami, which means "Saturday". In Ghana they name their children by the day when they were born, e.g., "Kwami" is Saturday and "Kofi" is Friday. Hence Kofi Annan of United Nations fame is really first named "Friday". I tell you this because when I mentioned it to Ginny she smiled. Kwami is a college professor and here to earn money doing aide work. He is as compassionate and caring as Cynthia who was here for two days previously. Kwami even insisted I take my run this morning when I offered to spell him as he had been up most of the night with Ginny dealing with her bowels. Bottom line? We are privileged to have Kwami here to care for Ginny, particularly so I can catch some sleep.

The Hospice people are all over our house at different times. Ginny's nurse Cynthia comes at least three times a week and Elvia, the Hospice aide, is here at least 5 days a week. I can reach anyone associated with

Hospice within 2 minutes at any time. Weekends Elvia is here or a substitute. Hospice continues to simply amaze me with their kindness, understanding, and expertise. They are concerned with my entire family.

Of course Ginny gets very teary eyed when she thinks of her death and thinks of missing the boys and grandchildren. What would you expect? Also, when a guest comes to visit (I control that like a jail warden) Ginny will tear up; ask Lo and she will tell you so! The Ativan helps, but I tried something different. A few days ago I had Chaplin Jim DeVries come and talk to me. He helped me a lot. So I had him here to talk to Ginny. I really think it helped considerably. He did mostly counseling and was not a holy roller about the Bible. He just spoke very soothingly to Ginny about what death was like and also about her presence thereafter. His kind tone and words really made me think and I know that Ginny felt so much better after he spoke to her. She mouthed him a kiss when he left. Whether you believe in God or not is unimportant to me; I care about your character. I know that good people have an ongoing connection and Ginny and our family will have that connection or presence in the future.

So, time passes very slowly. I have lots of time to think and that is good and bad. In any event I always come back to the moment when Amelia jumped up on Ginny's hospital bed and cuddled with her very ill Grandma, rang the Schwinn bicycle bell, ate strawberries, and slept for hours with Ginny. Other times she played so very often with Ginny and I can see Ginny hugging her. I do not know if there is a God, but those moments were just so precious and dear to me. Whatever forces are going on, there is not anger and strictness. On the contrary there is a sense of well-being and kindness. Those good forces are what are important to me. Ginny will most assuredly be in a better place when this is all over. In a sense, the Circle of Life will have been completed. Amelia did listen quite some time to "The Lion King" which with hindsight, was prophetic. In the end I will be so very sad, but so very happy to have had Ginny all these years.

So the care-giving continues a while longer solely with the thought of keeping Ginny comfortable and free from pain. That is as it should be. And as an aside, Ginny wanted me to send this e-mail out today and I do at her request and as my desire.

The process continues; Ginny has comfort.
Fri, Feb 10, 2012 09:29 PM

Contrary to my last e-mail, I have finally screwed up Ginny's medication today. I forgot to put the Fentanyl patches on at the appropriate time. Since I am a little tired all the time, I have to force myself to double check everything. And I do. Drat.

As the disease process continues, Ginny has developed a wound just above her bottom. It is being treated and we must recall to shift her in the bed every couple of hours. Also, a fancy new mattress was received today which is air-filled and moves up and down all the time. Hopefully it will help with this wound. It really is the least of our worries now, but still important.

It seems that increasing the Fentanyl patch to 400 mcg has alleviated the pain tremendously. Every three days I apply 4 100 mcg patches and it is no big deal--unless you forget to put them on! Also, Ginny is getting some morphine by syringe from me as needed. She has not asked for it much and the signs that were described to me by the Nurse re pain when a patient is unable to speak are looked for by me, every hour or so. Kwami is wonderful but cannot do medication; that is my main job. As of now, the morphine, 4 ml, is used about 2 times a day only. So, the bottom line is that usually Ginny is pain free which is the whole purpose of Hospice.

On Thursday the 9th of February we not only had the Nurse, Cynthia, but also a resident Doctor. Great guy and he gave Ginny the once over. So every day we have nurses, aides, a doctor once in a while, and calls from the Chaplin, the Social Worker, and volunteers for Hospice. Everyone offers to do whatever. When we run out of medication, they bring it to my front door; all arrangements are made by Hospice. They really seem to care that Ginny and I are both taken care of every day. So many of you have sent lovely e-mails to Ginny and I have read her every one. Friends of David and Mark have been so gracious and described her as a second Mom; as so wonderful for listening to their talk about their problems, and for just being her. That was so nice to do and all were unsolicited.

Ativan is needed for mood control and to try to promote a general sense of well-being. I will be increasing this often. No one wants to leave their family and friends; sometimes we simply have no control over these things as is the case here. Ginny is normal with reference to her feelings re these things and I can offer no reasonable explanation to her. Ginny's body is being terribly harmed by the pancreatic cancer but so far her thought process is usually good. At times she gets confused and that is part of the process. Her wonderful smile, nonetheless, is still evident often as is the twinkle in her eye. Unfortunately Ginny has slept most of the last couple of days. Nancy, Lois, Carol, and Paula have stopped by and I have let them in when I think Ginny is able to handle it or is asleep. Food keeps appearing at the door and someday I will have to repay these wonderful people; you know who you are.

My concern of course is that Ginny is getting weaker all the time and since she eats so little food and has so little drink, she has lost even more weight. About 60 pounds. She is extremely frail, tiny, and helpless. Rest assured that we are doing everything humanly possible to keep her comfortable. Comfort is what I think about every second of every day; when I awaken I ask what can be done to help Ginny; when I go to quasi-sleep, I ask the same question. Today Elvia not only gave Ginny a sponge bath but also washed her hair and did her nails. Ginny really seemed to like those things being done. I keep looking for these types of things. I do not know how much longer we will have the physical Ginny with us, but I have assured her that she will always be in my heart and the hearts of her sons, family, and friends. Sounds morbid I know, but it is true and there are no easy ways to describe what is going on. So, we go on in this amazing process of life and death. There is now sadness, fear, anger, and acceptance. Acceptance is the difficult part, for Ginny in particular, but that will come. Make no mistake about this; it is a very sad time. Unfortunately there is no pill for sadness. Ginny is and always will be the heart and soul of our family. No matter what, I know that I did everything possible to help my sweet lady, only I failed to keep her here.

February 12, 2012

Ginny died today. I was at Snap Fitness running on the treadmill when the call came at 5;00am on my cell phone from Kwami to get home quickly. David was at our home and Mark and Ang arrived shortly after I arrived. Ginny's breathing was labored and she was gasping when I arrived home. We were all crying and numb. I gave her an extra strong dose of morphine from the special red box we were provided at the beginning of Hospice care. And shortly thereafter her breathing stopped. It was over. We had all lost the good fight. Sadness pervaded all other emotions. Many people have the death of a loved one hoisted upon them in an unexpected moment. We were lucky in a sense as we had time to say goodbye and nothing was left unsaid. Goodnight sweet love, the world indeed was a better place because you were here. Thank you for your love. STD. I have absolutely nothing else to say. Period.

Al

CLINTON - Ginny Rylak, 65, of Clinton passed away on Feb. 12, 2012.

Her maiden name was Virginia Ann Campbell, and was she was born on Feb. 22, 1946, in Trenton. She resided in Yardley, Pa., a few years until moving to Pennington with her late father, Willard S. Campbell Jr., her mother Anna G. Campbell and her brother Willard S. Campbell III. Upon graduating from Central High School in 1964, she attended Keuka College, graduating in 1968 with a degree in elementary education.

While in high school Ginny began dating Albert D. Rylak, June 2, 1961, when she was 15 years old and I was 16. Their first date was at the Hiohela Bowling Lanes; she won the match by two pins. They were married, June 29, 1968, and were married for 43 years.

Ginny taught at Nutley and Hopewell elementary schools prior to raising her family. She was an active participant in Meals on Wheels during this time. Since she so valued education, Ginny was always so proud that her two sons, David A. Rylak and Mark C. Rylak both became doctors. David in emergency medicine and Mark in dentistry, but it was their values and the fact that they are just honest, competent, compassionate and caring adults that made Ginny most proud. Motherhood to Ginny was the most important responsibility given to anyone and she derived much satisfaction from it. She adored her two daughters-in-law, Lena Fairless and Angela Rylak.

Clinton and Harvey Cedars were her favorite places to live. Large parts of the summers were spent at the family summer home in Harvey Cedars and her favorite pastime was sitting on the beach admiring the ocean or sitting on the deck of her home gazing out across Kinsey Cove. All of her sons' friends were welcomed with open arms at the Harvey Cedars home and Ginny enjoyed filling their bellies with well prepared food.

In Clinton, Ginny was on the Parks and Playground Commission for almost 30 years and was for most of that time responsible for scheduling the use of the Clinton Community Center. She never minded calls at all times of the day or night so as to facilitate children using the Community Center when it was available. She believed that children had to have healthy active activities and deserved the best that Clinton had to offer. Ginny truly enjoyed living in Clinton and all the people in the town knew her for her wonderful smile and attitude.

Her two precious grandchildren, Amelia Ann, 3, and Benjamin David, age 5 months, of Staunton, Va., became the most precious people in her life and she willingly showered them with love and affection as often as she was able. They unfortunately will be diminished by her passing. Her 99-year-old mother, Anna G. Campbell, taught her well.

Ginny did not have a mean bone in her body and prided herself on being a homemaker, wife, mother and grandmother. Her homes were immaculate and always the center of activity for her children and their friends. She enjoyed watching the children empty her refrigerators and the sound of happy children was music to her ears. Until the time of her passing, many friends of her children kept in touch with her by letter, e-mail, and telephone just for affection and for advice. Without question, the world has lost a very wonderful and special person and the world is a much better place because she was here. Ginny will be sorely missed by family and friends.

In lieu of flowers, please take someone you love to dinner and tell them how you feel. If you feel you must, make a donation to the Clinton Fire

Department, P.O. Box 5062, Clinton, NJ 08809; Clinton First Aid and Rescue Squad, P.O. Box 5265, Clinton; or the Hunterdon Hospice, 2100 Wescott Drive, Flemington, NJ 08822, three organizations that she admired tremendously, particularly for the selfless service their members provide to their respective communities.

Private funeral arrangements have been entrusted to the Kearns Funeral Home, Whitehouse, N.J.

Al Rylak Remembers the Love of His Life, from the Pulse Express

Al Rylak has nothing but praise for the team at Hunterdon Hospice, who provided palliative care to his wife Ginny. When Al met Ginny, she was a freshman in high school. He was barely old enough to drive. Yet he knew from the start that she was "the one."

"Ginny was the love of my life; the only woman I ever loved," says Al Rylak, a 67-year-old attorney. "It's really something to be able to say that these days."

The Central High School (Pennington, NJ) sweethearts were married in 1968. They settled in Clinton, where they raised two sons and were active members of the community. The couple shared a love of life that lifted them through the most difficult of times. They worked well as a team, making nearly every decision together, including the most difficult of all: to stop treatment for Ginny's cancer after her doctors determined it was incurable.

"Ginny had stage 4 pancreatic cancer," he explains. "She received outstanding care at Hunterdon Regional Cancer Center, but once her disease progressed and spread, we began to question the struggle. She was in constant pain. Her quality of life was greatly diminished."

Al and Ginny were expecting their second grandchild when they received the news that she would not recover, no matter what medical interventions they might choose to prolong her life.

"It was very important to her that she see her grandchildren before she died. It's what kept her going," says Al. "She also wanted to live her last days free of pain as much as possible."

They met with Hunterdon Hospice to discuss their options. They could receive hospice care at home, to manage her pain and symptoms, but at any time could change their minds and continue medical treatment.

Through the compassionate care Ginny received from the entire team at

Hunterdon Hospice, she was able to die at home with dignity, free of pain. "My wife's last days were so much better than they would have been," says Al.

"Many people hear the word hospice and they are fearful," explains Anne Boyle, RN, Director of Hunterdon Hospice. "It's important to remember that hospice is about quality at the end of life."

For Ginny Rylak, hospice care meant being able to spend time with her three-year-old granddaughter, Amelia, and to share the family's joy upon the arrival of Benjamin, Amelia's baby brother.

"I wouldn't change anything," says Al. "I have total praise for the entire hospice team."

Hunterdon Hospice

For more than 30 years, Hunterdon Hospice has provided palliative/comfort care to individuals and families managing a progressive, life-limiting disease. The Hunterdon Hospice team includes physicians, registered nurses, social workers, certified home health aides, volunteers and a chaplain. "Under the direction of a physician, we provide pain and symptom management to allow patients to live as comfortably as possible," says Ms. Boyle. Hunterdon Hospice is licensed in the state of New Jersey, accredited by the Joint Commission on Accreditation of Healthcare Organizations, and a United Way member agency. For more information or to volunteer, please call 908-788-6600.

And so....

After Ginny died, my goal however was to have her cremated as soon as possible so as to destroy the last vestiges of her cancer. It became an act of necessity and defiance by me, essentially telling the cancer that although it may have won the battle, it had lost the war. I had her ashes placed in a plot at Riverside Cemetery in the Town of Clinton so I could visit her from time to time. We did not hold a memorial service for her until September 16, 2012 when a celebration of her life was held at our home in Clinton with a four piece Blue Grass Band called the Jugtown Mountain Stringband, led by Carlton Bridge, played on our front porch. Food and drink were in abundance, and many close friends attended. Many children even used the pool which Ginny would have loved. And after my two sons left our home, I did what I usually do when I am down. I ran.

I have run for over 35 years, missing only sixteen days during that time period. And so, I strapped on my sneakers and began running from Clinton, NJ to Washington, NJ and back. Four times. I just focused into myself and ran the total of 84 miles in a day and a quarter. I hardly remember the pain but I do remember being stopped by the police on two occasions and thereafter open bottles of beer being placed along the roadway on each trip for my benefit. I felt like an automaton or robot or at times simply cried, agonized, cursed, hated, felt mournful sorrow for me, missed my dear wife, and had every emotion you could have. After the run, I slept for almost twelve hours which was an eternity for me considering three hours a night had become the norm. I did not feel better, but felt cleansed in a very strange sense. So now I was alone for the first time in my life.

One of the more sentimental moments that happened to me occurred prior the Celebration of Ginny's Life which is reflected by the photograph of Amelia on the cover of this book. The Town of Clinton dedicated the gymnasium Ginny had essentially run for 30 years to her as a thank you for her efforts. What a wonderful thing to do. Clinton is that type of town. Amelia stands on the gym floor clutching the special gold necklace that belonged to her Grandma and which Ginny asked me to give to Amelia shortly before she died. You see, Ginny wanted to be remembered by Amelia and I know Amelia will remember her. I hope this writing helps. And even better yet, every time Amelia wears that necklace, she thanks her Grandma for it and I know she will wear it at her wedding.

The Beginning.

Being alone is difficult, particularly for this man. I think that women are as a rule, far more social than men. At least it is terribly hard for me. I visited the same old haunts "we" visited and I always felt as if I were the third plate at the dinner table. I tired so quickly of hearing the greeter at a restaurant say "just one?" I was not 'just one' but 'the one'. I had an identity and did not want to be deemed an intrusion since I was alone. I could always hear the second set of knives, forks, and spoons jingle as they were being removed from the table just as I was sitting down. Sitting next to the one large loud group in the restaurant was far from fun. I recall shortly after Ginny's death, on what would have been her 66th birthday, February 22, 2012, seeing a great horned owl in a tree behind our home in Clinton. It sat in that tree for hours watching me. Since it was Ginny's birthday and her pet name for me was Owl, I decided I should go out to dinner in her honor. Perhaps it was a sign. I went to the Clinton House Restaurant down the street and was greeted by, "just one". I said "no, two". After ordering dinner, sadness, a melancholy, came over me. Throwing a $50.00 bill on the table I left without eating and worse off than when I entered. So you see, trying to be normal in an abnormal environment is difficult. I knew what the loneliness of the long distance runner was in graphic and simple detail.

So many close friends in Clinton tried to help me, but I rejected most of their efforts. It was impossible for me to look into the eyes of my wife's best friend in Harvey Cedars. Food magically appeared at my door for another week. My dear group of "Al's Gals" from Harvey Cedars checked on me often and my best of all buddies, Susan, let me use her Upper West Side NYC apartment for a visit with my daughter-in-law Lena and granddaughter Amelia. I took up playing the guitar and learned James Taylor's "Fire and Rain" pretty well. And when I realized that the song was about death, I never played the guitar again. I attended one grief class session at the Hunterdon Medical Center and found it of no help as there were too many sad people around. Spending most of my time in the very same house where Ginny died was and is difficult. I loved going to our home in Harvey Cedars as that had always been a place of happiness. Each time I went to the beach I wrote STD in the sand near the water as a message to Ginny. Still do. But I had to make a change. I was even more convinced of that need after I gave away many of Ginny's clothes and personal effects. I took Ginny's wedding dress and had it cleaned and boxed. It sits in a closet waiting. Talk about a sad time; reality really set in and tears were plentiful then. It felt as if I were being disloyal. It also made me realize that I was not dreaming and that Ginny was gone forever.

And so I tried New York City, a place my wife actually disliked. I began taking the bus into the City often, going to everything from the Standard Hotel to the Metropolitan Museum of Art to the restaurant Robert at Columbus Circle to the Ballet at Lincoln Center. Zabar's, the Fairway Market, the Gourmet Garage, Chelsea Pier, and the Village were all part of my domain. I met August Shaw, also known as "Mr. Talented", who fancied himself to be a painter and a philanthropist even at a very young age and was a delight to chat with at a Subway Restaurant. The summer of 2012 in New York City was sweltering but so much fun for me. I learned how to ride the subways and buses, visited every museum I could find, and even the enjoyed the Naked Cowboy in Times Square. Often I would stay at the Cornell Club and liked it. I explored all that I could, usually alone but sometimes with a friend. It was shortly thereafter I realized that as Alicia Keyes sang in "Empire State of Mind" with JayZ, that I could exist in the City and indeed, the streets made me feel brand new; big lights inspired me. I was in a different place physically and emotionally while in the City. I had no past but only a present and an anticipated future. I was a new person whose grief did not hold him down but rather forced him to accept a brand new reality. I was Beckett who became my alter ego.

The View From Apartment 15T

It was on April Fool's Day, 2013, that I first met Linda who showed me my new apartment on the Upper West Side. I had no idea what effect the apartment would have on my grieving process and how life would later spring from within me again.

Peripatetic was the word de jure for me. I fluttered from place to place albeit our family home in Clinton, NJ, our summer home in Harvey Cedars, NJ and just for the hell of it, to New York City to get lost and to try to reinvent myself. The name Beckett became my alter ego and I kept trying not to cry, trying to feel some sense of hope, trying to feel a far distance from my loneliness and grief. My frenetic pace continued for over a year as I kept fleeing from my grief and my sadness, helplessness, and anger. Beckett was running away from everyone and everything that had happened since May 16, 2011. The faster I ran, the less distance there was between me and my circumstance. I could not understand what was going on in my psyche. At some point I realized that in order for my sons to heal I would have to set an example for them to follow. To wait for them to heal was pointless. I had to show them the process, but first I had to discover it myself!

It was then, at last, that I decided to try to minimize my running away from my grief and sought to embrace it by my alter ego, Beckett. Beckett was a new person that no one in Manhattan knew or gave a rat's ass about. He was one of millions in a city that simply offered a new life. This county rube who previously existed in his idealized 1960s life was about to begin anew and be inspired, challenged, dared, and enlightened by an island located between the Hudson and East Rivers. I was able to hide and grow in plain view.

One of the sad things about death, which we all shall face, is that you simply have a past but no future. My three grandchildren will little recall their dear sweet Grandma. One, Daniel, was not even born when she died. They are so diminished by her death as she had so much to offer. So what about me? What will my grandchildren know about me? What do I even know about myself? And so, I took apartment 15T and periodically wrote short notes about my experiences in Manhattan for the benefit not only of having my grandchildren know me, but also to show others how to grieve and go forward, uncompromisingly refusing to run away. I never again want to run away from anything but to run toward the future. Perhaps these notes will help others in their grief process. Perhaps these notes will help others just live. It does not matter. They are all true and here for you to view. This is what Ginny wanted me to do.

And so, on April 1, 2013, I spent my first night in Apartment 15T, Manhattan, NYC. Prior to falling asleep I drank a little cognac and watched the distant lights twinkle for me. Beckett had arrived. For the first three months, I commented by e-mail or not at all.   I had sent many e-mails to friends trying to describe what was happening to me in New York City, but they were usually short and disjointed as I tried to collect myself and understand what was happening to me. It was necessary to absorb my new part-time life in the City and after a while, these Notes set forth below appeared.

I guess I am really a New Yorker now.
May 9, 2013

Well folks, I promise that I will stop these incessant e-mails soon. What a day so far.

After awaking I decided to wash the bed sheets etc. and a few other things. Just for informational purposes, I make my coffee from a coffee press now. Somewhat metropolitan if I do say so myself. Afterwards I stripped the bed and with a white shirt and pillow cases proceeded to the basement of my building. Can of corn, particularly since this lovely Hispanic woman who was using 7 washing machines to my one made sure I did everything right. After loading everything up and using a special credit card, I read the scandalous NY Times as I awaited the end of the rinse cycle. Shortly thereafter I loaded everything into the dryer and I was off for my run as my items were drying. My route de jure was along the Hudson River where I now sit. Lots of people running in the rain with me. Knees okay. Plantar fasciitis okay. Foot okay. I still want to get a bicycle for use along the miles and miles of trails in Riverside Park. Yes, right in NYC. When I returned to the laundry room in my apartment my sweet co-washer had taken my items out and folded everything. We had a bond of some kind or another. What a dear kind lady. I guess this makes me a true New Yorker now. After all, most visitors do not do laundry.

Anyway, after breakfast I decided to go to the Metropolitan Museum of Art for the umpteenth time. When I entered Central Park, the skies opened up and I was somewhat drenched. Such is life. I actually sort of know my way around the Park now. Upon arrival at the Met things happened. Of course the place was packed as it was raining outside.

With my speedy yearly pass I just be-bopped in with no problem. I decided to take a Guided Tour as well as a Gallery Talk.

My guided tour was good, but I had seen much of the pieces of art in prior such tours. I had a good time looking at the Museum highlights again, realizing that the highlights were quite subjective. So, that was just okay.

Then I met Yana. Wow. Weeks ago I previously met a woman named Maria I had seen in previous talks and she remembered me as the fellow who had just moved to the City. Like I said, I have friends in the City now. Maria suggested that I do the Gallery Talk "The Art of the Book in the Islamic World". Yana Van Dyke was an associate conservator at the Museum and specializes in paper preservation. She was part of a team project entitled "Making the Invisible Visible. Conservation and Islamic Art". Yana led the talk. Did you know that parchment is made from animal skins? That papyrus is the first effort at paper and has nothing to do with parchment? That the colors used by the Iranian people in writing their Quran, Koran, or whatever, were made from natural minerals or elements like cyanide and gold? Most of the talk and show was about the Islamic Bible and language, but the writing and pictures were great Yana showed us the Blue Koran from 900 AD that looked as good as the day it was made I am told. All the pages were blue and all the lettering was gold. We looked at many things, but I was most impressed with the pages of a work entitled Shahnama (Body of Kings) which was created in the 1500s AD. It is worth the trip just to see these pieces of art and the precise detail. Bottom line? Yana has a wonderful essentially people-free job. She is a Conservator not a Curator. Her job is to preserve these wonderful writings that are really works of art and she has been at it for 18 years. On just one small item, Yana had worked two years. Without careful preservation, all of written history would pass into the wild blue yonder, forever. This is the type of job the Rylak men could never handle but which calls out to them. The stresses and strains of dealing with the public disappears and you focus on an object to restore for posterity. In a sense, all structures eventually disappear, but without preservation of the written word, we lose our culture. Sorry. Had to say that and I like the way it sounds.

Anyway, as I left the Met, the rain dwindled and I walked to my apartment, who do I bump into? My friend Pat Publik, the best Realtor around. When you start bumping into people you know, it is evident that you have arrived. When I entered my apartment, I decided to cook the 25 pieces of Brussels' sprouts I just purchased and following the lecture of Dr. Watson of DNA fame from yesterday, eat well. I also received a couple of calls from two clients, so I felt useful, at least a little.

The rain begins to fall.

Out.

Beckett

Graduation Day and three legged dogs.
May 22, 2013

Beckett arrived in the City early today. Overcast but beautiful nonetheless. Nice to see the apartment which I have missed. I was able to get in a very great 6 mile run and the knees and feet feel fine; so far.

The mirror in the apartment finally was fixed around noon today and I can state unabashedly that my intrepid pain in the ass attitude finally won over the store and installer. Glad that repair is finally done. I have learned unfortunately that the squeaky wheel usually gets the oil. Pathetic is it not? I do not want to be like that anymore. At least the installer said he was sorry for the delay.

Of interest as well is that while on the bus into the City I sat near a fellow named Jay who was a 'news writer" for CBS News. Interesting person. His day usually starts about 10 am and lasts past 8 pm. In view of the Justice Department's recent monitoring the e-mails of the Associated Press, you know I had to ask about that and I did. Although Jay was a tad too liberal for me, he was concerned about this new tactic of our government. It was a good talk. It never hurts to ask. In a week or so I may be meeting Jay for lunch on 9th Avenue, south of 57th Street which he says is loaded with tons of restaurants with all different national cuisines. So a new place to explore.

I did a lot of walking today as well. Since food needed the Fairway Market at 74th was a necessity and I also wanted to walk a bit around Central Park. It was interesting to see where a phantom park was supposed to be between Amsterdam and Columbus on 62nd Street. I think it is called Damrosch Park or something like that. Anyway, there is an article in today's NY Times it. The park really does physically exist and that is what a lawsuit is all about against NYC and Lincoln Center. So my legs tire.

I have seen quite a number of Columbia and NYU students in cap and gown at Pier One at the Hudson River Park. Many were with their families having pictures taken with the Hudson River New Jersey as the background. Cute. I took some family shots for a few of them. I apparently live in a nice location near all this good stuff which people like to photograph.

So I have decided to go to my first ballet at Lincoln Center tomorrow at 7:30pm. It will be fun. I am now going to paste what I saw on line:

Ergo, I will now start to continue a new trend of obtaining culture. I am advised that the opera season really does not start until September. So, ballet comes into my life in a big way now. Amelia should see some of this with me to supplement her dance classes. I will particularly let her know what I think.

Many of you know that two Thursdays ago I actually bumped into Anne Hathaway of Les Miz fame and a winner of an Academy Award. I have not seen her today and I doubt that she is looking for me; you never can tell. She is one good looker however but unfortunately looks anorexic. Skinny women are able to be beautiful.

To stem the usual feelings of loneliness, I am meeting a woman tonight I met when I listened to James Watson of Crick and Watson fame/DNA double helix stuff, last week at the Harvard Club. He gave a good lecture and I learned, even speaking to him personally. So tonight I will buy a lady with a PhD in speech therapy a drink and have a nice chat. I think I will enjoy it. Thank you Mary Ellen and Ken. Also, a number of clients have called today and that helps to pass the time as well.

For reasons I cannot explain, I have counted 9 three legged dogs today here along the Hudson River where I now sit feeling the sun emerge from a day of hiding behind clouds. It is getting quite warm so off comes the shirt so as to enable me to bronze this old skin. I love this spot even more so than Central Park.

Enough of this rambling. I am turning off all my fancy iPhone/iPad type of things now. Even though I stopped at the Apple Store today to see the new iPhone 6 version, enough is enough.

Out.

Beckett

Two Masted Boat
May 23, 2013

Well hello again. This will be my last NYC email for a while. Hope you all have a great day. You deserve it. Stay dry.

Last night was really nice. I am developing friends in the City and that is a good thing. I seem to have no trouble meeting people. I like talking about issues such as our how our language and speech has gone straight into the crapper. And it has. A glass of wine, a nice friendly woman, and me. Color that good. So I enjoyed my evening.

When I awoke this morning, I ran along in Riverside Park from 66th Street up to 92nd Street. It is a good jaunt from my place, but the cinder tract nearby around the Reservoir is superb. I took a couple of good laps and found that my knees and feet do better on cinder rather than cement. I asked four different runners what the distance was around the Reservoir, but got four different answers. No one seemed to know. I found that I really could turn up the speed which was just great. Felt like a kid again. Of course there were a large number of pretty ladies jogging so I sucked in my stomach and let it rip. What can I say? I was drenched when I returned to 66th Street, and it had not even rained yet.

I took a picture of the two masted boat in Riverside Park as I rested in my favorite spot long after my run. The two master is owned by the fellow that created Mad Magazine, Dick DeBartolo. It was tacking back and forth trying to go South on the Hudson River.

I find that there are a lot of people with dogs in the City. A lovely woman was walking a Pharaoh hound from Malta she advised as the dog was originally bred in Egypt. It was the exact dog you see at the Met in the Egyptian sculpture section, right next to the sculptures of the Pharaohs. Clearly an old breed. Worth a look.

I had a long chart during lunch at Riverside Park with a worker who called himself a structural painter. He and a few other persons were on lunch break from painting the metal supports under the West Side Highway, described by one woman as the way out of the City. All the metal supports are being painted a particular shade of green. The painter told me that it takes about two days to put up the safety wires and scaffolding for a distance of about 65 feet. Then it takes about one day for three guys to paint that 65 feet. The elevated part is miles long. This man and others have a job for life. He seemed a little embarrassed by the fact that the new union rules really slow things down, but he was okay with it. So, he hopes we all like the new color. His painting today was right in the Pier One area.

Tomorrow I am going to go over to Pomander Walk in the Upper West Side which is located between 94th and 95th near Broadway. There are these little houses on one alley or walkway surrounded by tall skyscrapers. This should be worth the jog. If you Google Pomander

Walk you will see what I encounter. So, no three legged dogs today but tons of mothers or nannies and even a few dads pushing their babies along in some rally fancy carriages. I like seeing that as it is emotionally beautiful. I did spend a lot of time at Riverside Park again. Love that place. My walks were halted in part because of some pretty severe rain. But, I did sneak into the Met for an hour to check out the Pharaoh hound sculptures.

So now my first ballet. I guess it really was my second as I had seen Shen Yun the Chinese Ballet production two weeks ago or so. Fabulous. Better than fabulous. It is such controlled motion that you really have to be an athlete to perform. I will go to many more ballets. I even understood much of it. Ironically, I sat next to a Japanese brother and sister at the theater. He was a medical student at Cornell at 70th and York where David attended, and he lived with his sister in Brooklyn. We had a lot in common and they were nice enough to explain what to expect. They knew ballet. I lucked out. It all made sense. Amelia is going to love this activity. I cannot wait to see my first opera in late September. The learning process continues. So much to learn. So little time left. Wish I had started sooner.

Well, Beckett says goodnight and wishes you all a good Memorial Day weekend. Heavens knows where I will be for the next week or so. It will all be good.

Beckett.

Phew two times over. And the rain never came
June 27, 2013

Well my friends, I just awoke from a short midday nap which is unusual for me. In a sense, I think I live the life that many might really enjoy; almost envy. After a lovely night last night of relative rest, relaxation, and enjoyment, I slept well for me. The day had been full of court and clients and was a little stressful. Then I took the early morning bus into the City. What a catharsis the City has become. After shopping for some food for the next day or so at the Gourmet Garage, I decided to run to the George Washington Bridge along Riverside Park and back; for fun. The sun was still shining and rain was predicted. My old legs eventually got me most of the way there and back which is about 12 miles in total. It really is tiring to run so far. Clearly I am wearing out.

It was then time to do something new. So, I took my new free woman's bicycle out for a ride. What an experience! I think I should wear a helmet to protect what little brain power I have left. After riding many streets next to passing taxi cabs and trucks, I decided to ride to and in Central Park. Now that was great. They have specific bike lanes for slow or fast riders. I rode for over an hour. Talk about getting tired! I was tired.

After my shower I cooked and ate my usual broccoli and then ate a lot of fruit. So, I guess my stomach Doc will be pleased with that. No rain yet. So I went to explore and shop. Beckett took a cab to the Morgan Museum and Art Gallery just to see the building which Robber Barron JP Morgan built. Ah, the decadence of conspicuous consumption. You have to hate those type of people, but without them we would have so much less. Walked a bit getting back. Still no rain.

At the Lincoln Center I found the David Rubenstein Atrium. Lots of free entertainment from time to time. Each week on Thursdays usually a free show is put on by Target. So that will be fun another time. I stopped at the New York Public Library for the Performing Arts called the Cullman Center. A great exhibit about Latino Music from the Tango to the Mamba to the Boogaloo to the general concept of Salsa was presented. They called it all Urban Hip Hop. Interesting concepts to listen to and learn about. I still fancy learning. No rain yet.

Since I could not get tickets to the New York Philharmonic, I purchased yet another ticket to the ballet. Yup, my seventh, and this one is called Sylvia. That is where I will be at 7:30pm tonight. In the nose bleed seats. Things do sell out in the City quite quickly.

Then I sat with tired knees at the fountain at Lincoln Center. Pulled the NY Times out of the recycling in the Compactor Room (I will not pay for the paper) and sat down and did the crossword puzzle in between dozes; it was easy today. I enjoy people watching and there were lots of people. Yup, the City has a lot of beautiful young women strutting their stuff. What rain?

So I ambled back to my apartment and intentionally placed this weary body on my couch. I slept like a log for about half an hour. So now I am rejuvenated at Riverside Park in the sun light watching the sail boats tack, the tug boats push, and the ferry boats ferry. I will enjoy my stay here a bit more, gather a meal to satisfy my basic hunger urge, and then treat myself to wine before the ballet. A lovely lady has told me about a spring bike ride through the five Boroughs and also suggested I go to the weekly Festival of Lights. It does not look like rain is coming at all.

To wax philosophical for a minute before Beckett signs off, I want to quote a very sweet bit of language I found on a stone near the firehouse on 66th Street and Amsterdam in the Upper West Side that lost twelve firefighters on 9/11/01:

No farewell works were spoken
No time to say goodbye
You were gone before we knew it
And only God knows why.

Not a bad dry day in large part even though torrential rains were predicted. And to my dear Amelia and Benjamin, I further quote a song I wrote many years ago for my sons David and Mark, "When it rains on the soil, it makes mud". Sing it for me.

Over and out,

Beckett

Shore-a side trip
Tue, Jul 3, 2013 07:51 PM

My friends,

Many of you have asked how things are going Down the Shore. So here it is.

Some of us have a friend who is very ill with a horrible disease. It is a sad time for many. Watching a friend deteriorate from ALS is so difficult. Anyone would be down. And the problem is that the disease is rapidly progressive. Sad three times over. He is a nice guy and his wife is as well. Can you imagine how he feels? His wife feels? There are rhetorical questions of course. Getting old is not for the weak of heart. Some of us have been "there" in some fashion or the other and "get it" more than most know. Bottom line? Do not be afraid to hug someone you love and do not assume the sun will come up tomorrow and bet your bottom dollar on it. Sorry Annie.

Yes, it has been very nice here at the shore. It is a special place and I am lucky to have it. I just want all of you here with me whenever you are able. The shore in a sense is a special gift that has been in my family's life forever, and this Harvey Cedars house since 1985 when Ginny and I built the house. Of course we came down here before the house was built for years. In 1984 I think, I was down the shore alone and saw this lot for sale. I bought it and called Ginny. She said, "You paid what for a sand box?" We laughed and then in a week or two signed the contracts to build the home. We never regretted this decision. There is something special about the ocean, the cove, the fact that you are on an island, the seagulls and the smell of the salt air, having a place on the water, a boat, etc. I so much want Amelia and Benjamin and the new grand baby I will meet in November to allow this place to play a large part in their lives. We have the perfect location in the perfect spot. It is all about happiness and memories.

You would enjoy what I have been doing. Two nights here which equates to almost three days. I see an entirely different group of people that I know. Different conversations. A whole different social sect. Last night I went to a part at Cynthia's (not her real name) house. It was for her family visiting from afar whom I met last year. I did not stay long but had a good time. Poor Cynthia divorced her husband three years ago because she was unhappy and now I think regrets that decision. It is too late. He has met someone else. So, I help her where I am able with her feelings of regret and sadness. Some decisions are irreversible. In a sense, you cannot go home again. I know all about that.

Most of the so-called Al's Gals are down here and I enjoy them of course. What wonderful friends I have in Harvey Cedars. They all make me feel so welcomed. Susan in particular is so special. She and her husband Russ approach being family. Susan even gave me a shore bike for Amelia to ride! I did some serious picking and found a cart of some kind for Benjamin to ride on the deck of the home. In spite of my very bad plantar fasciitis of the heels, the right heel in particular, I have been able to continue to run every day. My new Birkenstock sandals help; imagine me spending more than five for sandals! I have also taken long bike rides on the different bikes we have here. The cove has warmed up and I swim every day just to use infrequently activated musculature. At this rate I am liable to live forever – cannot do that as I have a nice new very large life insurance policy in effect which expires if I hit 105 years. I aim to beat the insurance company at its own game and shall. I think a lot here at the shore and walk the beach every day which is wonderful. You can tell where I have been because I write STD in the sand. When I saw the dolphins yesterday off shore it was magical. Of course I heard all about Mike Whyte's wedding from Larry Whyte (have not seen Ginny yet) and we had a nice talk. The Whytes and my family go back to when we were all virgins and even before! What with so much going on I have not yet taken by boat named "Amelia Ann" out this time but that will happen next time I am here. Lastly, I have been able to get a little client work done as well with reference to the Clinton Fire Department and its by-laws and another unnamed client. My crabs collecting in the trap have been fed with bunker and await Ang's arrival for a meal or release this weekend as I will be in the City with Lizette.

One of the things I think about a lot is whether to sell my Clinton house at this stage of my life. It is quite an expense to keep but very hard to let go of still at this time. So economically it certainly makes sense to sell it. Emotionally I just do not know. Therein lies the rub. Until I am 100% sure I will do nothing.

So there you go. Although Morpheus really seems to be trying to give me a rough time by not letting me sleep, I will head home to Clinton in about an hour or so. I want to get my fasting cholesterol blood test done to see if the Crestor is working. I suspect it is. If it is not, I say "tough". Thursday I will go to the City and begin another adventure of the Beckett. I think Lizette will meet me in the City and we will do all the fun things there are to do including fireworks over the Hudson. At least I will not be alone and have to answer the question "just one?" with "no, the one. Beckett." I know those greeters mean no harm, but you understand. I have explained this before.

Adios amigos y familia. I will shower and drive off to Clinton now. My run will be the Columbia Trail in High Bridge this afternoon. Have a great day and enjoy life.

Still Albert D. for now.

Soon to be Beckett, formerly Albert D.

A brief synopsis.
Saturday, 7/6/13

Run along Riverside Park past the NYPD car impound to about the Javitt's Center and back – coffee along the Hudson River at Pier One – bike ride toward the GW Bridge and back – breakfast in the apartment – did laundry – to Lincoln Center to check out stuff – dried laundry – to the Frick Collection via M66 bus on 5th Avenue at 70th Street (fantastic) – walked to Cornell Medical School at 70th and York – lunch at a French restaurant called Casimir & Company Café at 70th and Lexington (delicious) – back to finish Frick Collection – bus back to apartment – rest – dinner to be had at the historic Algonquin Hotel on 44th between 6th and 5th Avenues at 6:45pm – to Time Warner Building and cool down as well as looking at Center Bar for future use – walked home. Temperature today has been 90 degrees feeling like 100 degrees. To bed early. Tired.

Albert D. Rylak
7/21/13

I have to tell you that a bad day in Harvey Cedars is better than a good day in so many places. Particularly at Kinsey Cove. The heat yesterday was less than ideal, but toward the evening as the sun was setting, the cove was perfectly flat. The snapper bluefish began slapping the water at the surface creating strange rippling shapes. Then about eight Black Skimmer birds started doing their fly-overs. The birds have majestic reddish orange long beaks and flew like the Blue Angels in formation back and forth over the cove, with their lower beaks just touching the water. You could see their trail behind them in the water. It lasted for almost a half hour. I guess they we trolling for something.

So many neighbors and I just stared in awe from our decks at the sight. Such control in the air. Such a reaffirmation of nature. This was the first time I had seen this and hope to see it again. And again. The snapper blues kept slapping and the Black Skimmers kept in their formations.

It is a good thing to take time out of your life to just observe the wonders of nature. In the hustle-bustle of our silly little existence, we tend to focus on things that are meaningless in the broader sense. And so it is. God bless America.

Comments
July 23, 2013

After a very nice time at the Harvey Cedars shore for a few days as per my flapping fish Post, I ended up in Clinton and had a wonderful evening of food and relaxation. Thank you Liz. I guess I am just spoiled. After I saw a client early this morning, I got on the bus to Manhattan. Great move. Tomorrow night a friend is taking me to see Gordon Lightfoot at BB Kings on 42nd Street. Thank you Lida. Gordon Lightfoot wrote and sang such songs as "If You Could Read My Mind", " The Wreck of the Edmund Fitzgerald" and "Rainy Day People" to name a few. Old people like I will immediately recognize the name and the songs. I am flooded with memories. All good. So much is tied in with the Vietnam Nam War, the assassinations of President Kennedy, Martin Luther King, and Bobby Kennedy. Edward Kennedy, the hero of Chappaquiddick, and other poignant memories. My Ginny and I lived through all of these things and more.

So, since getting anywhere but particularly to the City early is my nature, I did just that; about thirty hours early; on purpose. I ran into a friend on the bus that I had not seen for years. Let me just say that her name is Cynthia and is an attorney of genius type material. You know these Yalies. A fortuitous and wonderful meeting. We Rutgers guys have trouble understanding them but it is all okay. Jeff Martin will know of whom I write. Getting from the Port Authority to my apartment is like riding a bike. A snap.

One of my goals is to learn the bus system here in Manhattan. I am pretty comfortable with the subways. So my dear friend Susan, I took the M66 bus to Madison Avenue and 66th and then the M4 bus to 80th from which I departed and walked to the Metropolitan Museum of Art. Putting aside the fact that my lips will not heal from whatever disease they have (or is it that I have) it was a smart move. I love that place and envy me for having the ability to go there so very often. Close to 25 times since April 1st when I got my apartment. There is so much to learn and so little time.

I decided early on that I wanted to take a self-guided tour of the Islamic Section (second floor, 450 and up) of the Met. I am in awe of the Persians. Previously I took a guided tour, but this time it was just me. With certain exceptions, it is usually just me. I am getting used to it. The rug you see below is from the 1500s in Tabriz, Iran. A knockout. The folio was done about 2,000 years ago and is on parchment. If you are able, try to get a really close look at the folio. It is so friggin crystal clear and sharp even with the passage of so much time. I really had a blast and after over two and a half hours decided to leave and really continue my bus riding experience. My knees can only take so much standing. So again Susan, I took the M72 this time. I made it to my apartment with ease. I am learning.

In an effort to remain as apolitical as possible, I keep silently asking myself why the Sunnis, Shia and Kurds in Iran cannot get along. Come on

147

people. Life is short. Enjoy the ride. Your culture is outstanding. Show me some brains. But I digress.

So as I now consume a very nice glass of white Bordeaux prior to 5 pm, I focus on where I will have dinner as it is Restaurant Week in the City. Tomorrow Lida and I will have a great time seeing Gordon Lightfoot. I will meet her at Penn Station and perhaps show her my apartment and a nice dinner. Lida has been gracious enough to water my flowers at the Shore while I am away, which is often. Thursday night if I am here, I will go to Lincoln Center to enjoy Mark Dendy's "Ritual Cyclical". Since I lead an unstructured life now, I have a freedom to do what I want when I want. And one of my wants is to take a course or degree program in Art or Art History. On the other hand, early onset Alzheimer's runs in the family so it might be a little difficult. So I can do nothing if I like.

Why have you wasted your time reading this tripe? It is just about a short period of time in the life of a man without a rudder, for the benefit of some dear friends that always ask how I am and what I am doing. So now you know far more than you wanted. Hit delete if you wish!

Zack and Pretty Women All in a Row.
July 29, 2013

Good day my friends. I am back in Manhattan for a few days now just sitting at Pier 1. After a great time with Lida at the Gordon Lightfoot session at BB Kings, I rested poorly as usual and then returned to Clinton the next day. Clinton is a great family town. Not a very good singles town. What with my current real estate tax bill, I guess the emphasis will continue to be on families. You really cannot fight the school union negotiators who have ruled the roost for years and years. Nor can you fight the State cutback in funds. I really feel sorry for people that pay Clinton real estate taxes but send their kids to private schools. Perhaps there is a conspiracy to drive old people out of the Town as well. But I digress.

I have just spent three nights in Harvey Cedars. So great to see so many friends there from time to time. Mark and Ang were down which is quite nice. I spent a large part of my time there working on my home. Painting and cleaning and similar jobs. This work was able to be done at a slow pace as I had nothing else to do. I am hopeful that next year, David, Mark, and I can have a weekend guy's thing to do this as a family. And, yes, our cove was just special (except for the jelly fish) what with the nice weather. Does anyone really not like to shower out doors?

I am going to do a remodel of my shore house. Many have given ideas and Mark and David have a few as well. Siding, windows, flooring, whatever. Or nothing depending on the price. I have just about thought it all out and now await the estimates. I hope Rick and Debbie will be gentle with me. Why? Why not!

So after I awoke in Harvey Cedars this morning, I drove to Clinton to pay bills, check on things, pay more bills, and then had enough. I should fill in the pool as that cost is steep and burdensome. Ginny used to take care of the pool. I do not need a large lawn. I do not need to central air the world. Too many houses. So little time. But I digress again.

So I met Zach while waiting for the bus. He just graduated from high school and will be attending Juilliard in a few weeks. What a class kid. Plays clarinet and sax. Learned a lot about Juilliard and music generally. Also realized that I know much more about the City and life than I thought. It is so clear that there is a whole world out there that I have to discover. Juilliard costs about $50,000 a year but due to a great endowment, there is help for needy students. What a place to go to school right next to Lincoln Center! Zach is going to send me a schedule of all the events put on by the students there most of which are free. The list will be used. One great point he made is that many of the students go to really fancy events such as the New York City Philharmonic and those folks who have to leave early just give their tickets to anyone so that person may see a portion of the particular show. I think it is jokingly referred to as the Juilliard ticket. Half a symphony is better than none. Anyway, we chatted almost nonstop until 66th Street. Zachary was excited and totally into his future. Please world, do not squelch that desire to learn and to live. There is hope for America so long as there are young people like Zach. I needed that reaffirmation and got it from him.

The moment I got into my apartment I felt alive. So I took an hour run along the Hudson River followed by a half hour bike ride downtown. As to the bike ride, you do get used to weaving in and out of the traffic. It really is a hoot. As to the jog, I know how to meet women if necessary. I was wearing my NYC Marathon shirt, my special one that Ginny had given me when I was a little younger, and a beautiful young woman stopped me and told me she loved the shirt. We jogged a couple of miles together before she turned off on 96th Street. Yes, I ran at her pace and now feel beat. I had no choice. She either took pity on this pathetic old man or, the shirt was a chick magnet. I prefer the latter. Of course I forget her name as my dementia must be on the rise again. Another interesting thing happened. A woman of more than a few years was walking her golden retriever puppy. For unknown reasons, she asked me to hold the leash when she attended to things. Fortuitous? Luck? Fate? Beats me. We live in the same building. She wants to buy me a drink! Her name? I forget.

Anyway, I have to say that the Hudson River is not very clean right now, mostly due to Hurricane Sandy. It will never be the location of the Annual Albert D. Rylak Quadrathlon. There is much debris along the shore and even out as far as you can see. Kinsey Cove is so much more civilized and safe. I know this will break the hearts of the O'Mara family. Sorry guys.

After my run, but before my bike ride, I stopped by the basketball courts again. A very tall woman was dribbling a basketball (dah). I guess I am attracted to height since mine keeps slipping away with osteoporosis. So I entered the court and retrieved balls for her after she began to shoot. We chatted a bit and then played a game of Horse. Actually, she was quite good and I protested that we should have played Jackass in lieu of Horse. She won. I know I was never very good at the game, but at least could hit a couple of shots. Women. Can't live with them. Can't live without them. I have no ego left. Gone with the wind.

So tonight I will treat myself to a really good dinner and then go to Dizzy's Club at 7:30pm to witness jazz, but in a "swing" mode. This will be just great. I do not even know what swing is, but I am sure to learn. A small group of musicians and one hundred of my closest non-friends. Alone again, naturally. A great song by Gilbert O'Sullivan as I have previously mentioned in another post. Tomorrow will be something at Lincoln Center at night if possible. The morning and afternoon will be at the Guggenheim. Never been there. Should be interesting.

Okay. My thoughts for today. It is good to meet new people, as they help you connect with life. Take a chance. The worse that will happen is you will be ignored. There is so much more to life than hard work; we have all been there. Since we only get one life to live, of unknown duration, enjoy what you have and do not count on tomorrow. Smile. Be happy. My sons have enabled me to do this by not objecting to my spending of their inheritances. They are so very capable young men and can take care of themselves easily. Certainly they were the pride of Ginny and me as well. Such fundamentally solid and good men. So, hi ho, hi ho, it's off to spend I go.

For now, Beckett

PS. Some friends wanted my thoughts on FB. And so it will be.

The Hand Modeling Seinfeld Episode
August 13, 2013

Beckett is back in Manhattan. After a very nice two nights in Staunton, Virginia seeing the southern portion of the Rylak/Fairless Family, I decided to take off for the City. Morpheus was good to me last night and all the stars made it so. I essentially arrived at the bus station and after a one second wait, got on the bus. Due to the rain, I anticipated a long trip into the City, but quite to the contrary, it was quick and pleasant. While in the Lincoln Tunnel I noticed a black BMW 535i with a large "Courtesy Car" sign emblazoned on its rear window, with the driver on his cell phone. Ten seconds later the front of that BMW made contact with the rear of a white Mercedes Benz ahead of it. Never saw an accident in the Tunnel before. I am sure traffic built up behind my bus, but there was no knowing for sure.

The 1 Train awaited me and I hopped on carrying my new small coffee maker that David and I purchased at a Target in Waynesboro, Virginia. That device is now pleasantly placed in my apartment kitchen awaiting use tonight or tomorrow morning. Anyway, the picture below is very relevant. For the record, and to all my gay friends, I am not gay. On the contrary the toe nail painting was applied by Amelia, my now 5 year old granddaughter. Everyone needs a good application from time to time she has explained. Much like George in Seinfeld, my nails look perfect; I could model my two large toes. Anyway, while on the 1 Train, I struck up a conversation with a lovely dark haired woman who was sitting across from where I was standing. She said she had a very unusual request and asked if she could take a picture of my painted toe nails as they made her smile. Of course I agreed. So on her camera are three shots of these magnificent nails. We chatted a bit and it turns out that Maria is from Italy and is in medical school there. Her last year involves a stay at Weil Cornell Medical School where my son David attended at 70th and York. We had a lovely talk and exchanged telephone numbers and e-mail addresses. Only in NYC. And you know these Europeans, they like older men even though I could be her grandfather. Anyway, we had gabbed so much that we both forgot to get off at 66th Street but closer to Columbia. So we took a cab to my place when she could get on the M66 crosstown bus to Cornell Medical which she had intended to take all along. Yup. NYC is not ready for me yet. I am a novelty.

Anyway, I decided to take a long run along the Hudson River at Riverside Park. It was pouring rain but wonderful. For the first 45 minutes I headed north. The place was deserted. No joggers. No bikers. Just me and the rain. Looking at the River, large boards were floating by and upon many of them were located Canada Geese enjoying their ride. I assumed the geese were surfing the waves. Reminded me of Harvey Cedars. The geese looked happy although none of them hung ten. That made me happy. On my way back to my apartment, South, the rain picked up even more so, and I began to see people running and bikers biking. Of course I was drenched/soaked to my skin as was everyone else. The rain forced a comradeship. Everyone smiled and said hello. Sweet. With about a mile to go, a lovely woman caught up to me and asked how I liked running in the rain. We ran together and of course the pace picked up. My testosterone would not allow me to do anything but keep up with her stride for stride. Phew. Tired me out but the rain helped me out quite a bit. And so I returned to my apartment where I now sit, having just vacuumed a bit and now get ready for some afternoon and evening activities. So much to learn. So little time.

In half an hour I will be at the Metropolitan Museum of Art for the afternoon and then Lincoln Center or a jazz club tonight. Life can be difficult. Just not today I hope. The sun is now shinning. It is a good thing.

Beckett

Four to Four
August 24, 2013

Well my friends, albeit e-mail or FB, here is today's 12 hour saga of Beckett, perhaps to be Phoenix, in the City. It has been one heck of a day, and much more is to come.

I awoke at 4 am in Clinton and felt somewhat tired as you might imagine. After coffee and the like, I went on my usual 5 mile run. Dumb idea based on what follows. Anyway, Liz was coming over at 7:15 am so we could catch the 7:40 am bus. After a pretty good run my esophagus issues reared their ugly heads again. Crap. Anyway, Liz arrived and we made an earlier bus into Manhattan. Quite a speedy trip in considering.

After our arrival we went to my favorite spot, Bryant Park. Got some coffee and tea, a croissant, and some kind of pecan biscuit. The temperature was cool, the park beautiful, and we sat and watched people and had a great bit of chit chat. Eventually we pulled ourselves away from the Park and took the 1 train to my apartment on 66th. All day the weather was simply perfect for the middle of August. We had already decided to take the free Staten Island Ferry to St. George, Staten Island and we did. I know Lisa's eldest does it all the time, but for an initiate such as me, it was fantastic. The photo accompanying this post shows one of a million great views.

Getting on the Ferry is like being in a cattle call. Seemed to be thousands of people and there were. A calm and smooth ride, excitement, perfect everything for the entire ride to Staten Island and back made things special. Saw the Verrazano Narrows Bridge where some years ago I started the NYC Marathon, tug boats, sail boats, barges, old replica boats from the early 1800s, tons of Muslim women all around me, lots of Spanish, German, and other languages being spoken from all directions, Ellis Island, the magnificent Statute of Liberty, Governor's Island, a lighthouse, and I think I will just stop there. It was a complete thrill for this rube from Hunterdon County.

Afterward we decided to go to the Brooklyn Bridge and walk over it into Manhattan. Due to a subway outage or repair issues, we had to do a lot of walking to get the right subway into Brooklyn, the Green 4, 5 line, and then figure out how to get to the Brooklyn Bridge. Tiredness and hunger were setting in so we walked from Brooklyn City Hall up to a miraculous street called Montague Street. There we luckily found a wonderful restaurant called Caffe Buon Gusto. What a great lunch. Perhaps because we were tired; perhaps because we were thirsty; who knows? Delicious food and drink, and a very nice conversation with others dining al fresco. We were told to walk the Brooklyn Promenade to the Bridge and we did so. Prior to finding the Bridge, Liz felt the female urge to shop and did so, purchasing herself a nice black sweater for tonight's activities. What majestic views of Manhattan. Just perfect again. Needless to say we were more getting tired. Eventually we got to DUMBO, which stands for District Under the Manhattan Bridge Overpass. Quite a nice area, right Ginny? And Ken, it was great to see where Pace University is located from the Bridge.

It seemed as if the entire City was outside walking due to the magnificent weather. We eventually found the walking entrance to the Brooklyn Bridge and did just that. Tons and tons of people. I guess this is the thing to do in NYC!! There is a bicycle lane and a walking lane, each filled to the brim with people. Somehow we got to the other side into Manhattan and then found the three different subways we were required to take to get back to the Upper West Side-the Green 6 to the Yellow JNQ to the Red 1 line. Somehow we hit each train just as it was about to leave. Made it here to the apartment at about 4 pm.

And so we are here in my apartment, listening to some Jazz music and preparing for our 6 pm dinner at Dizzy's Club where we will have a nice dinner and then at 7:30 pm listen to "Endangered Species the music of Wayne Shorter". Jazz is a good thing. Like ballet, it gets into your blood. I do enjoy it so.

So I guess you can see that this has been one hell of a 12 hours. Another 6 hours to go and then I will collapse and smile knowing that I have again enjoyed a small portion of what this glorious City has to offer.

Out.

Beckett, soon to be Phoenix?

Saturday Night Continuum
August 28, 2013

To those on my e-mail list or FB, I wanted to wrap up my Manhattan stay this past weekend. The jazz at Dizzy's was just great. A twelve piece group giving it all they had is just off the charts exciting. I had no idea, but there are at least four types of saxophones; the tenor, alto, soprano, and baritone. They were playing their hearts out the other evening. It is so much more fun to go with someone to such an event. I guess we are social beings and that is why we pair up so often. So a special thank you to Liz for coming along. It was well worth the trip. God bless America.

Sunday was a day of jogging, resting, and recuperating from Saturday, walking, and eating. We decided to get the 3 pm bus back to Clinton, but wanted to have lunch in dear old Bryant Park prior to our departure. From the time we left the subway we knew that something was in the air. Large groups of men with cameras or cellphone cameras surrounded something clearly important. So I/we moved toward the center of the pile and low and behold a very large number of women who had discarded their clothing from the waist up. It was obvious that they were protesting something. We later learned that the protest was part of the International Go Topless Day celebration. It was felt by many of the women there that they had equal rights to men in exposing their attributes and that same was legal in New York State. They were and are right. Liz accused me of knowing that the event was occurring before we arrived at Bryant Park. Of course I had no idea, but did make a point to take a few cellphone photos to document the event. For the record, I absolutely support and encourage all ladies to freely and unabashedly participate in the event next year or any other day. I would never deny anyone, particularly a woman, of her god given right to bare her god given attributes and to protest their constriction by any person or thing. Actually, it would make the world a better place. But enough of this chatter.

After a lovely couple of days in Clinton and Harvey Cedars, some of which involved legal work, I am now again back in the City. I do want to thank Karen for the great furniture and Susan for arranging stuff. The early bus brought me here and I immediately did a very long run along the Hudson River at Riverside Park South. It was very nice and there were tons of people running along much faster than I, getting in their runs before the sun really warmed things up today. As is my habit on this day, I read aloud Martin Luther King's speech that was given at the Lincoln Memorial 50 years ago today. It makes me feel good. Afterward, I cooked myself a cheese omelet and now I am fed until dinner. I am very good at cooking easy things. The air conditioning in my apartment is off until 4 pm for repairs, but that is NBD. No Big Deal. As I sit here typing, a new friend from a month ago has said hello and soon we will chat. He is a very nice man and is one of my new city buddies.

I have two primary goals today. Yes, I will go to the Met this afternoon and study art again for the 30 somethingeth time. There is no such word as "somethingeth" but I like the way it sounds. I just want to learn something new and different today. Perhaps something Syrian in view of what Assad is doing in that country now. Also, at 8 pm I am going to my first opera, which is outdoors at Lincoln Center. This should be a hoot as it is "La Clemenza di Tito" by Mozart which he wrote in 1791 shortly before he died. Should be interesting. Why are operas in Italian? Why have I never before been to an entire opera?

Anyway, I shall return to Clinton tomorrow as it will be my 69th birthday. Time flies. How did I ever live this long? Blind luck. I am sure that after my run I will be able to find things to do here that will keep me occupied.

Yes, I will return to Bryant Park before I leave, but it for sure will be less interesting this time! I would like to think that there still is fire in this partly gray-haired old body.

As an aside, I have been reading about how some parents hire others to write the college application essays for their little dears. To avoid this, might I suggest that colleges have applicants arrive, give them a piece of paper and a pen, and have them write about a given topic. That would solve that issue quite quickly. And finally, please Mr. President, do not only give a great speech today, but make the correct decisions on the issues that we face throughout the Middle East and the world. The lives of our children and grandchildren depend on it. Sorry for the political commentary. It just slipped out.

Ciao.

Temporarily Phoenix, formerly known as Beckett, formerly known as Albert, a recovering attorney

Tinkers to Evers to Chance. T to E to C.
September 5, 2013

To my e-mail and Facebook friends who have asked how I am, I give you a fine hello. Although my esophagus is having continuing issues today, T to E to C rules the roost. I seem to be running from Clinton to Manhattan to Harvey Cedars in three consecutive days. No problem. It is part of my psyche. You cannot change the spots on a leopard or the ways of an old person. My first grade teacher in Trenton, NJ hit the nail on the head when she said I had "ants in my pants" and wrote it on my report card, much to the dismay of my parents. It is still true today.

Yesterday was a very nice day in Clinton. I got so much done personally and with my clients, and topped it off with my first court appearance in a while. I have always liked going to court but in my semi-retired or Of Counsel state, it is even more fun because of its rarity. I guess I was always cut out to be an attorney as I seem to like challenges and also have the mouth that roars. And so it is. Also, some decisions will be made soon as to whether I wish to enter into the governmental/political realm in addition to my Hunterdon Healthcare Systems role as a Trustee and my Deni Law Group duties. So Clinton continues to have so much to offer to me at this time. So another T to E to C may occur in Clinton.

Today I was on the first bus to the City. I woke up early with bad esophagus/stomach issues that interfered a little with my daily run among other things. The sun rose as I entered the Lincoln Tunnel and all was good with the world. What a day I have planned. Today is the start of Fashion Week which is held all over the City, but is headquartered at Lincoln Center, just around the corner from my apartment. I have already seen some perfectly beautiful skinny women all over Lincoln Center and environs. Far more than usual. And, I intend to keep looking for more of them. They have an aura about themselves; a sense of self-assurance; a sense of command; a sense of strength. I have always said that the strongest person in the world is a beautiful woman with a brain. It remains true. Only the VIPs get into the shows, but I will enjoy my observations from afar nonetheless.

Anyway, after I stalk these almost anorexic woman and fill my old eyes with shock, awe and wonder, it is my intention today to tour Chelsea, Tribeca, and the Village. It is time that I grow up and get a little more comfortable in these locations. So that I will do. If my stomach holds up, I will find Cornelia Street in Greenwich Village where as a teenager my recently departed friend and high school classmate Bill H. and I consumed libation into the early morning hours and met a fella who later became Bob Dylan. I think I will fancy a great lunch or dinner in an appropriate café as well. I will need to experiment with the 1 and A trains for this adventure.

My day will end with my first ever attendance by invitation at the grand opening of an art exhibit at the Amsterdam Whitney Gallery at 511 W 25th Street in Chelsea. Feel free to Google it. One of my friends, Carole Boyd, is one of the exhibitors and has invited me to participate in the consumption of Champaign and other goodies while trying to learn and appreciate her art and that of others on display. So this is another first for me in my older years. I look forward to this my third event today. T to E to C.

Tomorrow I shall return to Clinton and Liz and I will go to Harvey Cedars after her day's work for a short time "down the shore". Saturday I hope to take some of my Harvey Cedars lady friends on the widow/widower Cruise in my boat, weather permitting. It is so much fun to tour the canals of Loveladies and see the beautiful waterfront homes. Conspicuous Consumption I suspect. There are too many widows and widowers in my shore neighborhood. So we are in a special club. We "get it" without saying a word. Walking the beach, seeing friends, eating well, drinking a little, and just enjoying Kinsey Cove are on the agenda. I am sure the weather will cooperate at least until we return to Clinton Saturday evening. Lastly, I believe the O'Mara family may seek to compete in this year's fourth running of the Albert D. Rylak Annual Quadrathlon, which event was unanimously sanctioned last weekend by the Albert D. Rylak Annual Quadrathlon Sanctioning Committee. T to E to C.

Well, that is about it. I did find the NY Times crossword puzzle for yesterday, Wednesday, in the recycle/ Trash Compactor room on my apartment floor. It was undone so I am forced by necessity to try to finish it off before my adventures continue. I get particular satisfaction not having paid for the privilege of doing so.

Have a wonderful day. Amelia and Benjamin, I will be down to Staunton, Virginia to see you on Sunday afternoon. Sweet. God bless America.

Albert D. Rylak, formerly known as Beckett, now known as Phoenix unless some better name comes along.

You Just Cannot Make This Stuff Up. I Am One Lucky Person
Sat. Sept 21, 2013 9:04pm

45

This is a story in part about the number 45. You cannot make this stuff up. I am one lucky person. At least in many ways.

My friend Liz and I decided to go to Gettysburg, PA yesterday and today for a few reasons. We left early yesterday morning, Friday, and arrived in Gettysburg before 11:30 am. Our goals were to see Liz's College, Gettysburg, to tour the Battle of Gettysburg Battle Fields, and to have dinner with four of Liz's college classmates. Having read up on the battle the past 10 days or so, we were ready for almost anything.

A fortuitous decision was made to see the College Campus first. We wanted to stop at the college bookstore in a building with a main auditorium where years ago Presidential candidate George H. W. Bush had spoken. A Gettysburg shirt and some paraphernalia were to be purchased. So off we went just enjoying the weather and anticipating a great day.

When we arrived and entered the auditorium it was clear that a TV show or documentary was being taped. On the stage was Chris Wallace, the son of Mike Wallace. Three gentleman sat on the stage with him wearing their Congressional Medals Of Honor, to wit, First Lt. Harvey "Barney" Barnum, Staff Sgt. Sal Giunta, and Staff Sgt. Clint Romesha. These recipients were in Gettysburg along with 42 other Congressional Medal of Honor recipients to speak to groups about themselves and their comrades as part of the 2013 Congressional Medal of Honor Society Convention. We were transfixed at the stature of these three recipients. You really become so proud to be an American listening to these heroes tell their stories. There is hope for this country. Some of the things said about our current politicians will not be repeated now, but someday I will tell you personally what they had to say. They are brave self-effacing heroes. We were honored to be in their presence. I even got to shake Barney's hand and nearly faint in admiration. They had so much to say. Each has their own web page and you can see them and realize what heroes they were and are. These men are truly exceptional in every way.

We then we did a tour of Gettysburg College and it was beautiful and wonderful. I love colleges and Liz gave me the grand tour. We also toured the Borough of Gettysburg which is an adorable small town surrounded by history. Some of the high lights would be the train station where President Abraham Lincoln entered the Borough to give his Gettysburg Address. We saw the Will house where Lincoln stayed and made revisions to the draft document. The Presbyterian Church where Lincoln worshiped. Musket ball marks on buildings were prevalent. I could go on and on but will stop here. History spoke to me. A delightful and inspiring place. So much to take in.

And then the battlefields. Unbelievable. I had not been to Gettysburg since my 8th grade class trip. There was and is a sense of awe and reverence. Culp's Hill, Cemetery Hill, Seminary Hill, Round Top, Little Round Top, Devil's Den, the wheat field, the peach orchard, Pickett's Charge, Generals Meade and Lee, the fish hook, the infamous General Sickles and so much more. It was a dream come true to see all of this over yesterday and part of today. Tiring but glorifying. And having just seen the Congressional of Honor Recipients, it made for an even more hallowed experience. We even hired a guide named Rick to drive our car with us in it and take us all over the National Park and describe in detail what happened on July 1, 2, and 3, 1863. On my jog this morning I went up to the Gettysburg National Cemetery and recited the Gettysburg Address just where Abraham Lincoln said it. I saw the graves of so many who died in the battle and the hair on my neck stood up. Liz was great as she knew the entire battlefield area and has a keen sense of direction. Having gone to Gettysburg, she had visited the battlefields many times. She kept getting us in the direction where we wanted to go. I could hear the confederate soldiers scream and their death knell as they were mowed down by the Union artillery. I felt a presence there. It was surreal.

But the best is yet to come. After breakfast at the Lincoln Diner, we were heading back to the battlefields when we stopped in front of the Presbyterian Church I previously mentioned. Lincoln worshiped at this church as did the Eisenhower family during and after IKE's Presidency. This could only happen to me. Police cars and sirens sounded and traffic was halted; certainly not for me. Two large buses pulled up and their occupants disembarked. Yes, all of the participating 45 recipients of the Congressional Medal of Honor had been brought to the tiny borough of Gettysburg to now worship and be honored at the Gettysburg

Presbyterian Church, the very same church Presidents Lincoln and Eisenhower had worshiped!! Liz and I saw each one wearing their majestic blue ribboned star. Some walking, some walking with a limp or with a cane, and some in wheelchairs. Clearly we had witnessed a special and precious moment. Rarely does one see 45 of the bravest and most heroic Americans in one spot at one time. We did, right in front of the Church. Yes, I am a very lucky man. I am honored. I will never forget that moment. I know Liz feels the same way. The United States Marine Colored Guard and rifle drill team topped off the majesty of the moment. You learned that the lowest ranking person always saluted first. Yes, and it was never the recipients. So, we stood on the sidewalk and saw all of this. Unbelievable.

Now I am very tired and probably should have written this Post tomorrow. I just wanted to try to let you all know of this special time in my life. From the Gettysburg College to the three special recipients to the Borough of Gettysburg, to the battlefields, to the National Cemetery and most wonderfully to the 45. May God bless you very special people?

And so Morpheus pulls me toward the second floor to rest, perchance to dream.

Albert D., formerly known as Beckett, and at times known as Phoenix

Foot Casts and Other Things
Fri Oct 4, 2013 4:52pm

Last night was not particularly good for sleep but I still felt rested and relaxed. I made a wise decision to stay in Clinton yesterday. And so, here comes NYC today, right at you.

I got the early bus into the City and on my way to the bus stop saw Megan, my Town of Clinton Councilperson predecessor. She is one active lady. The bus ride in was quite uneventful except for this large rock that came out of a truck and smashed a window along the side of the bus. That was novel!

Upon arriving in the City I went directly to my apartment and nostalgia swept all over me. So great to be back. I have only used my place three nights in the past month. Color that sad. Such a nice place so beautifully furnished by Linda.

So I decided to do my run. It was a long one as I had until 10 am as the Met did not open until then. Decided to head south along the Hudson as I wanted to see where than crazy maniac stabbed five people with scissors along Riverside Park South. I found the spot near the old retired train. To think the nut was trying to lash out at a baby being held by his father. I really think they should ban scissors just like guns although we all know that it is the nut, not the scissors, who lashed out and hurt 5 people. And Susan, that little child and his dad lived in your building at 185 WEA.

I am trying to be more rational with my runs and wanted to break things up a bit. So I continued south to the Port Authority and then headed up to the Met on 83rd and 5th Avenue. Needless to say I went through Central Park and saw all sorts of things of interest, including the one Civil War Monument in the Park. All the while I was thinking about what I would do at the Met; where I would go and what I would see.

At this point I had been trotting along for over 90 minutes and my knees were hurting. The lines into the Met were long so I cut across the lines, getting chastised by a few, and sat on the stairs. Thirst kept calling for me although I had no water and no money to buy water. I was stretching these tired OLD legs. They were tired and they are old. I was stinky and drenched with perspiration but when the lines subsided I went inside with my year pass.

I did not see one exhibit but had a damn ball. The last week or so I have spent hours studying the textile exhibit from 1500-1800 AD. Really neat stuff and I was amazed as to how the Persians, Chinese, and others had silk, made all sorts of clothing and draperies and rugs etc. for the wealthy. The exhibit stressed that the silk trade was tied into the spice trade from Iran and the Caspian Sea, east of the Urals, all the way to Italy and even South America. I learned a lot.

So when I entered the Met, I saw that there was a day long symposium entitled "Interwoven Globe" at the Grace Rainey Rogers Auditorium. An entire day of education on the exhibit I had recently studied!! Internationally acclaimed scholars from all sorts of great schools were exploring the impact of the textile trade in the above period called the early modern period, focusing on how trade textiles influenced global economics, social history, and the like. That was a mouthful! I stayed for four lectures and there were at least four more to go. One in particular reminded me of my Dutch friend Lida and was entitled "The Dutch East India Company and Asian Raw Silk: from Iran to Bengal via China and Japan". Those Dutch were very smart people. I guess what I am saying is that the learning never stops and I am so lucky to have stopped in at the right time. Absolutely great even though I did not stay the entire time. I had more fish to fry.

So I jogged back to my apartment. It took over half an hour and I was as beat as could be. Along the way I noticed that after getting out of Central Park, I found a McDonald's on Amsterdam near 72nd. I suspect that since my friend Liz might enjoy a birthday dinner there and I am not a big spender, that I will be frequenting McDs sooner than later. Anyway, I ate and then went to Riverside Park again to watch the ships and people. As usual I picked up my free NY Times crossword puzzle for today and worked on it. Quite easy for a Friday. The only person I spoke to was a guy who lived on 61st and gave me the info re the stabbing. This was not a lonely day so all was well.

Having time to spare I decided to go up to Lincoln Center. First I walked around Juilliard just to see inside. What a place. Then I saw these large metal objects that I guess you would call sculpture. They were all over the fountain area and quite attractive. After people watching a bit I eventually ended up at the New York Public Library for the Performing Arts. There were two photographic exhibits, one by a Hungarian fellow named Michael Peto and the other an English woman named Florence Vandamm. Really beautiful. These two people are long dead, but they took black and white photos of the Beetles, famous actors and actresses, and generally famous or well-known people. Vandamm is said to have invented the head shot. It was a good time. It was worth studying.

I have thought about going to Julliard tonight to listen to a cellist play at Paul Hall. Do not know if I have the energy for that. It is free which I like and the cellist is a fourth year student at the school. We will see.

As an aside, today was a day to also see men and women in boot casts. I counted 9 of them just on the Upper West Side. I guess a lot of people broke their ankles or other bones this past week. Usually the right foot. Heavens knows why. At least the three legged dogs were not around. At least the scissor guy is in jail or a mental hospital.

Tomorrow I head home to per chance be with people I know. There are so many millions of people in the City yet I usually speak to myself, in my mind. Since I write of my NYC experiences to answer the question I am so often asked as to how I am doing, I also copy these notes so my grandchildren, born or about to be born, will know something of me and of this great City. And that is all I have to say about that.

Beckett, formerly known as Albert, and also known as Phoenix, a recovering attorney

The Man in the Pink Dress and Other Glorious Abnormalities in Manhattan
Sun, Oct 13, 2013 7:26pm

Well Amelia and Benjamin and the soon to arrive new baby, I will give you a report on today in NYC which I shall also share with others. Sleep was difficult last night. It is a Rylak trait, so get used to it. You have me to blame for this characteristic and no one else. You have no choice, so live with it in the moment.

After a very nice jog along Riverside Park South, I noted that my knees had healed a tad from all the walking and standing at the Met yesterday. During my jog I passed a middle aged lady twice. Each time she asked me for the time. The first time I though she was just asking. The second time I noted that she asked anyone who jogged past her the very same question. So I told her midnight the second time. She said thank you and proceeded to ask the person behind me the same questions. Funny and sad at the same time. Things like this can stretch your tolerance at times. I am sure I will see her again tomorrow morning as well. At least she did not ask for money.

Liz and I took the 1 train mid-morning to 18th Street. Wanted to be outside a bit due to the nice weather. Stopped at the Rubin Museum on 16th just to see it and then went off to see Chelsea Market again. Every time I go there, I am amazed at how many different things are located in that building. Large bowls of spices and teas. Just amazing to me. The aromas of all the cooking foods was stimulating without causing difficulty. It was a nice place to be.

Then we went over to Chelsea Piers. Last time we were there was shortly after Hurricane Sandy and the place then was a wreck. It has been restored and I enjoyed sitting alongside the Hudson River with the assorted views of the Statue of Liberty (which by the way is in New Jersey), Jersey City, and Hoboken. On the way over, we stopped at the place where the naked ladies were being painted (they were not there) as per a previous post, an art gallery that I had visited previously which had this incredible large photo of Jackie Kennedy for sale for tons of money, saw fake cows at an abandoned gasoline station, and learned that most art galleries in Chelsea are not open on Sunday.

On the way down to Chelsea and on the way back to the UWS we had the pleasure of watching some pretty agile young men dance on the subway, "It's Showtime". I did post a video of that earlier today. It was quite entertaining although a few people did not like the idea. It is only in New York.

When we got back to the apartment it was time to rest. Our legs were a little tired. Wine helped relieve some of the pain. Since we had early reservations for dinner at Rosa Mexicano we travelled over to Lincoln Center to look at the outdoor fair. It was there I saw the man in the pink hoop skirt dress. Quite the sight. Saw him a bit later and snapped another photo, but he indicated he did not want that to happen. Heavens knows why he was wearing that dress but I guess he had his reasons. He was buying a pinkish kerchief to go with the dress. Needless to say, this was quite interesting. After seeing Joaquim Phoenix, Rooney Mara, Amy Adams, Spike Jones, and Olivia Wilde at a red carpet event at Lincoln Center Saturday night, I guess anything is possible in this City.

The pink dress photo will not be posted in deference to the wearer.

Our dinner at Rosa Mexicano was really delicious and now we are back at the apartment resting. After all that we did yesterday and today, it is time to zone in on a moment now for rest and relaxation. 60 Minutes is on and tea is brewing. Tomorrow Clinton will be in view as this short sojourn into the City will end. We have to see some of the Columbus Day Parade on Fifth Avenue prior to leaving. It is always sad to leave NYC. On the other hand, Clinton is a very lovely Town and I look forward to being in it until I head off to the Shore. Ricky Nelson sang it all with "Traveling Man" back in my high school days.

And so the sun now sets on NYC. She has done me proud again. These Posts will soon end as my time in the City becomes more ordinary. These things really do happen to me. Not a lick of falsity. I seem to be in the right place at the right time quite often.

Beckett, formerly known as Al, and soon to continue with Phoenix

Rubin but Not the Sandwich
October 19, 2013 7:50am

Amelia, Benjamin, and unknown third grandchild, I have a few more thoughts for you. My time in NYC was fantastic yesterday and will continue another day or so longer. I promise now that these epistles and reports will end on April 1, 2014, my one year anniversary of having my NYC apartment. By then I hope I have given you enough information to be able fall in love with this City and get to know more about the scrivener and life. Of course, when you are old enough to read!

Yesterday I awoke after a pretty good sleep. Sleep is a good thing when you get it. On the other hand, the big sleep will eventually impose itself on us all. I knew I would go into the City, but decided to take care of some Town of Clinton business first since I am now a government official type. A great run sealed the deal and then off I went to the bus station. The ride in was so fast. One hour door to door! I sat next to a really nice woman who was taking her niece and nephew from Oklahoma in to visit the City. We chatted and she asked ME for advice as to where to visit and what to see. The mouth that roared did just that. I almost knew what I was talking about.

The usual feelings of sophistication and happiness arrived once I got on the 1 Train. I notice that my Amelia-painted big toe nails glow through my sandals and that many people look down at my feet. I want to scream out "Amelia did that" but do not. Perhaps I have a feeling of what it is to be a woman in society what with men and other women eying you up and down. At least they just look at this old man's toes.

Having too many places to live can be a problem particularly with food. At my apartment the milk had spoiled and the lettuce had turned blackish. And I was out of Cognac!!! Since the weather was so nice I decided to waste no time and wanted to walk around and then take the 1 Train to 18th Street and walk to the Rubin Museum. And I did. People still looked at my toes on the subway but there were no dancers or singers in the aisles.

When I arrived at the Rubin, the experience was Zen-like. If you Google the museum you will see that it has mostly Himalayan and Tibetan art from Afghanistan to India to Burma to China. Nonetheless, it is mostly Buddhist art and artifacts. The first thing to think about is that the central interior six story circular staircase is art in and of itself. It is like a reverse Guggenheim effect. The soft music creates a first impression of calmness. And, since I am a senior, the cost was a mere $5.00 to enter and re-enter.

My goal was to spend a large part of the day at the Rubin and I did. My friend Ken had suggested this as have others. Until 1:30pm I was all over the six floors. Just before 1:00pm I took a tour of the basement floor with a very smart guide to study beads. Yes, beads. The first ever really found were from the Hindu people, then the Buddhist people, then the Islam people, then the Christians. Most of the beads were prayer beads and of significance the number 108 has great meaning to the Buddhists. Beads were made from everything starting with wood to human bones. Beads are cool. The interesting thing is that all this tied into my prior trips to the Met where I studied tapestries and art spreading throughout the world via the old trade and spice routes I have spoken about in prior epistles. It was as if all this art stuff from the Met to the Rubin came together in one large collection in my mind.

Anyway, I went off to have a very large lunch at a place Pat had me visit a year ago called Moran's on 10th Avenue and 19th in Chelsea. I ate outside in the glorious sunshine with vehicles whizzing by. I had had some wonderful conversations today with some clients and continued that a bit as I drank a much deserved beer. I only speak to clients I really like when I the City. I want to feel like I am helping someone when I take the time to chat, and I enjoy trying to fix things. A lovely young lady sat next to me, aren't they all at my age? We had a very nice talk for quite some time.

My ego loved it! At least it was not just "me" as is usually the case.

Then back to the Rubin Museum. I did stop and see Yoko Ono's "Wish Tree" in Chelsea on the way back. It was about 3:30pm and I was late for the general tour of the Museum I had hoped to attend. Anyway, I found the group and stayed until the end. Our tour guide was incredible. She knew more about Buddhism then I know about anything. I like smart people and particularly smart people that know how to communicate. She was just an encyclopedia of knowledge on what we looked at. After the tour my eyes were feeling a little askew and I continued with a headache I have had for a few days. Crap. Nonetheless, there are so many questions. What is Hinduism? What is Buddhism? Who is this guy Buddha who lived 2600 years ago? Is Buddhism a religion or is it a philosophy? Can you have a religion that believes in the afterlife in the form of reincarnation but has no central God? All this and so much more is reflected in the art and experience I observed at the Rubin.

Anyway, I took the 1 Train back to 66th Street and went to the Gourmet Garage to get some food. On my way back to my apartment at Amsterdam, I saw this forlorn man with two large grocery bags at his feet and using crutches. Our eyes met and I said "you need some help, don't you?" He smiled and said he did. He had broken his left leg and was trying to get his food back to his apartment near me. I grabbed the bags and walked to his place at 150 Lincoln Towers. A really nice man. He has a two bedroom unit. That is sweet. We had a nice chat as we neared his apartment and he thanked me of course. Turns out he was an ABC reporter who was head of his division and had covered all kinds of wars and even the World Trade Center bombing on site. His name was Bill Blakemore. You should Google this name. When I googled him later I realized that he was quite the big shot at ABC although he was really quite unassuming. Besides, it just goes to show you what happens in the City.

I promise this is coming to an end. Soon. Getting back to my apartment, my back was now hurting a little from carrying all the groceries. No good deed goes unpunished! I ate a little dinner and tried to watch the last part of The Five. After the recent debacle in Congress with the shutdown of the Government and our debt limit discussions and our $17,000,000,000,000.00 (did I add enough zeroes?) national debt, I had enough of TV so-called news. The TV chatter only exacerbated my headache so I went for a short run. The weather still was wonderful and I picked up a bottle of Kelt Cognac on my way back. It seems like everyone has either a dog or a child in a stroller in NYC.

The best part of my day then happens as I watch the buildings light up like Christmas trees in the night as I sip my cognac and relive my wonderful time in the City.
So today I want to go to Bryant Park to people watch and then the Neue Gallerie on 5th Avenue. Then who knows what I will do or what experience will befall me. You have to be open to change to get through the day sometimes. I guess I am as open as can be. Why? Why not! Time to run in Riverside Park.

October 29, 2013

What a day today has been and it is not over. Yet. Clinton is a wonderful Town, yet sometimes single older people such as I need more stimulation. Clinton gives you security and a wonderful family lifestyle. It cannot provide everything to everybody. And so, there is Manhattan.

Today I caught the very early bus into the City. Very special seeing the sun rise behind the Empire State Building from the bus. I did my run before the bus ride as I was determined to accomplish a lot today. And I did so far. After a short breakfast at my apartment I took the bus to the Met. Transferring on Madison to the number 4 bus, I broke the Metro Pass machine on the bus. Beats the hell out of me as to what happened, but I did it. All pickups after that event on 72nd were free. I apologized to the bus driver and he was a real sport about it. It must be the Rylak charm or lack of charm!

I did three things at the Met which tired me out quite a bit. First, I went to the Balthus Cats and Girls-Painting and Provocations exhibit. Cats are in most of the paintings, but too many young girls in positions they should avoid. Nonetheless, it was quite good. Balthus does have talent but seems to like teenage girls a little too much. What was especially useful was the fact that they had a booklet in large print that I could use to read all about each piece of art. My eyes seem to not be working right of late and that book was quite useful. Could it be that one is only allowed to see so much art and then your eyes shut down? Hope not.

Anyway, I then decided to see the exhibit on Medieval Treasures from a German place called Hildesheim. Wonderful artifacts from the 1200s. A small exhibit but the talent in creating crosses and other church items was splendid. And I did see the Golden Madonna. Sweet.

And then the music came. I took a tour of 18th and 19th century musical instruments. And many from an earlier time. Saw a number of Stradivarius and Amati violins; saw a harpsichord or ten, piano fortes, lutes, and lyres. The person that led the tour was outstanding. She went well over the usual one hour limit and everyone in the group was amazed, applauding after she finished.

From the Met I went off to Chelsea Market and had lunch. Of course I am alone as usual, but that is okay. This senior rate for the Metro Card is the best there is. Thank you Russ. Although I was going to go to the Rubin I decided that I was just too tired and came back to my apartment. Love my apartment. Thank you Linda. I do not know how much longer I can keep it but it has made a vast difference in my otherwise non-Beckett life.

And so, after another short rest, I went off to the David Rubinstein Atrium at Lincoln Center where they now sell discount tickets to many activities at Lincoln Center. It is like Tkts on Broadway at Times Square, but helps us un-wealthy see all sorts of performances at half price. Sooooo, tonight I get to see Macbeth at the Vivian Beaumont Theater, 15 rows from center stage, at half price. I knew Macbeth was playing this week, but never thought I would be able to see it. I cannot wait. I am a Shakespeare aficionado and this will be icing on my NYC cake. I am excited and happy.

So, I intend to "cook" dinner tonight, watch The Five, and then eventually end up at Macbeth. What a great day. I learned and will continue learning a lot. The weather is perfect. I will have a long run at Central Park tomorrow, go to Bryant Park for coffee and a scone, maybe go to another museum before getting on the bus back to Clinton, and then do some Town of Clinton business at my home in the Town of Clinton at 7pm. Today was a good day. Earlier last week I had a very nice time in Staunton, VA. Life is passable.

That is it. Amelia and Benjamin, and the yet to be born new grand-baby, live life to the fullest. I have miles to go before I sleep. And to my Facebook provocateurs, it was fun today to analytically deal with issues. It is good for the brain and a diversion while sitting at the Met resting my old knees.

Beckett

Walter Mitty and a Feeling of Nostalgia
Sat, Nov 2, 2013 9:28am

Amelia, Benjamin, and as yet unborn but loved new grandchild. I write this for you as always but also to see how fast my friends can hit delete! Do not blame them. These writings must get so old to them.

I arrived in the City yesterday afternoon and Liz was nice enough to join me. Liz knows the City and likes the City. It does not get much better than that. We spent most of the time just walking around aimlessly with no agenda. Lida will remember where we had that drink overlooking Central Park from the third floor of the Time Warner Building. And so it was again. Puts you in a New York State of Mind.

It was a beautiful day in the City. Warm as could be for this time of year. Yes a little wind, but many people in tee shirts and running shorts. So we decided to have dinner at the French restaurant Nice Matin on 79th and Amsterdam. Actually used my Open Table App to make the reservation so I felt technocratic. It was great. People in the subway while getting there were all happy. We even danced while a person in the subway at Columbus Circle played some really great music on his guitar. I tend to embarrass people. But no one knows me and I am one of millions. CCL. As an aside, I enjoy having friends in the City as my typical apartment dinner for one is half a head of lettuce, an avocado, and pretzels stuck in peanut butter, topped off with a glass of Borden's 2013, yet when I am with friends, I schmaltz it up a bit. My normal meal is filling however!

The meal was delicious and I over ate. At my age you have to be careful about calories. So we decided to walk back to the apartment. After a block there were loud bangs and fireworks. Scooting up to Central Park West, we saw many fireworks in the Park starting off the New York City Marathon pre-race celebration. Really beautiful and particularly so on such a clear and warm night. That was totally unexpected.

After working on the free Friday Times crossword puzzle, which we could not complete, and after consuming a tad of the moonshine I have left from my son David, Morpheus called. Upon awakening this morning I decided that I had to do something to wear off all the calories I had consumed at dinner. So, a little after 6:30am I hit the road to Central Park running full blast. I decided I would run as fast as I was able from my apartment, to Columbus Circle, Fifth Avenue and all around the Park and back home. It was dark and a little chilly. And I ran and ran. After I left the area of the Apple Store and got back into the park, I picked up the pace. Fartleks were the order of the day now. Google it! As I was sweating like a stuck pig, I just poured it on. No one was going to pass me. I then saw a sign across the Park road I was on that indicated that that point was the 24 mile point of the NYC Marathon.

Walter Mitty then kicked in. I remembered running the NYC Marathon when I was 57 years old. I had not trained for it and was supposed to walk the 26.2 miles with a blind person. When I arrived in Staten Island there was no one to guide, so I was told to just run it the race. And I did. I followed my friend Jeff's sage advice and started out slowly, and then went slower. It worked. Although it took me 4.5 hours, I accomplished my goal and felt like a king for days afterward. Unfortunately Ginny had hurt her back and was unable to witness this accomplishment.

And so Walter Mitty kicked in. I just took off full bore and few people were able to pass me. If they did pass me I just picked up the pace as much as I was able to punish them. I heard the nonexistent crowds cheering me on and I was a little teary eyed. I owned the road and since the race ends at 67th Street this year, I pretended it ended at Tavern on the Green as it had back 12 years ago. My cardiologist Ken would have been so happy. I was up at Harlem Hills and was passed by bicycles, elliptical, bicycles, wheel chair athletes, but few runners. I heard many languages as is customary in the Park. For one brief period of a little over 90 minutes I ruled the world and all was good.

So now I am back at the apartment and look forward to meandering around the City with Liz, seeing Central Park in the daylight, perhaps going to the Met to learn, and then after a late lunch heading back to Clinton. This has been a good time.

I really need to make more friends in NYC. Although in my mind I am an extrovert, my reality is that I am a fundamentally shy person that forces himself out of the box. No small accomplishment but one that truly makes life more enjoyable.

Beckett

Patrice, Charlotte, Reservoir Dogs Running Club, and other things that go bump in the night:
Wed, Nov 06, 2013 07:02 PM

I dedicate this to my soon to be born grandchild, knowing that she or he will be unable to comment or absorb this until after next Tuesday. So little person, here goes.

Last night was a great night which led me to decide to go into the City. The tiger did not sleep. I did not lose my uncontested election to the Clinton Town Council which would have been a real hoot had it occurred. The trip in was great and then things started to happen.

I wanted to run Central Park today. And I did. After arriving at my apartment I suited up and took off in the opposite direction to Columbus Circle. It was clear that my knees were having issues. But I persevered and even ran around the Reservoir. After getting up into Harlem Hills, I turned down Fifth Avenue on to the Guggenheim. Nice stuff. But I was pulled toward the Met and quickly changed plans deciding to do what I love best. I spent two hours at the Met. Took a tour of some of the Masterpieces but tired of it. Too many people asking too many questions. So I left the tour and took my own tour of the new and special Korean Exhibit of art from 400AD to 800 AD. Wow. Those Koreans knew how to do it. Buddha was there of course as he always is, but so much other great stuff-tiles, glass, gold, etc. I am glad that I was there. The spice and silk routes and other commerce really had an impact on Korean Art and so much other art. I love when it all starts coming together. And it does.

So I returned to my apartment. Since my knees were acting up, I rested a bit and iced them from time to time. I was going to a piano performance forum at 4pm but decided to go out and walk a bit. At the intersection of 66th and Amsterdam I saw a quite attractive woman looking a bit disoriented. So I approached her. Patrice had flown in from Chicago to visit her son (an attorney) who worked at 47th and 8th. She was in a sense lost. So I helped her get oriented. What the hell, I decided to walk her down to see her son. And we did, all the way to midtown. What a great talk we had. A woman with a brain is really sexy. Patrice has some fancy job that involves traveling and her husband is a law professor at the University of Chicago. They are all very smart and that was evident. I am just a Rutgers grad, both undergraduate and graduate school. I can hardly spell Chicago without spell check. We had a great conversation during the walk. She particularly loved that I know Justice Ginsburg and Justice Alito of the US Supreme Court as I have previously posted months ago. It was great. I had someone to chat with and I was doing something nice. I think I made points by walking her almost 20 blocks to her destination. As I have said, New York is not ready for me. Anyway, I gave her one of my Clinton Councilman cards and she said she had a fifty year old professor friend that is from Chicago who she wanted me to meet when that friend travels to Manhattan....which is quite often. I think that is hysterical. Almost like she was trying to fix me up. And I am an old man as is obvious.

Anyway, I did make it back to Juilliard in time for the free concert thing. There I saw a lady at least in her 80s wearing a silk bandana over her head and with painted eyebrows, lips, and cheeks. I mean really painted on. She and I chatted and in spite of her somewhat bizarre appearance, she was a sweetie. She told me all about the free concerts and the like at Juilliard and elsewhere. Her brain worked just fine. Her name was Charlotte. Amazing lady and we went in to the hall together. Old women like me. Excuse the prejudice, but the Chinese pianist, Nansong Huang, was amazing. He and a fella named Mikhail Kaykov played Prokofiev and Brahms. Never heard of Prokofiev before but Brahms was in my knowledge bank. It is inconceivable that one's fingers can move over the ivories that easily. There is pretty good free stuff in NYC! I am finding it slowly but surely. So when you come into Manhattan, you do not necessarily have to spend a fortune.

So now the Reservoir Dogs Running Club comes into view. I wanted to meet people here. The bar scene does not appeal to me and is costly. So a running club is just the right thing to do. And I did. Running is part of my milieu and essence. I think I am now a member of the Reservoir Dogs Running Club. Most of the running is up at the Jacqueline Kennedy Reservoir which is good as it has a cinder track and all. Too bad it is about a mile away. It will work. And I hope to meet nice people. There were other running clubs, but they took themselves too seriously for me. I am no longer training for a marathon. I am just happy to wake up in the morning.

Right now I am looking out my windows at a majestic view of the City. It is dark and the lights from the skyscrapers are all a twinkle. A cognac sits in my right hand. All is okay with the world. Although I am having serious vision problems off and on during the day, I can still see, and it is all New York. So little baby about to be born, and of course my dear Amelia and Benjamin, all is right with the world today. That is all we can expect.

Beckett.

A long morning in the life of Beckett
Sun, Nov 10, 2013 1:06pm

Well, I have recovered from the birth of my brand new grandson, Daniel Campbell Rylak. What a sweetie. He was born less than two days ago and I am as proud as I can be of the little fella. And so I have gone into the City and will report on my doings to Amelia, Benjamin, and Daniel. Has a nice ring to it. First time I have said that. Almost like my Posting on Tinkers to Evers to Chance. Amelia to Benjamin to Daniel. Ginny would have loved to meet Daniel.

Rather than spend a beautiful day in Clinton alone, I thought it appropriate to spend today and tomorrow with my NYC friends. I do not know their names, but they surround me and embrace me as one of their own. It is a warm and toasty feeling. So, the bus ride into the City was exciting for me although my eyes seem to continue with difficulty in seeing distance. What the heck. So it goes. Vision can be overrated.

After arriving at my apartment with some food from the Gourmet Garage, I got into my running clothes and took off for a three and a half hour experience. It was all good. My initial thought was to run in Riverside Park along the Hudson River which I did. Not a good idea as the cool water and wind made it difficult at best.

Hence, I changed my route and decided to explore Hell's Kitchen and Midtown Manhattan. Sweet. Not many people were out and about so I sang "Danny Boy" in honor of my new grandson. I did have trouble hitting the high notes. I stopped at the Walter Reade Theater at Lincoln Center to see if the Monday Morning Coffee Concert at 10:30am was to happen. It was, but the $22.00 per ticket price tag deterred me. So I continued on to 54th Street, and headed east. Low and behold I came upon the Museum of Modern Art, MOMA, and saw that the outdoor statuary could be observed free of charge for another hour or so. The works may have had great meaning although I have no idea why. It was a novelty to me. I stayed for 8 minutes.

As I exited the MOMA, I continued east and eventually got on Fifth Avenue. Lots of people and the sun had come out; there was very little wind. A totally beautiful day. I saw the Rockefeller Center Christmas Tree, sort of, as it was surrounded by scaffolding so as to enable the lights and decorations to be put up on it. Also, I noted that many Christmas Decorations were going up on 6th Avenue and environs. Really nice to see, albeit a little bit early in the season.

And so I entered St. Patrick's Cathedral. I am not a Catholic and actually have been excommunicated from the Catholic Church. The Lutheran Church as well. I am not a Saint. Nonetheless, I do enjoy a good church service at St. Pat's with many unknown friends. Too bad there is so much construction going on inside and outside the building. Stayed for the homily which was quite good. I did light a candle for my friend Anthony and wished him swift legs which he and his parents will understand. And the yellow Virgin Mary in the photograph below has a meaning which I am unable to relate as its presence was fortuitous. As I left the church early to continue my run, I heard "Al, is that you". Yes, it was me and I met Nancy and her friend from the Hunterdon County area. Small world. I continued my run inspired and ran as fast as the Kenyans could for about 300 feet. Then I tired, but continued my run toward Bryant Park.

It was necessary to go to Bryant Park today. Yesterday there was a shooting there and I wanted to make a personal point. I did. But as I approached Bryant Park from Fifth Avenue, I again was invigorated as ran as fast as I was able. Then in front of me was the New York Public Library and the Park. I watched the skaters for a few minutes. Everyone had forgotten the tragedy of yesterday and children and adults skated and smiled and were happy as if nothing had happened. I was happy as well. My unknown friends surrounded me. All around Bryant Park they had set up booths for the sale of merchandise and those booths will remain for weeks. Last year was the first year I had seen them. The park was crowded and vibrant with life. A happy place. I sat a few minutes as my legs were really tired from all this running.

As with most runners, once you get to your destination you have to get home. Should have thought of that sooner. Anyway, I pretended I was on a mission to get to the Apple Store on Fifth Avenue on my way home as fast as I was able or the world would explode. I ran and I ran and I ran.

The color of the light did not matter. I made it and the world did not explode. I had done my good deed for the day, but I sweat like a stuck pig and probably reeked the same as well. So anyway, I entered the Apple Store and sucked in the ambiance of the place. My friends there surrounded me again. Even spoke to a sales person about the Apple Company considering a Braille keyboard. He did not get my sense of humor, but he did show me some things to do on my iPhone.

So now it was time to get these old legs moving again in Central Park which I did. I travelled along the blue line painted for the New York City Marathon but finally just shifted my course of travel toward Central Park West and 66th Street. So many happy and friendly people. By this time I was spent and just headed home. When I post this Post (hah) on Facebook, I will add a picture or two of my adventure. I am showered and ready to go to the Met or Rubin, depending on my mood. I refuse to sit inside my apartment with all this beautiful weather awaiting me outside. My morning in the life of Beckett has ended. The afternoon begins.

Welcome to my world Daniel. You are in for an experience.

Beckett, formerly Grandpa (?) or whatever you eventually will call me

What a day.
Wed, Nov 13, 2013 08:02

Well Amelia, Benjamin, and Daniel, it has been quite a day. I will be brief as I am typing this from my iPhone. And I am tired. A good tired.

I awoke early in Clinton and got in a great run in the cool air. Wonderful. My friend Craig and I met and took the 9:30am bus into the City.

We then went to the International Center for Photography on 34th and 6th near Bryant Park. What a great place. Many different photographic exhibits. Of particular interest was the John F. Kennedy exhibit of events when the President was assassinated. Saw so much that brought back many memories. Seeing the Zapruder film clips was so sad and so real. The President's head was blown apart. For persons of my age, you understand. The whole place was a lesson in history. Craig was a fountain of good learning information.

Then we took the 1 Train to my apartment. We had lunch there and then took off for Lincoln Center. In a sense I felt like a tour guide as I know the area so well. Also I got to show off my place.

So we stopped at the New York Public Library for the Performing Arts. The initial stop was at the Michael Peto photographs of the Beatles and many others. I had seen this before but enjoyed it again. Then of course we saw the photography of Florence Vandamm, a pioneering poet of Light. She had taken wonderful pictures of famous people, mostly actors and actresses. Craig is really into this photography thing and was explaining much to me. I learned a lot here as well.

The final thing done at the NYPLFTOA was to see the most incredible exhibit I have ever seen, The Line King. Yes, Line, not Lion. Al Hirshfeld had for over 60 years drawn caricatures of thousands of famous people and Broadway shows etc. In many of these sketches he did for the NY Times was the hidden name of his daughter Nina. It was all good. To see so much of his art in one space was incredible. I will be back again soon.

Then of course we stopped at the Time Warner building at Columbus Circle. The view was great and I want to go to a new restaurant there called A Voce. We found it. So later we went over to show Craig my best restaurant Robert. It was closed and we could not get in as they were getting ready for a big private party. Well, I bumped into my pal Clair who is an aspiring actress and is in charge of reservations. She remembered me and let us in. She is my Beckett go to gal. Craig liked the place. I always do.

From there we went down the elevator to the Museum of Arts and Design. We took a tour for well over an hour and saw works by Maya Lin who designed the Vietnam Veteran's Memorial and also many three dimensional works of art all computer driven. Even had models of ourselves made, all by computer and then transferred to solid form. So much to see and learn. So little time. The jewelry was incredible. Try Coco Chanel for one.

So then we arrived at this great French Restaurant called Tout Va Bien on 51st between 8th and 9th. Best French meal I have ever eaten. Coco vin. I will be back. It is a gem in the city.

Now I am alone at my apartment and Craig heads for Clinton and a tryst with his lovely wife. I watch the lights twinkle and sip cognac. Not bad. I shall head home tomorrow and relax hoping my eyes rest and I will be able to see. Tiredness envelopes me as it should. Color that all good. Catch me if you can.

Beckett

ABD
Sat, Nov 16, 2013 9:27am

A lovely day in Manhattan Amelia, Benjamin, and Daniel. Yesterday I had the pleasure of seeing Daniel in Toms River in the morning on his one week birthday and also jogging all about the township as the sun rose. That was fun. I also miss seeing Amelia and Benjamin. After I returned to Clinton I had this great urge to have a French dinner in Manhattan. Called Liz to see if she was available on short notice, and we got the 4:30 pm bus into the City. Taking a bus into the City on a Friday night is a challenge. You see ribbons of red break lights from every window. Some ribbons stretch for miles. It is okay. Quite majestic on so many levels. We humans are part of the environment too. I hope.

We then walked from the Port Authority to the very same restaurant Craig and I had frequented a couple of days before. Tout Va Bien, which means "Everything is fine"; and it was. The Times Square area was filled with so many people, but the crowd dissipated after a few blocks. This restaurant is everything I had seen in Paris years ago. Filled with people eating coco vin and beef bourguignon and tripe. Yes tripe or the offal of slaughtered animals. Wine, desert, and sangria in a gallon container to ladle out at the end of the meal, topped off a great relaxed and delicious meal. It was wonderful to again have someone to chat with rather than just being "just one". When I go alone to a restaurant and I am asked if there is "just one" I always respond, "no, the one". Perhaps I am too sensitive.

The subway ride to 66th was its usual relaxed moment and getting into my apartment at night was perfect. What a view. The buildings were all aglow with white twinkling lights as the evening was clear as it could be. Almost as if the viewscape was one large Christmas tree. Cognac and the view were just perfect. As Morpheus called a sense of calmness enveloped me in a much needed way.

I awakened at 4 am, had my coffee, and started out for a long run in

Central Park. It was drizzling which was wonderful. To everyone I saw I said "hello" and most of them responded in a positive way. Running in the rain is a hoot and Walter Mitty can creep into your thoughts from time to time. You runners know of what I say. Since I had eaten such a large meal last night, this was going to be a long run in an effort to destroy calories. So, for the third consecutive day I ran for an hour and a half. Sweet. Although I am wearing out, I will continue continuing. At Wolman Rink the Zamboni machine was doing its thing and that black leopard stood in an attack position along the paved trail as I ran by in the Park. The pond near the Boathouse was misty with ducks floating and quacking. There were lots of people out there having a great time as was I. Running around the Reservoir was strange as the cinder track was moist to say the least. All was good with the world.

Anyway, I decided to listen to the sounds as I ran in the rain. Runners run in all different ways. Those that are flat footed have a distinctive "thud" as they pass. Many runners of a Kenyan-like tempo pass by without barely a sound. The majority of runners run in pairs or groups and chat loudly as they discuss their best times, colleges, and strategies. The sound of passing cars on the wet pavement and leaves is eerie at times. A toot or a siren is evident as well. Many runners breathe heavily as if they are making love to the roadway. Yes, birds even chirp in the predawn hours. We all have to just enjoy the sounds we hear and more importantly just listen. Sometimes we are so busy being busy that we forget to observe what is going on around us. I do not want to be guilty of that anymore.

So now I am back in my apartment having showered for the second time. The first was when the rain drenched me somewhat. Liz is out walking and will return with some fruit I hope. We will go and see the caricatures of Al Herschfeld again and then simply enjoy the City. There is no need to be a tourist. Been there. Done that. At last the sun is shining and all is right with the world once again.

And so another day do adventure begins.

Now Becket.

Apples and pianos
Wed, Nov 20, 2013 09:08

Dear Amelia, Benjamin, and Daniel.

Another day into the City to be with my unknown friends. As always, they embrace me and make me feel accepted without reservation. I like that and the peace and serenity of the City of Manhattan. On the way in on the bus, I did something to my iPad and could not fix it. Technology. We have to learn to live with it. And what amazes me is that it would be so easy for an enemy to disable all of our electronic gizmos pretty easily. What would we do if we lost them all? Anyway, I was able to get in touch with my friend Mike from Cornelia Street in the Village while on the bus and I am going to meet up with him next Monday at his place to listen to his band play. Never did this before. It will be good. Take the A train to 4th Street and there you are. And remember, it is the same street where Bob Dylan and Jimi Hendricks lived before they were famous.

Anyway, after I got off the bus and took the 1 Train to 66th Street, I went straight to the Apple Store on Broadway. Two hours later my iPad was working. What a pain in the derrière. But I was undaunted. While there, I learned more nuances about all this Apple Technology from the technicians. It is great to be a somewhat, almost, nearly, close to a Geek. If only........... So now I am downloading over a thousand pictures from my iPhone to my iPad. A lot of these are of a couple of years ago when times were happier and cannot be replaced. Some pictures are very sad but important to not lose. So happy to have my pictures on two devices and in the Cloud.

After arriving at my apartment I decided to continue not eating as I have put on a couple of extra pounds. And then I did my wonderful run along Riverside Park. The wind from the North made things difficult but I persevered and turned around South at about Columbia University. I have to point out that the tug boats pushing the large oilers and tankers were having difficulty due to the wind. Needless to say the run back was so easy it was almost as if I floated in the air. Went up to Lincoln Center and as I decompressed I looked at all the Aaron Curry "Melt to Earth" sculptures in the Josie Robertson Plaza of Lincoln Center. Good stuff.

Eventually I ended up back at my apartment (after a brief stop at the Gourmet Garage for minimal food) and took a nice shower and finally ate a little of this and that. Then I went off to Avery Fisher Hall and studied the art on the assorted walls. I liked being there as it was in that very same Hall that Cornell Medical School awarded David his medical degree and Ginny and I had happy times. I also noticed that from time to time, for a small fee, the New York Philharmonic has Open Rehearsals. Great. I shall go. Music is a good thing.

I decided to people watch a bit and that was fun. Nearly everyone had their cell phone to an ear; usually the left one. Why are we so connected all the time? There has to be time set aside to watch the leaves turn red and orange, to feel the wind, to see the sun set (or in my case, rise), and to in other ways enjoy nature and the natural order of things. But I digress.

As it approached 3:00 pm I decided to go to Juilliard and see what was going on. Was I surprised. The Piano Competition Finals were soon to begin and there were five groups of two pianists each playing Rachmaninoff's Concerto No. 2. And so I went to Paul Recital Hall, or as they say, Paul Hall.

Now all this piano stuff is new to me. As a Clinton rube, I have never heard Rachmaninoff played. The Hall was filled with people yet I noticed that people were not dressed up. They wore whatever. The ceiling and walls were wooden, I suspect to create a wonderful sound. The seats were luxurious and the people were quite pleasant. Upon the stage were two very large Steinway & Sons pianos which glistened. And then two pianists entered the stage and played their hearts out for about 30 minutes. And again two more and again two more until a total of five groups appeared. Amazing. So often we think of athletes only and forget the dedication and discipline of those in the Arts. You had to be there. Such emotion and at times you felt as if the pianists were one with the music. I liked it a lot. Of interest however were the names of the pianists--Sejoon Park, Penguin Lin, Wenting Shi, Hanbo Liu, Minggu Yao, Alexey Koltakov, Yungqing Zhou, and others. These were the best at Juilliard, which is the best in the world. There is a message here. You can figure that out if you like some day.

So I heated Liz's leftover and frozen brown rice, chicken, and some type of pod peas, and ate a very good dinner. Yes, it was Chinese from the past weekend. I am cheap and saw no need to splurge on a fancy dinner.

Now I sit in my favorite chair with a small amount of what some call moonshine, and I watch the twinkling lights. I can hear a little bit of traffic below, and feel at ease with the world. I am where I belong right now and it is a good thing. Tomorrow is tomorrow and I will return to Clinton to get ready for a short trip to Virginia for Grandparent's Day at Amelia's school. Since I will not get my new glasses until tomorrow and for other reasons, my ability to continue to focus on this computer screen has ended. As does this writing.

Beckett

Cornelia Street
Wed, Dec 04, 2013 08:36 AM

Well my lovely Amelia, Benjamin, and Daniel, I envy you three little dears for what the future will bring to you some day. Although the world will be so different from now, many of the places I write about will be around for you to explore. So do it.

The other day I went into the City to simply decompress. We had had such a wonderful Thanksgiving at Mark and Ang's place and our entire family was there. Wish I had taken a picture. You three were together for the first time. We were all in such good moods. Of course, Grandma was not physically there, but her spirit was evident to me. She would have been so very proud of you three.

So, after I was alone again, on Monday, I took the first bus into the Port Authority. It was early enough and dark enough to see this large red sphere emerge over the skyline of Manhattan. You realize how insignificant you are as you see nature at its fullest and best. There is so much unknown about the universe and seeing it from our little sphere makes it all seem more enormous and enigmatic.

So the 1 train took me to 66th Street and the hordes of people brought me tons of excitement. It was chilly and my voice had not entirely recovered from its issues, but it was fun. After I got to my apartment I headed out for a long run. This run was unscripted and took me all over Midtown, the UWS and the UES. So many decorations were out and people seemed in such great spirits. Since I am a novice in the City since April Fool's Day, I take particular note of silly little things--like these large pipes that protrude from the road with billowing "smoke" due to the cold; needy and homeless people sleeping on grates that push warm air toward the sky; certain sections such as along the East side of Broadway Avenue near Columbus Circle where the homeless may congregate but not the West side; dog after dog wearing little jackets; people walking dressed for Arctic weather but runners in shorts and a jacket; the streets not yet cleaned up from the prior evening's activities; the apparent disparity in wealth every place you look. I could go on but will not. The City is a place of many disparities which are so very evident.

Anyway, as I returned toward my place, I saw the Lincoln Center Christmas or Holiday Tree being unloaded. It will sit atop the second floor of the Metropolitan Opera House. Quite an operation as the tree is quite large. Also, all about Broadway were kiosks for the sale of holiday fare. The wealth of the UWS and the UES pales in comparison with the Midtown area. I wonder where the average people live in Manhattan. Or do they not live in Manhattan?

After my shower I spoke to a person about replacing and cleaning my apartment windows, I took off for The Village and Cornelia Street. At 7 pm I was to be at a band rehearsal. So I had seven hours to burn. I used my time well. My goal was to try to get to understand the lower section of the City. Of course I talk to myself a lot and I was all over the place. Yes, New York University envelopes a good part of Washington Square Park and the same with Union Square. I have a friend at 1 Fifth Avenue and candidly, her place is great to look at but does not compare to my place. I think I stopped in every shop I could find. The chess players in Washington Square will have me to take on or teach someday soon. What a great part of the Park. The arch is impressive and all the new buildings in the area for NYU somehow do not fit, but are gloriously beautiful. Bleecker Street is insane. Spent so much time trying to locate myself as off of Bleecker it gets a little difficult to orient oneself. The street grid does not exist in the Village. You should see the house where Edna St. Vince Millay lived. It is no more than 15 feet wide and comprises three stories. I could live there. At Murray's cheese shop, where do people get enough money to support a store that sells cheese for $40.00 a pound? Tea and coffee shops all over the place. And of course the pub called the Slaughtered Lamb.

Anyway, I stopped in a tattoo shop and had a long conversation with Will. Nice guy. His body was covered with all different colors of tattoos, his ear lobes widened by a large circle, and some metal protruded from his nose. Of course he was selling the mandatory hookahs and marijuana paraphernalia as well. I liked Will. He did not look like me or those of my generation, but he was well spoken and easily talked about his craft. I asked lots of questions and he answered them all. In my prior life as an attorney I had represented tattoo artists and understand quite a bit about them. We got along. Also, it was a place to warm up from the chilly air.

Then there was Gus. He served me at a restaurant where I went in for a mandatory espresso and warm up. Gus had worked on or near Bleecker Street for thirty years. He was very opinionated and tried to convert me to some sort of religion as things were slow. I just smiled and as my laryngitis was bad at this point I just let him chat to his heart's content. Gus lives on the UWS and hates the Village. Hell knows why. Nonetheless, he is able to make a living off of the people there. Especially at night as that is when the Village comes awake.

Stopped to look at real estate prices in the lower Manhattan section. Amazing. People are nuts. Now since NYC will have a new Mayor, deBlasio, perhaps things will change. The Manhattan of the wealthy may become more middle class; or not.

One thing that amazed me was how close I travelled to the former World Trade Center area and did not even know it. My Walter Middy impulse is to shrink in horror as I think of the feckless attack on our Country on 9/11/01 and being where I now stood. These poor people must have been scared out of their underwear. Smoke billowing. Sirens. Fear. Death.

Anyway, 7:00 pm arrived and I went to my friend's place on Cornelia Street. You have to be buzzed in to a gated alleyway and then walk to his three story house through a small park or atrium type structure. The building is red brick and quite old. It used to be a bakery of some sort and the basement story has walls and an arched ceiling (yes ceiling) of red brick. The ovens were once located in the basement area. That is also where the music and recording studio is located. The first floor has a fire place and reeks of charm. A large Christmas tree dominated the area. Did not see the second floor but that is where the bedrooms are located I am sure. It was like a little piece of the country in the City. Cornelia Street is quite beautiful any way, with perhaps 8 stores along its sides. It is also very short and goes from Bleecker Street to 4th Street. So I was on Cornelia Street but not. It was this area where in the very early 1960s that my late friend Bill Hausdoerfer and I met Robert Zimmerman. Google "Positively 4th Street" by Bob Dylan.

I had a blast to put it mildly. The band played all sorts of songs, many of which I knew. My foot was tapping and the cup of honey tea I had gotten on Bleecker Street eased my sore throat. So we had a guitar, a bass, a keyboard, drums, and a saxophone. All in a little section of paradise in a part of the City called the Village or East Village depending on your perspective. And this old man was just hanging out. Eventually I did leave and took the C train this time to Columbus Circle and then the 1 Train to 66th. It was there I saw those kiosks filled with buyers, heard music from every angle, saw the undecorated Christmas or Holiday tree on the second story of the Metropolitan Opera House awaiting decoration, and heard the sound of happiness all over the place.

But I was tired and it was off to my apartment on 66th Street and to bed; to look out of my lovely clean windows at a spectacular city glistening as I sipped my Cognac and eventually ended my day. Amelia, Benjamin, and Daniel, this is good stuff. Trust me on this one.

Then, Beckett.

Running along two rivers.
Sat, Dec. 14, 2013 4:48PM

Well A, B, and D, I am in the City again. After the accident at the Cornelia Street party last Saturday, I am surprised that I returned to this glorious place. The four bands on Cornelia Street were wonderful and as Lizette consented to attend with me, all was good with the world and I was not "just one". Food, others, decorations, and all that stuff were perfect. Until.... So I was sitting on a ledge near the East wall of the house when all of a sudden, a large heavy wall clock fell and hit the top of my right leg about a half inch from my knee. For about 30 minutes I could not feel my leg. I am now swollen and black, blue, and yellow in that area of my old body. Had it hit my knee cap, it would have shattered it without doubt. From my right thigh the clock then hit a young woman in the back and she was in obvious great pain. Luckily I received most of the weight from the fall of the clock. Over forty pounds from eight feet up. Anyway, I got over it and although I have had running issues since then, I do run.

So after I arrived here today at about 7:45 am, I got into my running clothes and took off to the Hudson River and Riverside Park. It was great but the wind was cold and strong. It was then that I got the idea of running along the East River on the other side of Manhattan. So I turned off to Central Park and meandered through the Park with some right leg pain. When I exited the Park at 72nd Street I just had to go to Cornell Medical School at York and 70th to relive happier times when David was a student there. There was a large pedestrian bridge next to the Hospital for Special Surgery that took me over the FDR Drive and along the East River. Quite cool, not in the weather sense. Nostalgia permeated my sweat. Not a boat on the East River for some unknown reason. Ahead of me was the Queensboro Bridge over which the 11th mile of the NYC Marathon was run, the Tram to Roosevelt Island, Sotheby's to the rear, Rockefeller University, and so much more. Although I was unable to find David's favorite Mexican Restaurant at 1-800-TACO, it was glorious to be there. I even went past David's old apartment. Memories. There are some really nice buildings all about the Upper East Side, particularly along Park, Madison, Lexington, and Third and Second. Then I backtracked home to 66th through the Park, cold, tired, sore, and happy. This silly little run had taken almost two hours so pain from running and from the prior accident were exacerbated. No big deal. A great way to get to know the City.

Now tomorrow I am meeting a new friend, Audrey, in Chelsea at the Cook Shop on 10th between 20th and 19th. So I decided to go to the Rubin Museum again and also to reconnoiter the area. A snap. 1 Train to 59th, then the C Train to 23rd. After I found the Cook Shop restaurant, quite nice if I do say so myself, I was in the Museum in as many places as possible. I did not realize that Moran's was just down the street to the South, and that Chelsea Market on 9th would beckon me. And it did. I was all over Chelsea Market which is just a great place to visit again and again. I also really like a place called Cushing's Way on 20th I think which had a large number of Greek Italianate row houses. That would be a cool place to live. At least the buildings were gorgeous.

After I tired, I got back to the UWS, and had a very early dinner or late lunch at a Chinese place called Empire on Columbus. It was the first food I had eaten today. Why? If you had my EE of my esophagus you could easily answer that question. Yes, I am slowly and inexorably falling apart. Even so, I feel like I have the heart of a 30 year old. Who knows?

So I am in my apartment now looking forward to watching The Five at 5:00 pm and snacking or noshing the rest of the evening if hungry. I also look forward to imbibing some moonshine or cognac, or both, after the sun sets and then trying to sleep well. Last night I attended the Deni Law Group Christmas dinner at Pauli's in West Trenton, NJ. Great time and great food, but Morpheus thought it was a bad idea I guess. I look forward to my brunch in Chelsea and then a ride home on the bus to try to beat the oncoming snow storm that approaches.

I do have a question however. How come the needy beggars who sleep on the sidewalk, look dirty and never emaciated, are always male? I would think that begging would be a gender neutral occupation. Just thinking. Perhaps women have too much class to fail to keep clean, and do not have to beg for money, but may obtain it in other ways. Perhaps not.

So that is it for now. Have a great evening. Oh, as an aside, to the hateful ex client woman that asked me "how can you live with yourself" in a somewhat sardonic tone, the answer is quite easily. Just read what I write if you ever receive a copy of it.

Beckett

What fools these mortals be.
Sat, Dec. 21, 2013 4:45PM

Good afternoon Amelia, Benjamin, and Daniel. After a wonderful time for two days in Harvey Cedars with a large number of friends, I did return to Clinton last night. And yes Daniel, my friend Liz and I did catch a look at you sleeping in your crib as we returned to Clinton. I have to tell you though that the sunrise yesterday was "island perfect". You have to awaken early to watch nature take its course and if you do not, you are making a large mistake. I will also tell you also that the contingency of the widow's and widower's club who were present on the Island did get together for wine and cheese at our home in Harvey Cedars. We toasted ourselves and our loved ones. I am the only male. Color that good.

So after seeing a client and taking a few calls, I took the bus into the City. This time I sat in the company of a beautiful young woman and that brightened up the trip quite a bit. I am a lucky man. She is a dear friend from Clinton. So I arrived at my apartment in excellent spirits. Now about the subway ride to my place. Always check the seat before you sit. I have mentioned this before, but if you do not visually check, you might be surprised at what you will sit on. I will leave it there. Rule 1 is to always look down and then sit or warn others of suspected danger. Many types and sorts of people ride the subway and bus. Not all of them are clean and spiffy. Rule 2 is that the same rule applies to the buses.

When I arrived at my apartment I had my arms full of enough food and drink to hold me through the middle of Christmas. I hope to see you sweet Daniel this Christmas afternoon. I saw sweet Amelia and Benjamin on some videos sent to me today by David and Lena via e-mail and text. Nonetheless, something must have gone amiss in my building as I noticed a slightly blackened film of NYC dust all over the place. I have no idea how it got into the apartment but it was there crying out to be cleaned up, which I did. Strange that I never saw this before. I am learning.

I have a special treat on Christmas Eve which is Tuesday. Thanks to my dear friend Tony and his connections with God or God fearing people, I will see world renowned opera singer James Valenti sing at the Christmas Eve midnight service at Saint Patrick's Cathedral. You need tickets for the event as a million people would want to be there. Thank you Tony. James used to play in our back yard and swim in our pool, shoot hoops, and play golf there with my son Mark. This is really above being great. This will make me smile and not feel sorry for myself. Yes, I do have a little humanity and self-pity left in my body at times.

So, as is my custom, I decided to reconnoiter the location where I would pick up my tickets on Monday AM first thing. The address? 1011 First Avenue which is the headquarters of the Diocese of New York I think. I have learned so little in NYC. I took the 1 train to 50th and walked and walked to First Avenue. Took forever. The crowds of people at or near Times Square and Rockefeller Center were beyond very large. Millions of people. Shoulder to shoulder. I had more people or parts of their anatomies brush against me than Carter has little liver pills. At times I felt molested. After I got up to First Avenue I headed north to 56th and there, just before 57th was my destination. Hours had passed by. People have to stop procreating if only for a short time. There are too many of us.

Upon arrival I was advised that my tickets were not down at the front desk and that the building was closed. I expected this, what with me having been excommunicated from both the Catholic Church and the Lutheran Church for nonattendance. So I am to return Monday AM first thing. I shall. My trip back showed me again what a rube I still was, in spite of my pseudo-knowledge of NYC.

My first effort was to get on the 41 Bus which would have taken me downtown. After a quick exit I got on the 57th Street crosstown bus. It dropped me off eventually right across from my apartment. Crap. Monday, I will walk across 66th and West End Avenue and just get on the 57th Street crosstown bus and be at my destination at 1011 First Avenue quickly and relaxed. And so it is. I do refuse to take tours and become a tourist. I am learning the City the best way possible and that is through trial and error. I am getting it although my learning curve is apparently quite steep.

I have a tendency to speak to people. So, as the bus neared Fifth Avenue, some people boarded with cellos and basses and were all dolled up in tuxedos and fancy black dresses. They took up tons of space and I gave them my seat upon which to place a cello. So I spoke to this nice lady who owned the cello. Turned out that they had just finished a performance with the New York Pops at Carnegie Hall or someplace like that. What a wonderful lady. She explained to me how to get to 1011 First Avenue from my apartment, took my card with e-mail address and telephone number, and will contact me tonight. She might even go to Saint Patrick's with me as a default on Christmas Eve at midnight. Yes, she will be enrolled in the widow's club and all of us with that special bond will meet in the future. Somewhere. Some place.

So now, I am ready for my trip on Monday AM to solidify my tickets to an extraordinary event on Christmas Eve. A new friend. A new experience. Life is good today.

Tonight I want to go out and treat myself to a great dinner and then go to Juilliard and watch some amazing people play piano. The sun is setting and the temperatures are in the upper 40s. I sit at Riverside Park surrounded by my friends whom I do not know and look forward as well to a wonderful run in 65 degree temperatures here just before Christmas 2013. If is all good.

So my sweet grandchildren, I hope you learn from this little writing and before I listen to the playing of the ivories at or near Lincoln Center, I will visit the San Remo apartments where a fella named Steve Jobs once lived and 320 West End Avenue which housed Joseph Heller of Catch-22 fame, a book you should read.

Beckett

The tickets were not just tickets.
Wed, Dec. 25, 2013 8:06PM

Merry Christmas sweet Amelia, Benjamin, and Daniel. What a glorious Christmas you shall have today and what a wonderful Christmas Eve I just lived through.

In a prior post I explained how I reconnoitered the area to find where I would pick up my ticket to the Christmas Eve Midnight Mass at St. Patrick's Cathedral, which pick up was to be the following Monday morning; the 23rd. Because of legal work, I slept very poorly the prior evening. When I awoke early on Monday I went right to 1011 First Avenue to meet with a lady named Jane Anne to get my ticket. After getting through security, Jane Anne came out to meet me on the 13th floor. She was very kind and I just gave her a big hug after she gave me my ticket to the event. These are as rare as hen's teeth and she said "you must be or know someone pretty important to get these seats". I told her no, that I was a nobody and that I only needed one ticket. Jane Anne smiled and said to keep the two. I laughed and told her that I was not even Catholic. She grinned even more. I hugged her again and said that I had been excommunicated from the Catholic Church for nonattendance. She laughed and said no big deal. I pushed it and said that I had also for like reason been excommunicated from the Lutheran Church. She joyfully said that I should have a great time and to listen to Cardinal Dolan as he would be speaking to me.

So I eventually got out of the 1011 First Avenue building and rushed to the bus station get to Hunterdon County to take care of some legal business. Needless to say, I did not want to leave Manhattan, but circumstances required an emergency appearance in court for reasons that are irrelevant to this posting. And that brings me to yesterday, Christmas Eve.

I arrived on Manhattan alone as usual and carried nothing but what I wore and my two very special tickets. Yes, I did a run in Clinton, NJ before getting the bus so all I had to do was walk around the City prior to the mass. Which I did. For hours and hours. So many things to see. So many languages, smells, attitudes, and yes, people. The weather was quite cold but street musicians of sort were all over the place trying to make a dollar or two. The Christmas Spirit permeated the air and people were quite generous with their dollar bills.

One acrobatic group of black men and one white fella were so funny that I laughed until I cried. They were performing acrobatic feats right in the middle of Central Park near Le Pain, the coffee shop. What spirit. They called themselves something like the "Hood Brothers" and engaged a crowd of over 100 people. They really got the crowd involved and joked about the fact that all the white people were safe as they in the group were vegetarians; that they had their token white acrobat; that they needed money and so many other asides that I cannot recall most of them now. At one point their acrobatic stunt required one of them to run a long distance and then was followed by a jump and flip in the air. The comment made by the leader of the group sticks in my mind; "ladies and gentlemen. This is the first time in New York City that you will see a black man running without two cops chasing him!". For twenty minutes this went on and well past when I left. What talent. What humor. We all need to laugh a little. Sometimes you just cannot take yourself or your plight too seriously.

Anyway, I went to my apartment and relaxed for a bit. My legs were tired as I am too old for all this physicality.

I needed dinner so just left my apartment looking for some place to eat a bit. Only had a scone early in the morning and food and drink were necessary to help pass the time until entry into St. Pat's at 10:30 pm. So I walked along Broadway toward Columbus Circle. It was chilly and crisp, joyous, music playing, people wishing Merry Christmas to others, and in general quite festive. It was at Columbus Circle that I met Leeza.

Leeza was a woman in great distress. In a prior post I mentioned that I never had seen a woman begging for money on the streets of NYC. Well,

Leeza changed that. She was about 23 years old or so, strikingly beautiful, dirty, shivering from the cold, sitting on the ground with all of her belongings, and had a little shoe box with two one dollar bills in it on her lap. I had to meet this lady and I did. We chatted for about five minutes and I knew what I had to do. Leeza got the extra ticket to the midnight mass, a cup of hot coffee, a $10.00 bill, and a promise of a meal and more money if she came to St. Pat's at 10:30pm. She did not know where the Cathedral was located so, I gave her pin point written instructions. I had no idea if I had just wasted the cherished extra ticket. I left Leeza and reflected on how lucky I was and how I hoped she would show up as she would be warm at least for a few hours. I had stressed that to her. Free warmth and then food and money. I felt good.

And then I went to a place I wanted to visit for dinner called Marea at 240 Central Park South. I needed to kill a couple of hours and I did. It is a great place and the bar area cannot get any better. Most of the people at the bar were alone like Captain Jack in the Billy Joel song. Emily, one of the bar tenders, knew how to do her job. I felt at home with all these solo people just out having a nice time alone with all their new friends on Christmas Eve. I shall go back someday soon, but think I was born to be at a spot like that. I felt I controlled the bar, the conversation, and the people there. Perhaps it was the Prosecco or wine that did the controlling, but whatever, it was a great time for me. Nonetheless, I could not get Leeza out of my mind. I went back to where she was previously, but she was no longer there. Sad.

And so I had more time to kill. I went to the Apple store and then to Rockefeller Center. When traveling in any City you have to find bathrooms that will accept non customers. Fortunately in Manhattan, one is located at Rockefeller Center. The drink, be it alcoholic or nonalcoholic, necessitated a few visits. As did the chill in the air.

Eventually 10:00pm arrived and I stood in line at St. Pats to witness a special holiday and time. Made a few friends in line who were school teachers, and actually met the Rector of the Cathedral named Richie. Nice fella.

At 10:30pm I entered St. Pats. Most people with tickets were escorted to the sides. My ticket took me to the arm of a fella even older than I who was wearing white gloves and who sat me down three rows from the main pulpit from which the homily was to be delivered by Cardinal Dolan. Holy crap. I was in a special spot in which I did not belong. I can only say the caroling before midnight was magnificent. It is easy to get teary eyed in one's widower hood. And I did. Twenty feet to my left, two rows up were multi-billionaire Mayor Blumberg, Governor Cuomo, and Police Commissioner Kelly and their families. I could have easily spoken to any of them. In front of me on the sanctuary portion were Cardinal Dolan and retired Cardinal Egan. Two Catholic Cardinals for crying out loud. I swear Cecily Tyson was sitting two people to my left as well. And these were just some of the people I saw. I am sure no one said "hey, is that Beckett over there?"

Catholic services are quite ornate. There must have been at least fifteen priests conducting the service. The head celebrant, Cardinal Dolan was an affable happy lovely person who spoke right to me. I love the ritual. I hate when everyone shakes hands and exchanges germs. But that is just me. Anyway, during the communion, in which I did not participate, the song "O Holy Night" was sung. It was beautiful. It was sung by James Valenti, the kid from North Hunterdon High School who played with my son Mark in my back yard. I have no idea where this kid got his opera voice, but it was breathtaking. He did himself and us all quite proud. A voice from the angels. I kept looking for Leeza, but she did not appear. She was nowhere to be found. I was disappointed.

So as I left feeling sad and inspired at the same time, I started walking home North on Fifth Avenue. On the steps of the cathedral in somewhat of a state of disarray she stood without her baggage. Leeza had come to St. Pats for a midnight Christmas Eve service, if only to keep warm. She did not sit with me but said she stood in the back. She was warm and refused a meal. I do not think much was open anyway. If I were to guess, I think she was high on something as she did not recognize me and her speech was slurred a little. Who knows? I hope her Christmas Eve made her life a little better.

So I walked home to 66th Street and tried to sleep. I just was not tired. I had Leeza on my mind. I should have stayed to try to help her. I did not. If this note is a little more disjointed than usual, it is from lack of sleep as well as lack of ability. Things seem to happen to me. Heaven knows why. You cannot make this stuff up.

Good night. Merry Christmas 2013.

Beckett

December 30, 2013

A dear friend just sent me the below e-mail. I cannot believe it. What are the odds? A feel good moment. As I have always said, I never exaggerate. I just tell the truth and things happen. I have led a very full and unusual life. It is not yet over. God bless America.

"Dear Al,

Russ and I just came back from a long walk. We ran into a friend of yours named Leeza sitting with all her belongings in front of the Folk Art Museum near Columbus and 66th. You described her well. She is very pretty and was very nice. I couldn't help asking her if she was Leeza. She got the most beautiful smile on her face and said yes. I told her she met a friend of ours on Christmas Eve. Another big smile came across her pretty face. She said she went to the church and had never seen anything so beautiful. She asked me to thank you for her. She told Russ she is working with two organizations who are helping her get off the street. Your kind gesture helped her more than you know. We gave her money for dinner and told her you, Russ and I will be back to see her again. God help her!

Miss you! Have a wonderful New Year!
Love,
Sis"

Dog booties and mink coats.
Sun, Jan 5, 2014 12:21PM

Amelia, Benjamin, and Daniel. Nice names for nice children. Good to have you three around from time to time. Wish it were more often.

Yup, I am back in Manhattan for the first time in 2014. I was invited to dinner by a friend, so why not. Despite the snow of the other day, the sun was shining as I left for the City and while awaiting for the bus to arrive, I spoke to a couple of kind and happy people. I like to start my trip that way. One woman in particular was an MRI technician from Easton, PA who took a job at NYU Langone Medical Center. Jobs are tight and she needed money. So, for three days a week she commutes into the City and works too long hours to make ends meet. Her friend accompanies her each time for moral support and works as a waitress on 34th Street on those days. Both must be so tired after three days of this travel silliness. But, you have to give them credit for working and not expecting the government to take care of them. But I politically digress.

After arriving at the Port Authority I hiked over to the subway station for the 1 Train. It dawned on me there that it was quite cold, and it was. At least the subway cars were heated. Not many people out on a Saturday afternoon. And yes, I got off early at the 59th Street Station and walked over to where my friends had last seen Leeza. Columbus Avenue near the Church of Latter Day Saints. No luck. She was nowhere to be found. I hope she got into a shelter for we were blessed with a pretty bad snow storm a couple of days ago. Actually, there were very few if any needy people sleeping on the sidewalks. That is a good thing if they were all in shelters.

So we had Japanese food down in the Chelsea area for dinner. Good stuff. I have to tell you however that Japanese noodles are in the shape of large earthworms. The ecru color of dough, but intimidating at first. The lady I was with was quite nice, the food different but good, and the conversation beneficial. So that was great. We will do it again. After assuring that my friend got home safely, I headed for the A Train to get home to my apartment. I guess I never really forgive easily. Kept thinking of Pearl Harbor which I visited last January and mentally saw the Japanese kamikaze pilots destroying our men and ships. Strange that that would come into my old but fertile mind. I forgive easily but never seem to forget. So, no more Japanese food for a while as stupid as that may sound. This is one part of me I do not want my grandchildren to emulate.

Sleep last night was my usual poor if at all, so after reading my digital newspapers and having some coffee, I decided to take a good long run before the anticipated rain arrived later today. As I ran up to Central Park, it dawned on me that the snow still lay upon the trails there which would make running dangerous. A quick hop over to Riverside Park confirmed the same. Snow can affect your running in the City and make for broken legs or arms. So, I decided to run, or in my case jog, an hour North and then an hour South on the sidewalks. The sidewalks were quite clean or at least not slippery. Since it was so early in the morning, I rarely stopped for any traffic lights. After I passed Columbia University the misty rain started falling, but that was okay. As an aside, I still do not like Columbia much as during the 1960s there was a hot bed of anti-American sentiment at the University which continued well into the time our President Obama attended. But I digress again. I did come upon the Apthorp Apartment condos near 78th. Wow with a capital W. More or less a very large complex, beautifully built, with a courtyard more than opulent. The likes of Rosie O'Donnell, Al Pacino, and Cyndi Lauper used to live there. I still like my apartment better!

During my run I noticed all sorts of things along Broadway as that was the street de jure. I have never seen so many Duane Reade Pharmacies! One on almost every corner. I know that Duane and Reade were two fellas from lower Manhattan that started the enterprise and that each has a street named after themselves near the site of the Freedom Tower. But really, do you need so many?! Restaurants of all ethnicities abound as well. I like Broadway as it is a central hub from Columbus Circle North; south too I guess. Speaking of Columbus Circle, the father of one of David's Haverford baseball buddies owned the company that build the fountain at Columbus Circle. I have spoken to them and they have an apartment nearby. How cool is that? Cool is a word from the 1960s.

I could not help but notice that no matter the weather, people walked their dogs. The large majority of the dogs were clad in coats of some type or another. I can accept that. The most amazing thing however were the dog booties that I saw. They were all over the place. Dogs of all types and sizes had their paws clad in little red booties. And, they stayed on as they walked! I understand why this was done; salt protection I suspect. But I just smiled and after counting 50 such animals with the booties, I ignored it.

In the City, it is difficult to get rid of the snow. It is pushed to the curb by the store owners but the sidewalks as I have mentioned are okay. So too the crosswalks, usually. The snow along the curb serves many purposes, but I determined one main purpose of interest. It stops jaywalking. Not a person wanted to cross at other than the crosswalks for fear of getting covered in snow or slush in the foot area. So you see, snow protects lives quite a bit. Not one jaywalker in over two hours of jogging. That has to be a record. But I will say that some of the crosswalks had enough snow and slush to wet my sneakers and socks and hence chill my feet. Such is life.

Since this is my first real snow since I got my apartment in April 2013, I also paid particular notice to fashion. Mink coats all over the place being worn by older women. Just amazing. Only rarely did I see a younger woman in a mink coat. I cannot help but think of all the minks that were sacrificed for warmth and fashion. Perhaps this is an Upper West Side thing. Whatever it is, you have to wonder what PETA would have to say about all of this. And I wonder what will happen to all those mink coats once their owners pass into the great beyond. Will they be discarded? Will younger women, then older and less moral, use them? Will they be retrofitted into fancy dresses for Lady Gaga types? Also, it is clear that the label North Face is prevalent all over the place. So to with UGG boots. It is funny how we dress to our age group like little automatons. Perhaps we feign individuality, but that really dress like our peers. Except for me. I just pull out of the drawer whatever is on top. I really do not care. Ginny used to laugh about that. Shakespeare said it best when he wrote "for the apparel doth proclaim the man". I guess sometimes.

Although during my run I did not see one needy person sleeping along the sidewalk, I did see at least ten really mentally ill people conversing with themselves and with passersby. How very sad. They were very poorly kept, in their 30s or so, male, unshaven, smelly, brazen, and had mouths that roared. I would hope that the F word could be stricken from their vocabularies. I do not know what their diagnoses might be, but they alarmed me and I would guess schizophrenia or something like that. Did I do anything about it? No. I viewed it as part of the landscape, whether right or wrong. I am not perfect.

Another thing Daniel, Benjamin, and Amelia, when you visit the City you will note that on the largest portion of Manhattan, the streets and avenues are set up to create great caverns through which the wind blows. Yesterday the winds came from the West and would certainly mess up a fine hairdo. Today the South was the culprit, particularly along Broadway. Some fancy architects in setting this up really assisted in giving the City a special and wonderful look, even if it makes you a tad unkempt. And the cityscape really is the landscape you will exist in when here. I like it.

After I finally arrived back at my apartment, I was a little tired and spent. And thirsty. I saw the cutest thing. Apparently the NYC thing to do when visiting some one's apartment in bad weather is to take off your shoes and leave them in the hallway just to the right or left of the front door to the apartment. The apartment next to mine had 8 pairs of shoes or boats sitting out there in the hall way. It was cute.

So, my tale of life in NYC now ends for a bit. Tuesday I go to Maui and Kauai for a couple of weeks. This pilgrimage will differ from last year when I did the same but to Oahu and Maui. I will be alone as always, but some friends living there will meet me for a meal and kayaking. To any burglars out there, all the things of value have been removed from my Clinton home, the most important thing on February 12, 2012. Just don't break anything going inside. And mercifully to all my friends, these epistles will soon end permanently after April1, 2014.

Goodnight Amelia, Benjamin, and Daniel

The Eagle has landed 1/7/14.
Jan 8, 2014

What a day. Yesterday at about 3:30 am I awoke in Clinton, New Jersey. After stirring a bit, I put on my jogging outfit and braved 4 degree temperatures and winds and ran for an hour in the dark. It was the only chance I would have to run as Hawaii beckoned me later in the morning. There is no way to describe the chill except it was almost as bad as when I joined the sub-zero jogging club one day some years ago in Neenah, WI. I kept waiting for my heart attack to deliver me more quickly to Maui but in a different dimension. You have never seen the color red that my face had collected. My dear friend Malcolm appeared a little after 5:30 am and after a tiny bit of breakfast he drove me off to Terminal C of Newark International Airport. All was good with the world. I love the frenetic pace and feeling of an airport.

Yes, my flight was at 9:30 am and I had lots of time to relax and people watch. And to read my assorted digital newspapers. Fascinating. All was good with the world. I sat next to a sweet young lady who attended

Rutgers. She wanted to hear all about Rutgers in the old days. I told her and philosophized a bit. Her friend from Montclair State and she were taking Spring Break at a friend's house in Kauai. How sweet is that! Then the 20 or so Blue Hens from The University of Delaware arrived. They were going to have it tough. A 30 day field trip on Oahu studying herbs and things. Yeah. What a deal. I told them all about wearing SPF-50 when and if they had free time. As people arrived it was evident that most of the flight consisted of couples or families. Very few people travel alone so in a sense I am and was an anomaly.

At 9:00 am they announced that boarding would begin on the large 767 jet. At 9:01 am they announced that there was engine trouble and that boarding would not begin. Drat. We did not take off until about 10:45am which caused me some trouble which will be explained later. I do like to fly but this flight had some issues. Their food menu was practically nonexistent. All they really had were drinks and snacks. With hundreds of people on the plane that can be a problem particularly when the flight is almost 11 hours to Honolulu. Other minor things do not matter. This was my second trip to Hawaii since Ginny died.

The people around me were just amazing on so many levels. I do not sleep on planes. Wish I could. Anyway, the couple sitting next to me spoke very little English. I think China was their country de jure. We communicated and I learned that they live 6 months on Oahu and the rest of the time on mainland China or New Jersey. Think of that connection! Across from me were six people and a baby. They were all from Staten Island. A young husband and wife with their 20 month old baby were flying to Honolulu with their parents for two weeks. Yes. Both sets of parents. Their parents had not known each other before the wedding but became best friends. And, what was even better, is that the parents, actually the grandmothers, took charge of the sweet little baby the entire trip which allowed child's parent to have some good time together as a couple. All that is so good. A bit behind me, near the end of the flight, I heard "Al Rylak, is that you?" And it was the Osowski or Okowski family whose kids went to school with David or Mark. I somewhat recognized them but like me, I am sure they have changed since my kids were in high school. I saw lots of men wearing crosses which meant to me that religion is making a comeback. They were not of a religious order but just ordinary people. Good. I people watched for my 11 hours of flying and it was all good. As time passed even the most beautiful people on the plane tend to look bedraggled. I do tend to gab a bit. When I asked one flight attendant wearing an orchid over her left ear what was meant as opposed to wearing it over the right ear, she smiled and said that an orchid over the left ear meant you were married and looking; over the right ear meant you were just looking. Hah.

After my flight landed, because of the late departure from Newark, I had to rush to try to find Mesa Airlines to fly over to Maui. I had 20 minutes. Crazy. Mesa was located at the far end of the airport in Honolulu. I had to go outside and find Wiki Wiki. That is what I was told by some fella that could hardly speak English. Had no idea what that was but it turned out to be a shuttle van. Somehow I got over to the Mesa area and heard my name mentioned on the loud speaker re the last call for the flight. Of course I had to go through security again which took some time. Yup. Where in Newark you kept your shoes and belt on through security, at this little place they practically stripped searched you. She was a nice lady though and it was okay with me. I kept hearing my name and eventually, half clad, carrying my sneakers and belt and other things, I was guided to my flight on the runway forgetting my knapsack. I was a little rushed. Just before the doors shut the nice lady who had searched me brought me my knapsack. Sweet.

The flight to Maui was 22 minutes and there were seven people aboard this puddle-hopper. The flight attendant was hysterically funny. She had to go over the usual rules about flying, personally introduced us to the pilot, and tried to sell us each a can of beer or soda. As the flight ended, she even walked down the short aisle looking for trash. There was none. So must have been a comedienne in training as during the flight she gave explanations as to where to get the cheapest gas on Maui, where to get good cookies, and like things. Levity is a good thing. She kept us all smiling. Even the young little thing that kept talking to someone on her cell phone after being told that that was not permissible on the flight.

After landing, my taxi driver from last year when I was in Maui, Alapake Heanu, was right there awaiting me as had been prearranged. What a relief for this tired old man. He got me to the condo and after a very short while I collapsed into a very large bed in my beautiful place at about 8:30 pm Hawaii time (a five hour time difference) and slept for about six hours. Feel like a million dollars and look forward to attacking Maui with a vengeance. May you all have a wonderful day. I shall. But first I need to jog along the ocean as the sun rises. There are miles to go before I sleep.

Aloha.

Al

Contradictions and knee braces.
Thu, Jan 11, 2014 2:56PM

Well, I have been in Maui for a time now and it really is paradise. The great weather is wonderful but at times can be boring. Even the best of things can get tiresome after a while. Nonetheless, it is a land of many contradictions and raises many questions in my decrepit analytical old mind. I will explain some of this below.

When I awakened from my much need post marathon flights the other day, I took a wonderful jog into Kihei. Kihei is the Surf City, NJ of Maui. Stores and shops galore and unrelentingly active in all ways. En route a rainbow appeared in the sky to the west; then another right atop, so I was looking at two distinct rainbows. Then a third and a fourth in the distance. Majestic as in the further distance you could see the Pacific Ocean and Molokai as well. A nice start to a day in the life of Al/Beckett in Maui.

Yes, jet lag existed that day and still does a bit. Clearly, as you age it takes a longer time to heal and recover. Anyway, on numerous days I have gone to many assorted beaches and all is well in those sections of the world. Along the so-called Gold Coast in Wailea there is a trail that is for the use of us low life's not staying in the crime de la crème hotels. It was created to allow commoners to have access to the ocean and enjoy the coast which is in reality owned by all the people and not the fancy five star hotels in the area. I have jogged it many times and enjoyed the vista as well as the opulence that surrounded me. I did go to the Small Beach once which is the nude beach in Makena. Tough to get to but hilarious once you arrive. Of course I tried my best to fit in but the place is full of assorted people, each one prouder of their assets than the other. It is a GLBT hangout as well as a heterosexual hangout. And yes, it is not just old fat people showing their stuff, although they predominate. There are a number of very nicely endowed and good looking young ladies and gentlemen as well. Okay, the smell of marihuana abounds and even a beer or two. Different. The NSA will probably note my activity or lack thereof at the Small Beach.

Unlike last year when the neuro-virus played havoc with my body, I have been swimming quite a bit. And snorkeling. Even came upon a green turtle the size of my car. A very big sweet and docile animal. Yes I have seen assorted fish of all sizes and colors. I do like the pre-beach replenishment beaches of 80th Street and its environs in Harvey Cedars better than here, but I am not complaining. The sand is so fine in Maui that it simply clings to your body. The water is clear with a bluish hue and warm. It is good stuff. I like it here.

Most of my stay on the beach is sitting alone however and watching the multitudes of people walk, talk, jog, sun, and in general be societal. I am an anomaly as I have my lone chair. After walking on the beach I can always find my spot as it is the one with just one chair and a green towel. I am not complaining, but I think most people are unable to vacation and play alone. So I set a new bar for achievement. Yet, I am a social animal. So, I have spoken to many of the people on the assorted beaches. So many are from Canada. So many from Canada love their national health insurance. So many Canadians asked me about Governor Chris Christie. Many foreign languages were heard. Yes, the beaches of Maui are interesting and beautiful.

One fella I met named Peter soared in the sky on his kite board. I was helping him get the sail ready, and swoosh he went out into the air and water as if propelled by a jet. The entire process looked very dangerous, He and I are now fast friends. I help him whenever I see him. He asked me if I wanted to try kite boarding and told him that as you age your sanity level increases, so I would have to pass on the offer.

And oh the sunsets. Ellen and Bob asked me to view the sunset with them at the Five Palms Hotel near Kihei. I did and it was simply irresistible. While there, two other people from Long Beach Island, NJ joined us,

Don and Marcia. They are building a house overlooking the ocean in Kapalua. Nice to have some folks from down the shore around. We all have a special connection as do most people from 80th Street, Harvey Cedars, NJ.

About the day I arrived, a man had been fishing right off the place I usually swim, Keawakapu Beach. He was in a kayak and chumming for fish. His legs dangled overboard. Unfortunately for him, a tiger shark bit off his leg and he later died. You so not mess with the Pacific Ocean. There is a life in the water which includes tiger and other sharks. That was sad. I guess you really are not 100% safe anywhere so you have to think and be prudent always. In other words you cannot leave your brains at home.

I have noticed that amid the alohas and mahalos, there are many homeless. Being homeless in paradise is better than being homeless in the cold of the East Coast, but a tragedy nonetheless. So many look spaced out and were filthy and emaciated. One fella who gave me a rough time while on a jog, had a fishing lure hanging from his lower lip. There is an urge to help, but a very real fear that harm could come to you. Paradise. Poverty. It is all part of the same.

Anyway, there seem to be many knee braces about the richer section of the Gold Coast of Wailea. Either they are being worn for style or a fashion statement, or many people simply have bad knees. I have seen at least 50 people with these black or tan knee braces walking for exercise. I also notice that the older people hold hands while on a walk. Younger people usually do not as they have cell phones or other devices in their hands or are way too serious about exercising. I prefer what I see with the older people. A closeness and a connection forged over time. We can all learn from that. They seem to be more connected and focused on the person with whom they are alongside.

Rather than a scooter, I have a real baby car this time. It is a Ford C-Max hybrid. Great car. Forty two miles per gasoline of gasoline. Sweet little car. May have to get one. Not a lot of pickup, but it gets me around.

Yes, I have seen humpback whales, but not as many as last year. I came to Maui a week earlier than last year and that may be the reason. On the other hand, perhaps their mating and baby care has been delayed for other reasons. But the green turtles abound. I will see more of them in Kauai in a few days.

I think I should let my clients know when I am away. Since I use my cell phone as my office phone, I have received two calls at 4:00am HST which rattles ones sleep. I do not fault them at all. Yet, I did offer advice as if nothing was different and I was at my home office in Clinton. They deserved that. After all, but for my clients I would not be here now.

Amelia, Benjamin, and Daniel, there are little critters here called geckos which are little lizards. They will not hurt you and they are just part of the ambiance of Maui along with birds, the likes of which you have never seen. The lawns are immaculate and await your playing on them after the sand has tired you. You must come here someday. Even though the price of everything is OTC (off the charts), it is something you must experience. The good and the bad.

Last night was special as I had the pleasure of going to dinner with Annie and Tracey. Very nice people I met here who have a connection to my brother Frank and his wife Julie. It was like homecoming and the food and conversation great, particularly the latter as I needed some of that. So you see, I have a collection of very nice people that I know in Maui now.

Along with Kat, the bar tender, who put me onto the big party at the Small Beach last year. To my surprise, she remembered me when I saw her the other day. This time she may accompany me to the festivity. That would be interesting.

Today at 3:00 pm I will be in the sky taking a personal tour of the entire island of Maui and Molokai area by helicopter. This shoot be a hoot. This is the only official touristy thing that I am doing on this trip to Maui. I do not want to be a tourist. Just like my life in Manhattan, I need to just be myself and discover my status in life and location on my own. I am making some very important decisions about my remaining time on this planet which is all good. I will not continue as I have since February 12, 2012. I am learning to be alone and getting more used to it. In that sense this trip has been beneficial. And no one knows where I will be next year.

So this post ends. I need to go on a long jog to wear off some of the food that I seem to over-consume while here. I need to look at people and again note the vast income disparity that seems to exist here in paradise as well as the differences in appearance and attitude. Actually I will do that throughout all the places I have been. I need to question my value structure and analyze the why and where of my life and life in general. All this is good.
Mahalo.

Albert D., formerly known as Beckett possibly to be known as Phoenix

Sometimes reality is wonderful. Other times we perhaps invent a "reality" which does not exist.
Thurs, Jan 12, 2014

Well Amelia, Benjamin, and Daniel, good day to you three little dears. Another day in Maui and another experience or four. This post may contain a tad of commentary as is my nature.

Because I was typing (you may know it as keyboarding) another post yesterday, my long run started out later than usual. That was a mistake. A matter of an hour or two impacts your run here, all due to the heat and the glorious hot sun. After about an hour and fifteen minutes of jogging along, I began to feel slightly dizzy and short of breath. Color that bad. I pushed on until I found some water and slowed my not so rapid pace a little. I continued on to my condo at The Palms at Wailea. All in all, it took about 30 minutes to return to normal after my run. I was beat. Bottom line? Do not be an idiot and run in the sun without water unless you are a youth. Even then it is stupid. Dehydration can be an issue here in Maui particularly when you drink caffeinated coffee just before your run. Drink, drink, and drink. Water that is. As I was feeling somewhat disengaged during my run, I was not fearful at all but stoical. Que sera sera.

After my recovery I decided to go and take a nice swim and snorkel. This time I went to Ulua Beach Park. The cooling swim was great. Snorkeling was equally great but I was caught in the tide. Before I knew it I was out at least a football field from the shore. Other people were not out as far, but had Boogie Boards to support them. My first thought was that I was like my soul buddy actress Anne Hathaway and that I had been caught in a rip tide just as she had a few days ago. My second thought was "oh crap". Anyway, I managed to get in to the shore line after about 10 minutes. It would have been a good way to go, having seen so many beautiful fish amongst the coral reef. At least I could breathe now. When you travel alone, there is no one to check your whereabouts which is a reality. The worse thing however is that there is no one to apply suntan lotion to your back!!! I mean you cannot ask a total stranger to do that to you.

I decided to go back to my condo again and get ready for my helicopter ride on Blue Hawaiian Helicopters. It was my hope to leave early and see some sights. Walking along the beach and then up the trail, I came upon a beautiful bride and her Mom standing near a wall close to some green grass overlooking the ocean at the Andaz Hotel. She knocked my socks off and I spoke to her. To the west was the ocean. A makeshift simple altar and about eight seats lay behind. A harp was playing and a small wedding cake and about seven or eight glasses of Champaign sat on a separate table. Yes, I stayed afar for the entire wedding, transfixed. So often people will spend so much money on a wedding so as to be queen and king for a day. About half of all marriages end in divorce anyway. This wedding was simple, small, beautiful and full of love. The bride and groom were health professionals of some kind and the minister spoke of that. Apparently the bride's father had died as had the groom's mother. Everything was just perfect however and you could not help but become teary eyed. Perfection does not have to be big and grandiose. Anyway, I learned of an amazing ritual after the pronouncement of their union. The bride and the groom went over to the altar where there had been placed a quart sized clear glass beautiful jar and two smaller clear bottles of sand. In one the sand was blue and the other, white. The newlyweds took these bottles of colored sand and simultaneously poured them into the larger clear bottle. Of course the sand mixed together. Quite a bit of symbolism there. I had never seen that before. It was so wonderful. So Hawaiian.

And so I showered and cleaned up this old body as best as I was able. That gets more difficult each year. I drove to the heliport in Kahului just to find the location. Now knowing where it was and having some time to burn, I went traveling to Paia (Willie Nelson loves this place) and wanted to make an effort to get to Haiku and the Jaws where the surfing is supposed to be magnificent. I never got beyond Paia. Because of a surfing tournament or other reasons, the two lane road along the coast was packed with cars. I am talking a five mile back up. I know. I measured it. It was like Saturday trying to get onto Long Beach Island, NJ through Surf City, NJ to Harvey Cedars. Yuck. Those in the traffic were more likely to honk horns, give one the bird, or take like actions. My thought was that we from the mainland had ruined this area. Nonetheless, I eventually found a parking space and had fun looking around that small town. A very eclectic place on the ocean however. Because of the traffic I gave up the thought of trying to get to Haiku and learned that getting to Jaws required special permission or something else. My plans changed. So for the first time I had stopped at a shop and had shave ice which was different and quite good; like eating cold tasty air. Saw some art galleries and shopped a bit or two, buying nothing. It was disturbing to see 7 youngish people sitting around the side of a building smoking pot and looking bedraggled. I did not feel sorry for them. I did not pity them. Today I would not carry the guilt of having a few shekels and watching people ruin their lives. That was their problem; their choice.

Then I reversed my direction and arrived early at the heliport for my flight. I had ordered a solo ride but the aircraft had an issue. So they put me on a fancy helicopter with 7 others at a much reduced price. It was all good. Due to clouds and hence weather, I could not tour the entire island of Maui, particularly near the Haleakala Crater. But Blue Hawaiian made up for it by covering all of southwest Maui and the northwest section including Kapalua, Lahaina, and most importantly the mountains of the island of Molokai which you can only see by air. They also gave me a DVD of what a previously flight had seen during their travels around all of Maui. A classy thing to do. I will not even begin to describe the flight as it was totally spectacular. Over the ocean we saw humpback whales and their babies. The 4,000 foot plus mountains of Molokai took your breath away. We were right down in them. I saw the location of the old leper colony and the filming sight of the waterfalls scene in Jurassic Park. Clouds, cliffs, and majestic mountains. I will leave it there. Worth the cost and the memories of which are forever emblazoned in my brain. I do however have a few cell phone pictures.

During my flight I met another group of couples. This couple thing is getting a little old. One was from Chicago and they were in Maui for a week escaping the cold chill. Another from Austin, Texas, likewise in Maui for the week. The final couple was from mainland China, having flown to Maui for a week via Minneapolis. All had travelled a long distance for a short vacation but all were pleased nonetheless. The couple from Chicago were staying at the Four Seasons in Wailea. Seven hundred dollars a night for their room. Sorry, but even if you have it, that seems a bit extreme. For that price for me, they would have to throw in a naked woman along with a mariachi band. I am not cheap. I just do not get it. But that is me.

So I ate out last night at the bar; fish as usual while here. Sat across from the fella shucking the oysters and making the assorted shrimp and the like dishes. A great fellow from Ecuador. He was good and never stopped working once. He told me that too many of the native Hawaiians simply did not want to work, but collect from the State. His words, not mine. Since it was Saturday night some neighbors were acting like college kids when I returned to the condo, getting louder and louder as they got more and more drunk. Yet I guess they were all big shots in Maui for a day or a week. I hope we do not ruin this paradise. It may be too late.

So now I go off and run again, hoping that the clouds are covering the sun and with a bottle of water in my hands.

Al, aka Grandpa

The eagle has landed again.
Thurs, Jan 15, 2014

Well Amelia, Benjamin, and Daniel, the eagle has landed again. This time in Kauai. It was sad to leave the hustle bustle of Maui, yet I knew a real paradise awaited me on the most northerly island of Hawaii. From the moment I landed I detected a different sense of lack of action and serenity. Except for the one highway around the island which near small towns was bumper to bumper with traffic. Otherwise, all was a go.

Upon getting my rental car I drove north toward Princeville. After stopping at a food store for some basic victuals in Wailua, I found my condo unit at a place called The Cliffs at Princeville at Hanalei. Yes, "Puff the magic kingdom, lived by the sea, and frolicked in the autumn mist in a land called Hanalei". I learned that most of these condos are time shares which I will look into, but my unit had nothing but grass between it and the ocean. Yup, an ocean view is a good thing. As I entered the unit I looked at the ocean and there, just awaiting my arrival on cue, were humpback whales leaping into the air with their calves, splashing all about. It does not get any better than that! It went on for about 30 minutes. I think they were very happy to see me.

And my condo is quite nice. Two bedrooms and two baths in case I find a lovely wahine to join me, all modern and all very well put together. Everything I need I have. The Pinot Grigio I bought was useful as I sat on my lanai looking at the whales play and chatting on my cell phone with a few people. Reality set in and I unpacked and decided to have a meal as the sun would soon set. Ironically, in December 2013 my brother Frank and his wife Julie stayed at the Sea Lodge about a quarter of a mile or less as the crow flies from my location. We should try to be here at the same time some year! And I later learned that my son David and his wife Lena stayed at the very same Sea Lodge on their honeymoon!

The road around the island is not only small, but somewhat treacherous at times. No big deal. It makes people drive slower. After asking around I decided to go to the Hanalei Dolphin Restaurant on the river leading to Hanalei Bay. A couple of hairpin curves and a scenic lookout at the mountains later, I arrived. But first I had to travel over a tiny one lane bridge with rules. The main rule was that as a local courtesy, up to 7-8 cars would go over the bridge from one direction, and thereafter the other direction would do likewise. Etcetera. Everyone obeyed the local custom. Can you imagine that in New Jersey?!

Now the fellow that suggested the Dolphin was very correct. So typically Hawaiian. So out doors with a roof. So full of people laughing and having a good time. Such great food and such great prices (meaning high). It was all okay. I sat at the sushi bar where singles are usually placed along with a couple who lived on the island near Anini Beach Park and Kilauea Lighthouse in Kilauea. Great people and great conversation. I really did not want to bother them but they sensed I was alone and took me into their dinner time. My meal was mahjong fish and vegetables and they bought me sushi of some sort as a welcoming gift. All great. Washed down with a martini, all was good with the world. To say that the people of Kauai are friendly is an understatement. Thank you Walter and Dale.

Before returning to the condo, I travelled to see Hanalei Bay. Wow. Half of a circle of sand carved into the shoreline. It does not get any prettier than that. Putting aside the movies filmed at Hanalei Bay, it awaits my arrival today. I did return to my condo eventually and slept pretty well for a chronic insomniac. I am now awake, drinking coffee, and look forward to a long run around Princeville and ending up on the sands of Hanalei Bay for part of the day. It seems that Route 56 would be difficult to jog alongside as shoulders do not really exist to any safe extent, so the interior roads of Princeville will do me proud.

The mountains to the interior were visible from the airport in Lihue and all 28 miles to Princeville.
I mean real mountains and not hills. Even the Blue Ridge and Allegheny Mountains would pale in comparison. This island seems to have it all which I will see from a helicopter someday soon.

And so, as the sun also rises (sorry, but I could not constrain myself) it is time to strap on my running sneakers and get these old legs moving so as to enjoy what I have never seen before. This is going to be a very long run as well as a learning experience. Since relaxation and calmness is the focal point now, this will be my final note or post. As my Buddhist friends would say from the old Sanskrit texts, Namaste. Peace, be well, honor you, honor earth, good health, and good being. Not a bad philosophic concept. Although I miss Ginny terribly, I am doing much better in Hawaii than last year.

Albert D.

Welcome home Al. Or is it Beckett!
Wed, Jan 29, 2014 4:47PM

From Clinton to Hawaii to Virginia to Clinton to an ER in Flemington to my first trial in a very long time, to Council, to NYC. What a month January 2014 has been. I color all of this good. And it is not over yet.

I awoke this morning after an unusually long and restful sleep. I must be sick or something! Whatever. After a short run, I took the bus into the City which was great. Passed Met Life Stadium where the Super Bowl will be played on Sunday. Actually, although the event is in NJ, all of NYC seems to be in hyper-football mode talking about how lucky NYC is to have the Super Bowl in their state. Hah. The bus driver and I hit it off. He and I began telling jokes and anecdotes which helped pass the time. I loved his "how come we are told not to judge all Muslims by the actions of a few lunatics, but on the other hand, we are told to judge all gun owners by the actions of a few lunatics". Love logic and anti-logic. Nonetheless, a very good point. To my politician friends, please do not run again. Two terms and out is enough. I will stand by that posture. Period.

As soon as I got on the 1 Train to my apartment I realized how much I had missed the City. It has been 27 days since I last visited. I felt like I was coming home. It is a good place to be alone with all your non-friends. After getting some food from the Gourmet Garage, my apartment made me feel even more welcomed. I jogged a little and then did what I really wanted today. I walked over to the Met and spent fours there in my jogging outfit and aroma. Yes, my knees hurt but my brain has been used which I like. I refuse to stop using it.

I love the Met. It is like going to Haverford College or Bucknell University, two places that provide a wonderful education. I always leave, albeit tired, feeling like I have learned so much and usually I have. Today I wanted to see some specific exhibits and I did. Antonio Canova: The Seven Last Works was just wonderful; Early American Guitars introduced me to guitars that were built by C.F. Martin with rosewood and other woods, all from Nazareth, PA; Silla: Korea's Golden Kingdom gave me a total respect for the art of Korea in the 500-700s AD; Cleopatra's needle was all about obelisk's; and Jewels by JAR should be googled as it was my favorite. I also had to return to the modern art exhibits as the Picasso's excite me. All of art excites me. The bottom line is that I walked out of the Met feeling educated, sophisticated, special, lucky, and happy. I did not just sit around and continue aging.

So as I walked back to my apartment who do I bump into? Leeza. I have written about her before and you will recall I gave her a ticket to get into St. Patrick's Cathedral on Christmas Eve. She was as pretty as ever, but also as homeless as ever. What a tragedy. I bought Leeza some lunch/dinner and she was very thankful. She even remembered me giving her the ticket and remembered two friends who have met and helped her, Susan and Russ. When asked if she was getting help, she said a little. That meant none. I will check on her tonight. I want to help Leeza because she deserves it and because I can. On the other hand, I am a man and she is a twenty year old woman. I have to be careful. So anyway, tonight I am going to find her some hand warmers and hot coffee. It is going to be so very cold tonight. And she is so very vulnerable.

Anyway, I am going off to dinner now and then need to rest and have some wine. My legs are oh so very tired. I bet I covered a half marathon today in terms of distance. So I stop this epistle early which is good. An unexpected pleasure will happen tomorrow as Liz is going to come into the City for a while to see me. Great. So much to do. So much to see. Today life is good. I am in an Empire State of Mind.

Be good sweet Amelia, Benjamin, and Daniel. You are missed.

Beckett

After Midnight
Mon, Feb 16, 2014

Well my dear little grandchildren three, old Grandpa, aka PeePaw, has gone off to the City again. Liz was nice enough to join me and as we took the bus in we were undecided as to what to do. The snow was to fall later in the morning and the apparent snow from the last seven snow storms was along the street, curb, and parts of the sidewalks. Although new snow is exciting and rapturous, old snow mixed with the dirt of the City and salt and sand and et al is not particularly attractive.

I love to listen to the people around me. The bus driver was a dear older man, younger than I, who was funny and as nice as could be. Many people were tired of the winter conditions. The usual 1 Train was delayed, so we took the 2 train to 72nd Street. This turned out to be fortuitous as we stopped at Trader Joe's to get breakfast food and a few other victuals. It is interesting to note that the shelves were not filled with food. We were able to get what we wanted, but due to the series of snow storms that have impacted NYC and environs, many items of food could not be delivered to the store. So I learned a lesson. The food supply on this Island called Manhattan, because it is an island and because it is so congested and easily impacted by bad weather (think snow) can be adversely impacted. To my terrorist non friends out there, take note.

Anyway, we walked back to 66th Street and my lovely apartment opened its arms, embraced me, and I felt happy to be there. I know this apartment is a luxury, but it is a good luxury. Liz made some fancy breakfast which was delicious and we talked about what to do. Jazz was in the offering as I love jazz but we also talked about going to a Broadway show. I also made my usual trip to the Compactor and Recycle Room and smiled as I found an undone copy of the NY Times crossword puzzle for Friday which we were able to complete. I do not buy that paper for many reasons, but I love to get its crossword puzzle for free. I feel satisfied having kept the cost in my pocket. Just one of my many quirks. It was also good to speak to my dear friend and see that she was okay. And so then we left the apartment.

Trying to be a little more non-rubbish, I suggested we take a bus. We did. Right on West End Avenue you can catch the 57th Street crosstown bus. As we waited for the bus, we chatted with a couple that invited us to the Museum of Modern Art (MOMA) as their guests, but we were intrepid in desiring to go to TKTS and get tickets for a 2:00pm matinee. And then the snow started falling. It was coming and coming.

Liz is not a big bus person, she is an anti-rube, but the ride was fun and we got off at 57th Street and Broadway. The snow kept coming. Walking down to TKTS at 47th, the crowds did not lessen and the City was filled with people, noises and smells. It was alive. I was alive. Times Square is a special area in which you feel large and small. It is a conundrum and an enigma at the same time. It is wonderful when taken in small doses.

And so we got in line to buy our tickets. The line went on and on and on. Must have been three hundred people waiting for tickets. I guess it is because TKTS sells half price seats. It was almost 11:30am. And we stood with the snow falling. A wet snow. Chatted with a father and his teenage daughter behind us from San Francisco. They had come for a five day stay in the City and were living la dolce vita. They were trying to take in the entire City in those five days. Cannot be done. They were lovely nonetheless and we had a nice chat. And the snow kept falling. All the people around us were in the same predicament and everyone was in great spirits. Believe it or not, I had a great time waiting. The crowd became individuals and we were all chatting and laughing and cold and wet. It may sound strange, but groups of people in a similar situation change after first being stressed. They loosen up and enjoy their circumstance.

Well, by 12:30pm we were at the front of the line and bought half price tickets to "After Midnight" playing at the Brooks Atkinson Theatre on 47th Street. More on that later. It was a great choice. So we had an hour and a half or so to kill, so off to the Long Room on 44th Street for a late lunch, which I call Linner. Yes, Linner. Cool place. It is like an Irish Pub with a dining area. Many beer selections and darn good food. So we dally a while to avoid the snow, and leave for the Theatre just before 1:30pm. And the snow kept coming. When we arrived at our destination, the line was quite long and around the block. This pleased me as I felt that all these people could not be wrong. It must be a good show. The line moved quickly and we entered the theatre to finally sit in the best seats in the house. Close to the stage and practically in the middle section.

And so we saw "After Midnight". Absolutely great as it was a musical that combined Song, Jazz and Dance. The infamous Wynton Marsalis picked seventeen of his best Jazz players from trombone to trumpets to saxophone to whatever, who performed all the music for the performance, on stage. And when they played and the cast sang and danced to twenty-seven fantastic musical numbers famous in the Harlem of the 1930s you just knew this was special. Holy crap was this great. The star was K. D. Lang who sang her heart out. Dule Hill of The West Wing on TV was the narrator of all that was going on. The songs at times were risqué and brazen, the dancing ranged from tap to swing. Everyone and everything was just perfect. There was no let up for an hour and a half. The music simmered and I felt I had missed a lot as I had never seen Duke Ellington perform. And, what a place Harlem must have been in its heyday. In short, I am glad I went. The audience gave a standing ovation at the conclusion of the performance.

And so we left the theatre and the snow continued. Apparently Woody Allen was sitting nearby us as everywhere a noted person goes there is a stir. And there was a stir. Getting to the 1 train which was now operational was a relief and eventually we got back to the apartment. Relief and warmth. Dinner was to be in store for the evening. We relaxed looking at the snow fall from my 15th floor window and watching the 2014 Winter Olympics at Sochi on the television. The snow seemed to rise to the sky at times as if it were falling upward. Eerie. At 6:00pm we decided that we were not going out for dinner and put together a dinner of canned soup, salad, fruit, and bread. It was a wise decision. I may be old, but I am not stupid or senile.......yet.

I had never seen the City from high up when the snow was falling heavily but last night I did. Strange and surreal. I loved it from the warmth of my apartment. Lights still peeked through the dense falling snow for hours. And then, it all stopped and the City lights became clearer. As the sky cleared, a white full moon appeared between the skyscrapers and all was good with the world.

After watching the last exciting Olympic women's event of Sweden v.

USA in curling, I tired and fell asleep awakening just a short while ago. Grandma has been gone two years and two days sweet Amelia, Benjamin, and Daniel (and of course any other that fortuitously may come along), and she certainly misses you. Life is good here in the City. Grandpa is doing okay. Time to run. Literally. I hope it is not too icy. As they said in "After Midnight" break a leg......or not.

St. Patrick's Day Parade 2014 and Veniero's Pasticceria
Sun, March 22, 2014

To my little sweet grandchildren, I finally bid you hello. I have been derelict in relaying my NYC experiences as I have not been in the City for some time. Humanity entered the equation about four weeks ago as this old man had the flu, followed by shingles, followed by esophageal EE making me unable to eat, sleep, or drink to any extent. But Becket, heretofore to be known only as Al, has returned. I have reached the point in my life where I no longer need an alter ego.

Last weekend I came into the City to just get out of my home in Clinton. I had been stuck there for weeks what with my assorted maladies. So I picked the weekend of the St. Patrick's Day Parade to return. I have to tell you that when I arrived, spending just two nights, I simply relished my magnificent nighttime view of the world. Eschewing my usual Cognac due to esophagus medical reasons, I just sat in my chair looking at the twinkling lights and trying to imagine the thousands of stories being lived in those thousands of apartments. That view sustains me in many ways.

When outside, I did see the usual bootie clad dogs, my poor friend Leeza about whom I have previously written, the beautiful people walking around in their pricey outfits living in a self-imposed surreal world, and on my so-called runs now merely a slow trot I nodded to my usual contacts. It was just so very cold.

So anyway, I decided that I needed a haircut and went to Barber Shop 72 on 72nd Street on Sunday. Quite the place. First of all, it is open on a Sunday. Yes, a Sunday. And then you see six chairs with six barbers and a full house awaiting needy hairy people like me. When you arrive, they take your jacket. And then you wait and listen. Two little boys were getting their first haircuts; from tears to happiness with a lollipop. Benjamin, you came right into my mind. My barber Mike was funny and asked if my hair had previously been cut by a lawn mower. He and I got along as he gave me a layered cut of some sort or another. I left the establishment about 3:00pm and the place was still packed. So now not only do I have a tailor and dry-cleaner in the City, but my own personal barber. And the total cost for the haircut was less than the cost in Clinton, NJ. Go figure.

The Parade was on Monday at 11:00am. The temperature was in the upper teens and the winds were up to 30 miles per hour. I stayed about an hour and a half shivering. Having underdressed for warmth, I paid a dear price as after the parade I sat in the tub for over half about trying to feel my fingers and toes. It still was great. Prior to the beginning of the Parade, a very short leprechaun of middle age, ran past my station on 5th and 56th with a soccer ball. The police tried to stop him but eventually gave up and let the crowds cheer the little fellow on. I loved the mounted police, the celebrities (absent Mayor deBlasio who boycotted the parade), the very high security, the Irish music, and most of the frivolity. The most impressive thing to me however were the soldiers that were part of the 69th Battalion marching from as far as the eye could see. There were all these soldiers in formation, well over a thousand. You get a tiny touch of what war must be like and a deep appreciation for the logistics of it all. To see this brings Afghanistan and Iran into a clearer focus and reality. The only things that were upsetting were the usual. Too many young people drunk out of their minds, too many people using four letter words beginning with the letters F or S, and too many people just having a good time and not respecting the flag and the soldiers passing. It is a reality of life and I guess I am not just old, but old fashioned. It is interesting to note however the real anger exhibited by the GLBT groups that were barred from marching with their banners. I mean, many of the representatives of the GLBT groups were mad and let you know it. If I thought my rights were being violated I guess I would do the same.

I then left after my soaking and went to what I thought was an Irish Bar called the Amsterdam Ale House looking forward to corned beef and cabbage. Turns out it was not Irish (cannot believe Google all the time) and did not serve CB and C. The closest I could find to an Irish meal was Shepherd's Pie. It was good.

I did return to Clinton Tuesday after another look at my view, feeling refreshed but also feeling exhausted and somewhat ill. My assorted illnesses had returned with a vengeance. If only I were not so human.

And that brings me to yesterday when I returned to the City. Liz came to visit. It is always so great to have someone here, if for no other reason than to have someone to talk to as I explore the City. Some people are good alone. Some are not. I am trying to be the former but mostly fit into the latter category. Liz is part of my widow and widower's club where we periodically see each other and understand each other. Anyway, upon arrival we took the 1 Train to Columbus Circle and went to my newly discovered Sara Beth's on Central Park South. I thought it was new to that location but it turns out to have been there for 8 years. We shared muffins and the most delicious jams ever made by human hands. Chatting with some folks sitting next to us from Florida, we all had a lovely conversation about Broadway shows, grand kids and the like. Then off to the Time Warner building to Whole Foods. Wow. I should have been there before. The finest super-duper market I have ever seen. We stocked up on sushi and assorted other victuals. And yes, I did bump into Dana Tyler of CBS news. Our eyes met and she smiled at me and I nodded at her. She is one pretty lady. So, another celebrity sighting.

After getting to the apartment and relaxing a bit, we decided to go to the East Village. I had never been there before. We went to Washington Square Park and Union Square Park. Both places were vibrant with vibrancy (I like the way that sounds). In other words, they were totally alive. From guitar players to mimes, to tarot readers, to "hood gymnasts", you could not help but feel alive. The City brings life. Even the subways are alive with musicians, singers, acrobats, evangelists, and crazy people. Anyway, we stopped at Grace Church on Broadway. A majestic Episcopal Church with stained glass windows second to none and wooden carvings so realistic that you want to say excuse me if you bump into them. The church is on the National Historic Register.

And then we went to Veniero's Pasticceria. Now this is a bakery on 11 St. started in 1894 and has been under one family ownership forever. If you walk into the place you get pimples or if older, just by breathing you gain 5 pounds. There can be no finer bakery in the world. I sampled the cuisine and did not want to leave. But did.

We then headed off to the apartment which was a little tricky doing the subway thing. Tricky for me at least and I am an old Eagle Scout. I will have to improve my map reading skills. And that was it. I guess I over did it as I was quite tired. So dinner was had at my NYC home. I have to say that cooking in is so much less expensive then eating out. That is so obvious, but true nonetheless. I will avail myself more of that in the future.

And so now I am sitting typing this epistle or remembrance if you will. First thing this morning I ran along the Hudson River for a little over an hour at Riverside Park. I have missed doing that as the running portion of the Park has been snowed and iced over since January and too dangerous on which to run. And so this was a special run. The first thing I see and 20 minutes into the run is a fella on a paddle board going up the river. I could not help but laugh. Then a little further along I saw about 30 ducks whose bodies were white and the tops of their heads looked like they had fans on them. Then I got so very lucky. A BYW (beautiful young woman) wearing orange sneakers, bright lime green pants, and a shocking pink top ran next to me and we chatted. The 45 year age difference did not matter as I did not want to hold her youth and inexperience against her, and I ran a fast as my little legs could go talking and laughing with her. She was a new attorney and that coupled with our running made for an enjoyable run. After a goodbye, I hobbled back to my apartment having again overdone it. Totally worth it!!

So today Liz and I meet Ken, one of her Gettysburg College friends, who lives in Washington Heights up near Harlem. We will go out for a drink or late lunch assuming my EE allows me to drink other than green tea and to eat real food. I want to show Liz Marea tonight which is a high end bar/restaurant at Columbus Circle and then sushi for dinner. I will have a new friend in the City which I need. Tomorrow back to Clinton and then Harvey Cedars.

And so it ends sweet Amelia, Benjamin, and Daniel. And should there be another, you too. My epistles end as promised as I do not expect to be back in the City until after April 1st, my one year anniversary date. I hope that you have some understanding of my experiences in New York City. The City has helped me heal a good bit from the loss of your dear, sweet, loving and beautiful Grandma who misses you so. Life was totally unfair to Ginny and candidly, to you too, as she would have loved you and taught you about love and happiness and the things in life that are so very important and really matter.

Do not be afraid to try new things. Live life like you do not have forever. Do not put things off for tomorrow as tomorrow may never come. Be strong and never compromise your values. Be forgiving as no one is perfect. Be kind because not everyone is as lucky as you. Help people when you are able because so many people are in need. Be bold and try new things as if you shy away from life, you will miss so many fun and enjoyable things. Do what makes you happy so you have no regrets. Be responsible and not self-centered because there is a big world out there. Be trusting to an extent because that is how you may get to know the soul of the people you meet. If you are shy, do not worry about it. You are what you are. Just do the best you are able. At one time I was so very shy but just let nature take its course. You are perfect.

The end.

Love, Grandpa

A Town of Clinton, NJ Council Meeting

Well, last night's meeting made the Star Ledger newspaper. Good. I like to cause trouble. A person running for Congress wanted to use the municipal building for a "meet and greet". We said no. Yes, he was a

Democrat, but would have said the same even if he were a Republican. Let him rent a place in Town. Will send you the article if I remember.

So glad Daniel is into peaches now. The little dear will now see some of the nice things in life....like pureed peaches. Cool. Wait until he tries prunes!

Amelia and Benjamin will now have a picture of Daniel join them in my NYC apartment. I still would like a picture of the entire Toms River family there as well. Speaking of that apartment, I am off to the City again now. I want to spend a few days at the Met, reading Killing Kennedy, jogging where appropriate, and eating sushi. Of course my nighttime view is what it is all about. I find that very relaxing. If I did nothing else but look at the view it would be worth it all. I do like the frenetic energy of the City and feed off that. Hard to believe I raised two sons with Mom who hated the City. C'est le vie. Are you sure I am your father?!!!!!!

I am on the bus now bouncing around. Making this commute every day would be difficult. Still, there are a variety of people near me, all whom seem pretty nice.

I look forward to Amelia's birthday party on the 19th. Hard to believe the little dear is going to be 6 years old on the 20th. And my analytical and talkative Benjamin, I look forward to seeing him as well. Daniel does not love me yet, but that will come in a few months.

In my final e-mail to my grandchildren, I neglected a couple of important things. Like to keep trying to find happiness. Like making sure you take care of yourself individually and as a family. Like spending even 30 minutes a day just resting or meditating in your own space. Like accepting people for whom they are no matter what they believe or do not believe, provided they are good people. Like not only living within your means, but even below your means. Yes, I have lots of things, but the things are irrelevant in the broad picture. Like trying not to feel trapped in any situation, be it a job, circumstance, location or whatever, unless you are handcuffed to the wall by the police. There is nothing that cannot be improved. I could go on. As I age I try not to judge or be pedantic. Yes, I like to use a big word or two. Bottom line however is the first premise above. Mom always stressed that. Be happy. Smile once in a while. Life is short as we know......unless you were Gra who died only because she tired of living.

And so another adventure begins. So much to do. So little time. After a cold and windy today, spring will truly be in the air. Have a great day.

Love and hugs,

Dad, who in the future may be called Trebla

Anita and Misandry
Thurs, April 3, 2014

I have been back in the City for a few days. Wonderful. Yesterday I decided to see the movie "Anita" which was playing at the small film center at Lincoln Center less than a block from my apartment. The movie was all about Anita Hill and the issues that arose during the confirmation hearing of Clarence Thomas to the U.S. Supreme Court and the testimony given by Anita Hill. If Anita Hill was telling the truth, a tragedy for her. If not, a tragedy for Justice Thomas which continues even today. I went into the theater with a totally open mind but recall vividly those events of about 1981.

I know that the movie media can sway so many people as that is the job of the Producers and Directors, which they do quite well. I do not know what the truth is with respect to those events. I was not there and it happened thirty plus years ago. This movie had a point to make and made it very well. The fact that a black woman was attacking a black man for what is now known as sexual harassment and the further fact that the black man viewed the confirmation circumstance as a high-tech lynching is interesting but secondary to my thought process. Actually, Hill and Thomas are really irrelevant to this writing.

Misandry is the hatred of and prejudice against men. I experienced it yesterday. The theater was filled with only about 20 people at most. When I walked in there were maybe 15 middle aged people sitting in their seats, all of whom were women. So I said to myself, I may meet a nice lady, who knows. The first words I heard from three women sitting near me were "what are you doing here?" A few others laughed. I feigned ignorance and asked why. The comment made was "you men". Another person coming in just behind me reiterated that comment and said, "You men. You just don't get it". I suggested that I did not understand, but let us hope the movie was good. I knew no one in the theater. I am just Al, no longer Beckett.

As the movie unfolded, it was clear that I, and another man who entered to the rear, were in a place in which we were not wanted. I will only address me. It was clear that the men who sat on the Judiciary Committee re the confirmation process were portrayed as chauvinistic angry stupid white males. Maybe they were what with Joe Biden leading the charge as the Hero of Chappaquiddick, Teddy Kennedy, sat to his left. Anytime a man was portrayed, the theater as a whole made snide comments and loud guttural noises. It was embarrassing. Since I had paid my $9.00 senior citizen rate to see and hear the movie, I wanted to do just that. After about 10 minutes of interrupting grunts and groans, I finally had enough.

So, I shushed the fine women and blurted out that I could not hear the movie. I did that perhaps four times until they all shut up. It was clear that my presence was not appreciated. I cannot help but feel that these women were out for an afternoon of male bashing. After all, TV commercials make men out to be stupid, certainly not as smart as their children, and whose primary role is to work like worker bees to support their families; no one caring that they miss so many wonderful family things and the stresses hoisted upon them in that role.

So the movie ended with Anita Hill receiving treatment on the screen worthy of Mother Teresa or Martin Luther King and a standing ovation. As I left, a woman said to me, "you must have a lot of guts to have stayed in here". I said no, I enjoyed the movie, at least what I could hear. I have no respect for most of the women I saw in the theater. I am not an angry white man. I simply seek knowledge. My genitalia have no bearing on my thoughts.

The irony is that I concluded that Anita Hill was probably being truthful based on the presentation. Why would a black woman attack a black man who could ascend to the highest court in the land? Why would she subject herself to the vicious attacks she received during and after her testimony? Why did she immediately tell others of the events soon after they occurred, although her testimony was seven years later?

So I believed Anita Hill. I did not deserve to be treated as I was in the theater. Those antagonistic women were guilty of the same ignorance and intolerance as Clarence Thomas. Maybe we can all learn to not prejudge and to be civil as we are not today. Or maybe I am just getting old and chasing windmills trying to fight for the constitution I so love and a kinder and gentler nation where tolerance of all types prevails. Or maybe I am just too sensitive? Never.

Al/Dad/Grandpa/a recovering attorney

And so it was.

Madame Butterfly.
Thurs, April 10, 2014

A number of people have asked me to periodically relate some more of my Manhattan experiences. I will do so from time to time with the understanding that these epistles are not necessarily for the benefit of my dear grandchildren as I have inundated them with too much of me already. They, as most of you, need a break from me. My writings are like hemorrhoids; they never go away. So hit delete now if you like.

Ergo, yesterday, Wednesday, April 9, 2014. I was in Flemington, NJ and learned that James Valenti was staring at the Metropolitan Opera House in Puccini's Madame Butterfly. I was going to the City anyway, so I decided to try to get a ticket. That was difficult. As I drove to the bus stop I finally reached Lincoln Center and got one of the few remaining seats. This was a treat just meant for me. And it is much cheaper when you pay for one.

If you recall, James is a graduate of North Hunterdon High School near me and was a friend of my son Mark. He actually used to play with Mark in my back yard. I have previously written about him and he is the fella that sang so beautifully at St. Patrick's Cathedral at the midnight Christmas Eve Mass. Anyway, I got into the City close to 5:30pm and the Opera was at 7:30pm. I wanted some food and after I learned that James' parents and others were eating at Shun Lee on 65th, I went there to say hello. Great to see the family and friends but did not want to impose on their dinner.

So now I am sitting at the water fountain at Lincoln Center watching people as I usually do. Some Opera personage observations are appropriate. I was dressed in a suit and tie. Seemed appropriate. Many men wore turtlenecks with or without jackets. Others looked like that had just come home from coal mining. Most women wore jewelry of some sort or another which always gives a dressed up appearance. I realized that there is no real dress code. On the other hand, so many of the young girls (12-16) were dressed to the nines. Hard to describe, but they were playing adult and looked wonderful; this was a big night for them. I long to take Amelia to the City for an Opera or Ballet and to just watch her reactions. I think I was the only uncoupled person in the house but that was fine today. I am learning and really getting used to it. And even more importantly, since women attend in groups it is easy to find a friend. And that is how I met Janet, a sweet lady with a British accent from Brooklyn attending with friends. But I digress.

So the lights come on at 7:00pm and I enter to a better seat than usual, but still high in the stratosphere or nose bleed section. I e-mailed James Valenti and congratulated him on having the lead male role which becomes relevant later. I may post a photo or two later to my Facebook account.

Now, the simple version of Puccini's Madame Butterfly is that a poor Geisha girl named Butterfly is selected to marry Lt. Pinkerton (James) and after the marriage Lt. Pinkerton leaves for America claiming he will return. Three years pass, Butterfly has his child of which he has no knowledge. When he returns now married to a Jersey Gal (sorry, had to take liberties here) and renounces his Nagasaki, Japan wife, she is somewhat upset. Divorce is easy in Japan. Madame Butterfly commits suicide eventually and Pinkerton and his Jersey wife take the child away to the United States.

After the first of three Acts, I received an e-mail from James asking me to come backstage and meet the cast. Holy crap. Did not expect that. And then I was invited by him to the Empire Hotel for drinks thereafter. This is all pretty cool for an old Polish/German rube from Trenton and Hopewell Township, NJ. What an exciting moment in my life.

The Opera was just great and my new friend Janet met me at two intermissions and insisted on purchasing me some wine. That did not help my esophagus issues. Query? Am I meant to be a gigolo? I could always do worse things I guess. Anyway, she was very nice, and yes, a widow.

I sat next to a couple from Colombia. She was a singer and he a director of a play in mid-Town. They invited me to attend tonight, but I am tired and weary now. So that is out. They spoke very little English. So I conducted the conversation in Spanish. You would have laughed your head off at my pigeon-Spanish. Somehow we communicated.

I did advise James that his Pinkerton role angered me and that I wish Madame Butterfly had had a good divorce attorney. She would have avoided death and been treated fairly. James understood. What a scoundrel!

So it was a late night and after little sleep I did my morning jog up to and around the Jackie Kennedy Onassis Reservoir. Got my NYC style haircut and I have spent the rest of today so far reading Gutfeld's book "Not Cool" which expresses my point of view more clearly than I. When you read this book you understand the Left and bullying. Loved it.

So that is it for now. It was a "this could only happen to Al" type of day. Yup. I just exist and let it all happen.

Al

Do the best you can with what you have.
Sun, April 13, 2014 3:18PM

Well, we are about to leave the City in a bit. What a great four nights. The first two nights I was alone in the City and I am still so excited about my Madame Butterfly experience which dominated the entire time. Liz came for a visit the other day and it was fun to continue my NYC travels with company, albeit very nice company. After she arrived we did eat a glorious dinner at Shun Lee. Never had lotus root before. I like that place.

I truly believe the best way to see and understand the City, or any city, is to just walk or run it. No tour buses and the like. Did this technique in Paris, London, other Cities, and likewise Manhattan. You see the people as well as the scenery. And, it is no big deal to get lost, which I did not today. You also get to feel the pulse of what is going on. Color all of this good.

Just today proved my theory correct. After I awoke today I took a very nice jog along Riverside Drive. So many new things to see. In days gone by, Riverside Drive must have been quite the place for the wealthy to live. The views of the Hudson River are amazing. Up until today I have run Riverside Park South innumerable times. It is great. But today I was actually on the sidewalk. Passed so many hotels, now condos, such as the Dorchester, and many others whose names I forget. Some of the mansions, although now surrounded by large buildings, are/were so beautiful. So many well-known and famous people once lived in this area--like Babe Ruth. The Drive ends at Grant's Tomb and begins around 72nd Street. A glorious statute of Eleanor Roosevelt is found right at the start of the Drive. Note how I have nicknamed the location "the Drive".

I was most impressed with the Soldiers' and Sailors' Monument which honors those who served in the Civil War. I stopped to take a look around and since I am a Civil War aficionado, I enjoyed the stop. Could not help but imagine what the area was like a hundred years ago. I would never move from my current neighborhood, but Riverside Drive is an area to visit and revisit.

I did make a few interesting observations. The homeless still are found sleeping on tennis courts and park benches. There is the usual assortment of dogs being walked but there were three or four breeds I had never before seen. The streets and sidewalks are quite clean and well kept. Dog walkers are up early, 7:00amish, and I think that most of the residents are not up and about at that early Sunday hour. There are few food stores or shops in the immediate residential area, so I guess you have to head east to find sustenance along Amsterdam or Broadway. The daffodils are popping up all over the place. Pigeons enjoy every flat place available. It is Spring Time in New York.

Yesterday we did stop at the Beatles exhibit at the Lincoln Center version of the NYC Public Library. I felt that to be lots of fun. To see the instruments that the Beatles actually used was great. Overall, a nice visit. Central Park was as busy as ever earlier in the day. We had stopped at Le Pain after our run in the Park for iced tea and since the place was saturated with dogs, we sat and chatted with many dog owners. Lincoln Center is always vibrant and alive and continued to be so. So many languages being spoken. So many really attractive people hanging out near the large fountain. So much frenetic activity. Right next store to Lincoln Center is Damrosch Park where we read and sunned. At Columbus Circle, large Easter eggs all over the place; I mean like three feet or so tall. Sitting along the Hudson River and reading is a real hoot. Nannies walk their baby charges and little children ride their three wheeled scooters. The crowds were out and the Pier One Cafe was now open for business. The ladies were showing their assets. The men were smiling. The joggers were jogging and the dogs were walking. The ships were floating by either alone or accompanied by a tug boat. I am surprised people do not walk their cats. Just wondering.

So now my knees are tired as this entire trip, but particularly yesterday, I overdid my run and later long walks. The price you pay for getting old. We are sitting at Bryant Park with a scone and some tea watching the people parade. It is a beautiful day and the sun is shining. Since it is Palm Sunday, well dressed people walk by carrying foliage which I assume are palms. I have mixed feelings about leaving the City soon, but there is much to do in Clinton today. And so is life in the fast lane.

Have a great day.

Al

Sometimes I overdo it. Such is life.
Sat, April 26, 2014 4:13PM

Well, it has been quite a couple of days. I arrived in the City yesterday and it was a glorious day. I had some personal business to take care of which took up the morning. Afterwards I got in a wonderful long run along Riverside Park and environs. So many different people. So many three legged dogs. So much to see and enjoy. As is usual, I eventually ended up at the Met and spent hours studying ancient Southeast Asian Hindu and Buddhist sculptures and artifacts. That is a mouthful. I did not have a docent but I did the tour myself. Too bad my pre-dementia does not allow me to remember too many specifics, but everything I saw was from the 6-8th century AD. Made me feel young. Someday I will really understand the difference between Hinduism and Buddhism. Dinner was sushi and an avocado. Believe it or not, that is a great meal. Then I spent lots of time by the Hudson River reading Brian Kilmeade's book on the Revolutionary War spies that supported our side of the revolution, risking their lives and property for our soon to be new country. Fascinating. I love to read, particularly since I now use a Kindle, but it seems my eyes are fighting a battle to prohibit that joy. Of all the senses I do not want to lose, I agree with my late mother-in-law, Gra, that I do not want to lose my vision. Yes, I had a full day.

So Liz, her son David, and her brother John are coming into the City today to see the Beatles exhibit I have mentioned in a prior e-mail, check out the Dakota and Strawberry Fields, and have dinner. That is great. I believe they are going to stop by and see the apartment if they have time. It is worth a look. I happen to love it.

On my way to the Met yesterday via the 66th Street Crosstown bus, I met a very sweet lady named Beverly. I am apt to do that now. Anyhow, she told me of a free Tai Chi class in Bryant Park on Saturday. So, after I awoke today I jogged over to the Park arriving at 8:00am. The class was not until 10:00am. So I ran back to my apartment, showered, ate breakfast, and then later took the 1 train over toward the Park. Candidly, I was quite tired from my run as I overdid the speed thing. I went from a normal trot to a real runner. Stupid. Anyhow, when I arrived at the Park I was advised that the event was not until 11:00am. I had time to spare. Yup, I saw a lady with a Rhodesian ridgeback dog and we struck up a conversation for an hour. Jeanette was a fascinating conversationalist and we hit it off. As her parents-in-law just moved to the City, I gave her my card and hopefully they will contact me. The entire time, this lion killing dog just lay near me and slept. Cool dog.

And then 11:00am came. I have never tried Tai Chi, but for an hour today did all the motions, helped by a number of instructors. How hard can this be, right? Well, my legs were already tired from my earlier five mile run and at first the Tai Chi made my body feel quite at ease. As it progressed, the slow motions and deep breathing exhausted me. I clearly had overdone it again. I stress the word "again". I might sign up for classes, but note that they are free at 7:30 am on Tuesdays and Thursdays at Bryant Park. Had the pleasure of meeting two very nice ladies, Pam and Kim. They encouraged me to join and go to classes with them. I still have "it". The only problem is the age difference. They are in their late 50s and much too old for me. And so it goes.

So, I am anxious for this long and active day to end. Looks like dinner will be more sushi as I have become a sushi addict. Could be worse. As you can tell, I lead a very active life here in NYC. Liz may spend some time here after the Beatles tour, so-so called, as she is on a short vacation. Whatever the case, just before bed, I will sit in my favorite chair, enjoy a small glass of cognac, and watch the skyscraper lights twinkle me to sleep. Not half bad. It could be worse.

You never know what hand life will deal you. You simply have to make the best of what you get. Sometimes it sucks. Sometime it is okay. I prefer okay. Hug your lady or guy tonight if you are lucky enough to have one. Leave nothing unsaid. Assume nothing. Enjoy the ride. So to all of you that so frequently call, text, or e-mail and ask how I am, I am okay. I get by with a little help from my friends.

Albert D.

You've Got Mail
Wed, April 30, 2014 7:59AM

I like having guests at my NYC apartment. Liz arrived with her son and brother Saturday afternoon and it was fun showing them my apartment. In the late morning I had taken the Tai Chi class in Bryant Park and after my run etc. I was quite tired. Anyway, after they all went off to see the Beatles exhibit and other associated things, I relaxed and then met them for dinner at Nice Matin which truly was off the charts good. A tad expensive I suspect, but still good. We had desert at the Cafe Lalo on 83rd Street which was highlighted in the movie "You've Got Mail" with Tom Hanks and Meg Ryan. Liz was able to spend a few days here so that was great for the rest of my time in the City. Ironically, I had jogged and rested in part on Saturday along Riverside Park and one of my high school friends apparently was there as well watching her granddaughter play soccer. It might have been on Sunday, but whatever the case, it was wonderful. I have not seen Marlene for at least 50 years and I hope I can see her someday. Small world. I was so tired Saturday night that I literally slept like a log.

Well Sunday arrived and it was time to get off and do things. I took a long run and Liz went on a walk wherever and we met up afterwards for breakfast at the apartment. Tired to do some old crossword puzzles but they won; my old brain just could not focus. Then a very long walk was taken up to the Reservoir and back to Whole Foods for supplies. Just before sitting by the Hudson River, I, yes, Albert D. Rylak, made a great pot of chicken, barley, and cabbage soup. It cooked all day and was better than good. I am not a cook so this was an experiment in insanity by me. What a great dinner. After dinner we took another long walk to Riverside Drive to see the most beautiful residential type of area in the City. The views of Riverside Park and the Hudson River simply are majestic. You pass the statute of Eleanor Roosevelt and go up beyond 97th. I could not afford to buy a door knob there. We continued the "You Got Mail" theme and saw where Tom Hanks lived at the 79th Street Pier, Meg Ryan on 89th Street I think, and then Tom Hanks again on 93rd Street. We saw where in the movie Hanks and Ryan finally met at Riverside Park. I arrived home and this time literally collapsed into sleep.

So then Monday came. For reasons known but to Buddha, the beautiful weather continued and we refused to stay indoors. After breakfast I took my run to visit the site where Nathan Hale was hanged by the British at 66th (my street) and 3rd Avenue and Liz went on her on reliving of the "You Got Mail" route and we met up at Riverside Park. I had to find the hanging location as I just finished the Brian Kilmeade's book I previously had mentioned and it was prominently mentioned in chapter one. After finishing more off my homemade soup, we went to Central Park to just do the Sunday Times Crossword Puzzle and watch people. The sun was ablaze and it was just a perfect day. We sat and puzzled for hours. These were some of the things we saw: dogs wearing pink booties; people sunbathing in Sheep's Meadow, a few clad only in their underwear; many pregnant ladies; people rowing boats at the Boat Basin; more foreign languages than English; musicians all over the place; happiness; so many flowering trees; tulips and other bulbs blooming; lovers walking and holding hands; dogs and more dogs. In short, Central Park was at its most beautiful. Forcing ourselves to leave the Park, we ate sushi at the apartment. Apartments have so many advantages as it is so much less expensive to eat in. And then, yes, another walk. This time we went south from Lincoln Center to the projects, into Hell's Kitchen, and eventually North at Riverside Park to Pier One. Only in NYC could you see all those lovely statutes (one of an apple in a ring with a bite out of it) and then a man tightrope walking on a strap suspended between a fence and a seat and a man filming acrobatic males leaping over chair and pillars and exercisers exercising and.................. Morpheus soon called and I cannot remember anything else.

Now it is Tuesday and the weather finally failed to cooperate. Liz and I walked over to the Nathan Hale hanging site as she wanted to see it. Stopped at a map store on Park Avenue and looked at some maps valued over $500,000.00 each. I particularly liked that. Then over to the Met. I had the pleasure of seeing the Lost Kingdoms of Southeast Asia again but with a friend. It really is so much more fun with a friend. Worth a trip as the sculptures were all over 1,400 years old. From there to the 79th crosstown bus to a large lunch at the Chirping Chicken on Amsterdam. Then naps were in order as all this exercise and activity has a tendency to tire one, particularly someone of many years such as I. When I awoke, I ran for almost an hour and Liz made omelets for dinner. I now sit feeling tired and wondering how I got through the last few days without having a heart attack or worse. Bottom line? All is good. Wednesday will be a very rainy day and a return to Clinton or the shore is in order. This treadmill just will not stop!!

On a philosophical note, I cannot help but wonder why some people seem just mad and tense most of the time. They usually are self-absorbed and cannot see how lucky they are to just be alive and to have the things they do have. Perhaps it is because there is a lot of mental illness around or perhaps because we no longer have the coping skills to exist in the "instant" technological society. Whatever the cause, it is so much more fun to just smile, relax, and take things less seriously. We may think we are the focus of the universe, but we are not even a pin prick out there. Enough said.

Albert D.

From Planned Parenthood to michaele with a lower case "m".
Fri, May 16, 2014

I sit in my favorite chair this morning at my NYC apartment looking at the twinkling lights in the fog. Soon I will do my run and then catch the bus back to Clinton, all before the rains come. Yesterday was a good day and night.

While on the bus into the City I pontificated via Facebook on the fate of Rutgers University and its latest series of embarrassments, the last having protestors force a more conservative graduation speaker to cancel an appearance at graduation. I did so civilly and it helped to pass the time. I like civil discussion which in large part is absent in today's society.

While getting to the subway underground, I decided to enjoy life underground for a while. A fella playing two flutelike instruments was playing "Time to say Goodbye". I just leaned against the wall and listened while 1,000s of people rushed by me to their appointed destinations. He was quite good, even had CDs to sell, and as lachrymose as I was, I was able to eventually forget my past sadness and enjoy the beauty of his music. So $5.00 went into his hat. Another part of the City had given me pleasure and I had just started my adventure.

And so I arrived at my wonderful apartment. The air conditioning had recently been activated. It was on full blast. Polar bears would have enjoyed things there. After I turned that all off I recalled that most apartments in the City have either heat or air conditioning in any given season; not both. So, on went the gas oven to try toward things up. It took a while but all went well.

So my run along the Riverside Park and Hudson River began again. Not the warmest or pristine of days, but still, nonetheless, perfect. Two sailboats were out on the River which brought me much pleasure. On my way back south I noticed a magnificently beautiful young woman jump roping with a really muscular fella nearby setting up a training station on the Pier 1 pier. After receiving a smile, not uncommon for good people to smile at pathetic old men relishing their youth, I asked her when she came to rest how she was able to jump rope backwards. She explained that it was just easier for her. Then she put on boxing gloves and the muscular guy, who was quite nice, had her punch at the large gloves he held up. She was boxing. When she tired I asked if I could try and he anxiously said yes. That surprised me. And so I did. For about two minutes until I tired. He would move the gloves around and I tried to punch them. Not an easy task. And no, I did not jump rope backwards. That is for another day!

And so I wanted to cool down from my run and the pseudo boxing, so I continued jogging up to the fountain at Lincoln Center. There about 50 students from the Shenandoah Middle School of Clifton Park, NY were about to perform at the fountain. I stayed a bit and I listened. They were wonderful and drew a crowd. Yet another pleasure moment in the City. And it did not cost me a dime.

And so I took off for the Gourmet Garage on 66th to get some victuals. En route I was asked by a young man with a sign if I supported Clean Water and he had a petition on that for me to sign. After telling him I was busy trying to run, he continued the topic and told him I preferred dirty water. That ended that. Less than a minute later I was literally blocked by a young woman with all sorts of Planned Parenthood material wanting to give me literature and seeking a donation for her group. So I stopped again and told her that although I fully supported what she called a woman's right to choose and fully supported massive distribution of birth control, I was conflicted as to abortion when I saw the heart of a six week old fetus beating. She kept stressing a woman's right to choose and I kept stressing my uncertainty based on experience. I was already out of law school when Roe v. Wade came down in 1973 and she was not even born. I could not resist saying something I regretted later as she pestered me over and over---"You are bothering me. Stop or you will make me wish your mother had aborted you". I wish I had not said that but it did stop her pestering me.

And so to the Gourmet Garage and enough sushi for lunch and dinner and a few other things. After eating I took the 66 crosstown bus to Madison and then the number 3 bus to 82nd Street to get to the Met. En route I met two lovely ladies and chatted at length with them. You see, even in this cyber age, people want to talk to people and I suspect that is a large part of being human. We need social contact. And I will give it right to them.

So I get to the Met and a tour of the Egyptian Sculptures is about to start. Only four people on the tour so I jumped in. This docent was simply outstanding. She took us on a 90 minute odyssey through ancient Egypt. Since I age rapidly and dementia undoubtedly enters slowly into my brain, I forget more that I recall. Some things really stuck out re that tour. The magnificent structures, idols and whatever were carved with stone tools. Yes, stone! Most of what I saw were between 4,000 and 5,000 years old. The Pharaohs were called Kings and were male until a few came along like Cleopatra which led to the name change from King to Pharaoh. At times precut beards were placed on the Kings and Pharaohs, male or female, and tied to their chins. Mummification was not reserved to the elite as the sand and sun practically mummified everything. Egypt during this period did not have slaves to build their assorted monuments and pyramids, but craftsmen. At first and for a long period of time slavery did not exist. When the Nile River, which as an aside flows North, overflowed, the farmers would leave their Fertile Crescent until the waters subsided and during that time work on the pyramids. When the Aswan Dam was built an effort was made to save many of the temples etc. of Egypt; they were only partially successful. It went on and on and I wish I were still there enjoying this wonderful
Teacher. But the tour eventually ended.

And that is where michaele (correctly spelled) came into play. He is my hair guy and I went for a haircut on my way back to the apartment. Now michaele is a little different than your ordinary barber/stylist. I still like him. He tries to make me look pretty. Yeah. He suggested a blue or pink streak in my hair. I may take him up on that next time. Perhaps mauve?

Throughout the day I received assorted cell phone calls and texts from friends and even clients. It was all good. My son David was nice enough to FaceTime Amelia and Benjamin with me so I could see their beautiful little faces and tell them a story about snapping turtles and helicopters that go swoosh swoosh swoosh. I do not want to lose out on my grandchildren. I need them. They need me and do not know it yet.

President Obama was in town for the dedication of the 9/11 Memorial. Although it will not be open to the public until next week, it was great to see finally a bi-partisan moment in this crazy upside down world in which we live. It was worth the traffic jams and security all about the City for this event. So many people alive today were not even born when that horror occurred. Islamic Terrorists murdered so many innocent people and forever changed America. You can see how fragile freedom and life can be. At first I thought all the security and traffic issues were for me, at least in my Walter Mitty moment but that was not to be.

And so at the end of my day yesterday after using my Kindle for an hour or so, I sat in my favorite chair as I do now and watched the very same lights I watch now twinkle and glow in the fog and mist. The circle was completed and I had a great time.

How Not to Relax and Rest
May 29, 2014

My friends, I have lived through a very busy time in my life since last Wednesday evening at 8:15pm until now which is Thursday evening, a week later. A dear friend received a call that required immediate care in Naples, Florida. So as she was dealing with the issue, I was arranging flights to Florida. We left the next morning and arrived in Naples before 4:00pm on Thursday. A whirlwind trip via Charlotte, NC, attending to things in Naples, and then driving a car back to New Jersey, arriving in Clinton very late afternoon on Sunday, was physically and emotionally exhausting. We did spend one night in Fayetteville, NC the home of Fort Brag. In the end it was all good and that is all that matters. I must relate that while on a jog in Fayetteville, (yes, I jog every day, even when exhausted) I passed an Embassy Suites Hotel where a number of weddings were taking place. You want to feel small? The groom and all the groomsmen in one wedding party were all over 6'7" tall with one being at least 7' tall. My being height challenged due to osteoporosis comes to my mind. Had to be a basketball team type of wedding reception going on. I wonder if anyone there was famous. Also, on the ride to Clinton we had to play a game to keep sane as more than 20 hours in a car over two days is a little much. So we espied license plates and found some from 45 states and three Canadian provinces during the trip home. Not half bad. Naples is wonderful and the food off the charts good, but we were not there long enough to relax and enjoy. Memorial Day was uneventful in large part and restful and then eventually Wednesday arrived.

So NYC beckoned me again. Feeling a tad sad and depressed for obvious reasons, I took the 5:30am bus into the City. Although so very tired, I livened up as I was returning to my newly found paradise. I was going to relax and read, but my Kindle died so that was not possible. Yup. So I reverted to the old Al and did all the usual stuff I do, including the most amazing jog I have had in years, sushi for lunch and dinner, a trip to the Met to see an exhibit about European art from the 1200s AD until the 1600s AD, and finally a long bus ride anywhere it wanted to take me. Yes, I had great chats with wonderful young or older NYC women who took pity on this old man. What a hoot. What an educational experience at the Met as well. I also received some correspondence via e-mail from a course I took on Domestic Violence a couple of weeks ago. I criticized the scrivener as she had make the course about Domestic Violence as it pertains to women only, and not men. Since the course was supposedly presented to assist hospitals and their workers in dealing with Domestic Violence issues in a medical sense, I got into a mood and rebuked the entire program for not recognizing that Domestic Violence is gender neutral and not just a woman's issue. I am sure I will hear back about this in the near future. CCL. Still not having recovered from my trip to and from Florida, I was quite tired and required Cognac and rest which came as the evening lights presented themselves to me in pure magnificence as I sat on my couch just staring at the view.

So today is Thursday and I awoke early as usual. Sleep is for the weak of heart. The big sleep will come soon enough. My free Tai Chi class was at Bryant Park at 7:30am and I ran there in about half an hour, arriving close to 7:00am. It is fun to know where you are going in this City and even more fun to dodge buses, people, and cars. I have always felt that I was in reasonable shape for an almost 70 year old, and stretched as much as my old muscles would allow after I arrived. Yup, I did forget to bring money and water. A big mistake I would later learn. At 7:30am sharp our Tai Chi Master started doing his thing and I did likewise. After an hour and twenty minutes my muscles ached and I reverted to my previously mentioned exhaustion. Nonetheless I loved it and did the best I was able. Everyone should try Tai Chi. Made some nice friends, had a gay guy ask me to join him at the gym which in a sense was different, and saw Beverly whom I had met as per my prior Tai Chi post.

But now the problem. I had to get back to the apartment on 66th. Duh. No money and no water. What happened to my brains? Not a good run back if you can call it a run. I was not only exhausted, but thirsty and hungry. Eventually I did get back to shower, eat, and drink. Afterwards I felt like I had restored my energy level and ergo, back to the Met for the second consecutive day. It was easy for this weary elderly person to take the 66th Street crosstown bus to Madison and then the M1 bus to 83rd Street for a short walk to the Met. The place, inside and outside, was packed again. Love it. The usual five singers and bass player were near the steps singing and trying to hawk their CDs. They were great and I recorded some of their stuff with my iPhone. The sun felt good but I knew my time there would be limited. I was simply just flat out tired and had an appointment. So, upon entering my most holy shrine, I located the first docent I could find and took a tour of 5,000 years of the art of China in 75 minutes. I know that may sound a little overwhelming, but we did it and it was simply fantastic. A couple of facts: Early on the Chinese used tempera to color their pottery. You know what tempera is? I did not. It is egg yolk and pigment. And what was so amazing is that the Chinese calligraphy (at least five types) was in large part their art and not just their writing. I am too tired tonight to dwell on this, but the docent was more than exceptional and I learned a lot.

Going to the Metropolitan Museum of Art is like going to college or graduate school. Perhaps even like taking on-line college courses. You get from it what you put into it and you realize how little you know but also how important it is to learn. I have been there at least 50 times. It is important to try to keep the body and mind in good shape by exercising both. Well, perhaps I overdo it, but you get the idea.

And so I returned to my apartment for a 4:00pm conference call on hospital business since I am on the Board of Trustees of a local hospital. It was relatively short and sweet and I continued my sushi dinner, watching "The Five" on television, and chatting with two clients as I ate. Be still my heart. I so tried to rest my weary knees and legs. No such luck. So I went over to the Hudson River at Riverside Park to watch boats, pretty girls, joggers, and assorted dogs. On the way I did something good and for which I am pleased. Near the entry to the Park, a two plus year old adorable little girl was running way ahead of her parents. As she passed me on the sidewalk, I heard them yell "stop" and looked around. She had no intention of stopping and I ran to her, grabbing her just as she entered the street and as a car was bearing down on her. Crap that was scary and close. Her mom and dad were screaming. All was well. I got a big hug from two strangers, a big kiss on the lips from the mother, and a "sorry" from a little girl coupled with a promise to obey her mommy and daddy. Tears. Brightened up me right up right away. Shortly thereafter Liz called and we chatted a while as I hoped to see the Manhattanhenge. You will have to Google that one. Missed that.

Now I anticipate leaving the City tomorrow and heading to Clinton or Harvey Cedars for a bit. I came to the City initially to rest and relax, but in the end it was just my usual very active and happy time. I again sit with my Cognac looking at the same view as always and yearn for Morpheus to carry me away soon as visions of the twinkling lights mesmerize me. Could be worse.

The end.

Harvey Cedars to Clinton to Manhattan
June 11, 2014

I get around. After a lovely weekend in Harvey Cedars with Liz, Mark, Ang, and Daniel, I have come into the City again. I was able to witness Daniel's first boat ride at age 6 months and took the Widow's Cruise with a couple of my widow friends. The boat has paid for itself!!! Also was able to see the sunset from my boat as I sped along on Barnegat Bay. All of this is simply off the charts good. Harvey Cedars is what Ginny used to call the "happy place", and it is. Just a nice place. I am also having a good time in Clinton teaching a lovely young lady the mystical art of running. Just like Andy and Jeff Martin helped me 34 plus years ago I am trying to make her enjoy the thrill of feet on the pavement. She is willing and able to give it a go and has great potential if she keeps at it. This is also good for an old man.

So this morning I awoke at 2:00am and eventually exited my bed at close to 3:00am. Yes, sleep is not in my DNA so I embrace the lack of it. Yawn. I had some things to do in the City. So after a nice run, I got on the bus and arrived in Manhattan close to 6:30am.

And so my dear friend who invited me to the Harvard Club for a luncheon meeting of The National Institute of Social Sciences did me a great favor by the invitation. I thank her profusely. Not only did I have a great meal at a great place and meet lots of people, I heard a fella named Ambassador William J. van den Hehvel speak about Theodore and Eleanor and Franklin Roosevelt. What incredible people they were. His stories were spell binding and candidly, I wish the Roosevelt family were in politics now. My search for knowledge was totally fulfilled. So tomorrow I shall jog to the Eleanor Roosevelt statute on Riverside and 70th to just meditate on the wonderful lives of that family. Eleanor was a leader that did not play the victim card ever and was just a great person. I attended the same event last year when the DNA fellow named Watson gave the major speech. He was here today and I had a long talk with him as well. Cool. I also had the opportunity to speak to a Bishop from Arkansas who was the spiritual counselor to Bill and Hillary Clinton. Bottom line, this was a good time for this Clinton rube to meet and greet. Sometimes I do that well. Sometimes I do not. Today was a good day.

A really fascinating thing happened at the Institute meeting. I sat near a man named Nick Case. Does not seem like much, does it? Well, it was a very big deal. He and I graduated from the same high school although I am older than he. Nick works for Citi Bank in Camden County, NJ and graduated from Rutgers as did I. We knew all the same people. Nick knew my father-in-law Bill Campbell who was vice principal of my high school and the teacher connection was incredible. For my CHS followers, the teachers' names of Guthrie, Hutchinson, Udy, Krieger, Archierie, Willever, and many more came forward. He also knew many of my classmates including the entire Clark family, of which Judy was our class president. Billy Howe and Barry Arch and Bill Cain. He knew Knuckles' Park and the location of the old Boy Scout House. He knew where Nancy Nelson lived the importance of which being that it was there where I had my first real kiss while playing spin the bottle. It was like a class reunion with all the good stuff. We do live in quite a small world.

So I am now back in my apartment waiting for my food to digest so I may eat the sushi I purchased earlier at the Gourmet Garage. I look forward tonight to my Cognac or moonshine and the twinkling lights from apartment 15T. Tomorrow at 7:00am I will jog to Bryant Park for a 7:30am Tai Chi class and then head back eventually to my apartment and then Clinton as I have a Hospital Board meeting at 5:00pm. I really wish I knew how to sleep but that is a trait I am unable to change.

So, for all of you that ask so frequently, all is well. Moments of sadness appear at times, but good things happen as well. The good exceed the bad. Beckett refuses to be defined by tragedy. I hope that you are all relatively happy and that you have found peace in your lives. I am getting there. My next future City goal is to go to Four Freedoms Park on Roosevelt Island. Just take the tram at 59th Street and Second Avenue to the Park. If I have no one to go with me, I might jog over the 59th Street

Bridge in the opposite direction from the NYC Marathon. Time will tell.

And by the way, my book should I ever get it finished, is going to be called "The View from Apartment 15T". Time will tell.

Namaste
Al

I know Manhattan has a dark side but I refuse to accept it. Someday, but not yet.

June 17, 2014

The famous Canadian singer Gordon Lightfoot has a song about "There's a kind of restless feeling" which permeates my air space at times. Beautifully written and relevant to how I feel about the City. I get that feeling every time I enter Manhattan. Maybe it is because Morpheus does not allow me to sleep more than minimally or maybe it is because I am simply Polish carrying feelings of centuries of being beat up by assorted others. Whatever the cause, I embrace it and it has become part of my persona.

Although I want to relate the events of this past day, I have to first tell you about a wonderful new friend I have made who lives in the City. Barbara and I met as seat mates last weekend as I returned to Clinton where I live and she to Pennsylvania to do a photo shoot. Typically people on the bus ignore each other and just pretend to be asleep. For reasons known only to a higher authority, we simply hit it off and talked the entire trip until I exited the bus. Barbara has created a great business concept that involves harmonizing music to your meals. If you have time, go to her site at www.musicalpairing.com. You will be impressed. The point I wish to make however is that you have to be open to meeting and greeting because the rewards far outweigh the risks. Now Barbara may be a mass murdered or stalker, although I suggest that that is highly unlikely, but rather than simply resting or reading, I met someone and she had a fascinating story. By exposing my vulnerable side, I have grown from the experience. We cannot be afraid to make fools of ourselves or to be rejected.

So yesterday I came into the City. This time I read the NY Times on my way in as the bloke next to me took up more that his fair share of the seating arrangement and pretended to be asleep. A gentle nudge was of little consequence. There were some good stories, purporting to be news, to be read.

After arriving at my apartment I got over to the Gourmet Garage to get some food which sounds unexciting but which I love. The sushi chef who knows me as a buddy made me the best and freshest sushi I have ever eaten. She tries to take care of me. And she does. The mundane laundry chore had to be accomplished and it was. I do not particularly like doing laundry as it takes too much time and the laundry machines are in the basement of my building. With careful planning it gets accomplished. Wish I had thanked Ginny for always taking care of that chore. Our homemakers are the most unappreciated people in the world. Afterwards it was time to jog Riverside Park which I did noting the so many beautiful people along the route. The City has so many young professional looking people that seem to be quite physically fit. I cannot keep up with them. So I bump into my dearest friend Susan and her husband Russ and grandson Harry at the Pier 1 Cafe. I love Susan and she is like a sister. Susan is without question one of the nicest and most giving people I know. In my darkest hours she helped me. When I brought my granddaughter Amelia to the City she let me use her apartment. When I need a rug or a lamp or whatever, she gives me exactly what I need. Nonetheless, this is the first time since I have had my apartment that I have seen Susan in the City. I intentionally did not want to pester her but also simply ran into her. This attests to how large this Cit is!!! We live part-time a block and a half near each other, and yet never have bumped into one another until yesterday. Amazing.

During my run I saw one amazingly intrepid person whom I see periodically. She is physically challenged with an illness that makes her arms flail about and her legs are stiff and inflexible as she trots along. Yet, this unknown person is always running along Riverside Park. I always say hello to her. She always smiles back. She is an example to all of us. I would never interrupt her run, but someday when and if she stops near me I want to go up and say hello. You never interrupt a runner mid run. She is certainly on my list of people to be emulated.

So now it is time to go over to Central Park. I seemed melancholy today so I decided not to go to the Met as usual. As I crossed the Sheep Meadow, the beautiful people were out sunning themselves. I am still a guy. Half naked ladies sunning themselves is still fun to look at even at my age; and there were many. Since the World Cup of Soccer 2014 is going on, some men and women were juggling soccer balls and many wore their favorite soccer team's shirt. It was a happy place and I wanted to draw on that happiness.

And then I heard it. It sounded as if the NYC Philharmonic was putting on a symphony in the Park. I was half right. When I arrived, there indeed was beautiful music being played but by a group of about 35 high school students who were from Columbus, Ohio. They were a symphony orchestra and had arrived by bus to play later that night at Avery Fisher Hall. This was their warm up and they played for at least a half an hour as

I watched and listened. While they played a lady dressed in a skimpy bikini skated in circles wearing her on-line roller skates and bubble man used his lengthy string to make large bubbles, all to the delight of the little children. A lone saxophonist sat in the distance trying to collect some money for his playing efforts, but he was disappointed as the orchestra drowned him out playing one march after another.

But it was not yet over. A group of high school students from Bangkok, Thailand then took to the outdoor stage. All dressed in white, they played their stringed instruments and I said to myself, self, how many of these young people will go to Juilliard? They were even better than the Ohioans and were also to be at Avery Fisher Hall tonight. What an abject thrill two times over.

So I am not done yet in this new adventure. Tavern on the Green has reopened as of about a month or so ago and has a window on the side that serves/sells drinks without the necessity of formally entering the restaurant. After I re-crossed the Sheep Meadow, I stopped there for some libation as it was hot and sunny and I was dry and thirsty. A very nice addition to the Park. Expensive but nice.

And so I returned to my apartment to have my usual early dinner and eat that sushi I thought about off and on all day. It met my expectations and it was time to go for a long walk. And I did. As I crossed West End Avenue there was an old man sitting in the island between the north and south lanes and a woman next to him. So I stopped to see what was going on. It seems that Paul as he called himself, had somehow hurt his left hamstring where it attaches to the back of his knee. He was in great pain. I asked if I could help and he said he wanted a taxi to get him home. Apparently he was on his way to babysit his grandson when this happened. Since my kids are doctors, I feel empowered, knowledgeable, and suggested that he should move out of the street and over to where the 57th Street Crosstown bus stops. He agreed. Two perfectly wonderful students with skateboards in hand and who attend Martin Luther King High School on 66th Street, stopped and asked if they could help. And so we carried the old fellow over to sit at the bench at the bus stop. A police officer stopped to ask if there was anything he could do such as call an ambulance and I told him all was under control. The nice lady went and got her car and the two fellas got Paul into the car (a damn Prius) to take Paul home. I then continued my walk. Putting aside the fact that I am sure I was older that that old guy Paul, I mention this as my life in the City is full of incidents like this. More importantly, those two young people and lady who stopped restored my faith in the youth of America. Two African American teenagers, a Jewish woman and an old Polish American male helping an older gentleman of unknown origin in need. A good picture.

And then my City experience ended even though I was still in the City. It was necessary to watch World Cup Soccer or Futbol if you will. The USA played Ghana and won 2-1 in a very exciting game. And then the show "24" was on later. So I was "forced" to stay in my apartment. Still, watching the twinkling lights as I sipped my Cognac and drifted close to much needed sleep made the end of a perfect day just that. Perfect. So after Tai Chi in Bryant Park in a few minutes I will return to Clinton do some needed things and long for my return to the City. Peripatetic really does describe me.

Beckett, now known as Al, sometimes known as Phoenix, a recovering attorney

Harvey Cedars to Clinton to Manhattan
July 3, 2014

Yesterday will go down in the Beckett history book as one busy and wonderful day. So much seemed to happen and all of it good. I guess the more you forge ahead the better it is for your sense of ego and purpose. It was with me.

My entire family arrived last Friday at Harvey Cedars. David and Lena and Amelia and Benjamin. Mark and Ang and Daniel. This was a very good thing on so many levels. We all get along so nicely and it is important that the cousins know each other. I will not brag about the little dears, but they bring me great pleasure and their parents have done a wonderful job of raising them. I enjoyed the fact that David and Mark got to surf and watch World Cup Soccer just as brothers having fun. I am grateful for being able to help with the little people when possible. Amelia is so into being an independent sweet little girl and found a new friend in Rory with whom to jump in the ocean waves and play on the beach. Benjamin is just nonstop very sweet, logical and independent thinking and melts my defenses, and Daniel has a smile that lights up the world as he deals with trying to crawl and understand his new world. Lena and Ang had some "girl time" and that was good for them both. Since the weather was perfect and the food and libation plentiful, I could not have asked for a nicer time. Yes, what would have been my 46th wedding anniversary passed with a degree of sadness, but Ginny completely would have wanted the family time together and enjoyed it through me. Some of the kindness of people simply overwhelm me. Susan gave me three practically new bicycles for the grandchildren to have as their own, Liz visited for the day and spoiled us with a wonderful desert, and Ginny and Larry treated my grandchildren as their own.

And so yesterday the first party ended and after everyone had departed from my shore house. I drove to Clinton early in the AM and met Liz at the bus station to go into the City, ostensibly to see Bucky Pizzarelli at Jazz at Lincoln Center. En route from the 1 train, we stopped at my usual Gourmet Garage and stocked up on some sushi and other great food. We then took a long walk through Lincoln Center and environs. Tried to get a haircut from my friend michaele (yes, no capital letters) but he was unavailable. Just felt so urbane with all the people around and the frenetic activity. My New York State of mind had arrived. We decided that we were going to watch World Cup Soccer where there would be excitement and activity and stopped at the Amsterdam Ale House. A much too sophisticated crowd. Then I asked a stranger where to go and he suggested Blondi's on 79th. And so it was. We sat at the bar in front of a television, one of many, and watched the US team play Belgium, losing in Extra Time. I guess a tad too much beer flowed but the patrons were chanting USA and otherwise having a very friendly and exciting time. Always wanted to do this and we did. Tim Howard is the best goalkeeper in the world. I think he thought he was being shot at!

And then the time for main purpose of the trip arrived. Bucky Pizzarelli. Lida and I had planned to go to see this legend and icon of jazz, but for many reasons, she was unable to attend. And so substitute date Lizette was available and willing to venture into the City for the event at Dizzy's Club. What a great time with dinner tossed in and with a majestic view of Central Park to boot. Bucky is now 88 years old but still has it. His bass player and drummer were off the charts great as well. It was all good. I hope my grandchildren listen to jazz and realize how important it is to American culture.

Leaving to walk back from Columbus Circle to my apartment we stopped at Midsummer Night Swing at Damrosch Park. Wild and crazy.

Last year the music was Swing. This year the Merengue. Very sensual Latin music and any woman that can do the crazy steps is one big turn on. I felt as if I were in a Spanish enclave of happiness and frivolity. The evening was loud, vibrant, alive, and the skies were clear and breezy. It does not get any better than this.

And so this man of many years, eventually left Damrosch Park and although tired, returned with Liz to his apartment to look at the lights twinkle as he always does. Sleep came quickly and for the first time in months it was for more than three hours. Sleep disorders are difficult things to deal with as are other matters involving the human psyche. But I still get by with a little help from my friends. And today I will get my hair cut or as I say, the gray portions removed so as to improve my "look" so as to be more to my liking.

So all is good in the alter ego called Beckett, formerly known as Al who is now really Al. Life goes on at a pace that is somewhat fast, but how else can one do all that has to be done? We are not meant to sit and vegetate. There will be plenty of time to do that later. Attitude is everything.

MANHATTANHENGE
July 12, 2014

Yesterday afternoon was fascinating and enlightening. As I think through what I shall do with the rest of my life, I am reminded that things certainly are closer than they appear in the rear view mirror. Life is finite and our thoughts are infinite. So we have to make difficult decisions with that thought in mind. And so as I struggle with the final portions of "The View from Apartment 15T", I try to do what I am able so as to not just sit by idly and wish if I had only..........

Liz had suggested that we go into the City to see Manhattanhenge. I will discuss this at length soon, but we hopped on the 12:20PM bus in Clinton and arrived in the City for that purpose. Anytime I come into the City I seem to try to do all there is to do. That is my personality and there seems little purpose in trying to change that now although I do make such an effort from time to time.

And so we went to Riverside Park to sit and enjoy doing the free Sunday NY Times Crossword Puzzle from some time ago. I like the challenge of the puzzle although neither I nor we were completely up to the challenge this time. It happens. I noticed for the first time as we sat at Pier 1 a rather unusual odor coming from the Hudson River. And just think that a week or so ago that very same water had splashed all over me in the speedboat called The Beast as we traversed the River to the Statue of Liberty. Funny how beauty and ugliness can coexist. Anyhow, I do love to look at the people and what with the beautiful weather they were all over the place.

While at Riverside Park, a very elderly man using a walker came up to us to converse. He must have been a retired comedienne. One one-liner after the other was presented to us. Even though his body had become frail, his mind was as sharp as a tack. I played along with him for about 10 minutes and then we departed. He was a nice man who clearly wanted to talk to someone. We were his victims! I hope I see him again.

Liz then put together a dinner which was just what was needed. You know my friends, not only is much less expensive to eat in than out as I state often, but the meal is so much better for you. I typically have Polish sushi for lunch or dinner which consists of peanut butter dipped pretzels or I eat out. I am part Polish so I can say that! I hope my grandchildren handle eating better than I have the last couple of years except of course for my sushi.

So now it was time to get over to the Upper East Side to see Manhattanhenge. The M66 bus greeted us just outside the apartment and off we went. I do not profess to have a good sense of direction but we got to where we wanted and began a walk to 57th Street. The walk was interrupted by a ride on the Tram to Roosevelt Island. When my son David was at Cornell Medical School here in the City I had taken the Tram over one time to jog the Island. I had forgotten the thrill of the ride. Below is a photograph taken mid-stream. What a hoot. Many now live on Roosevelt Island and commute via Tram or subway into Manhattan proper. It was just a fun thing to do. I expect to go back very soon to enjoy the FDR Four Freedoms Park at the southern end of the Island.

And then we returned to enjoy dessert at Off The Wall. Reminded me of Just Chill in Clinton. There is apparently a caloric difference in non-fat and lo-fat yogurt. Why can't they stop silly advertising games? A calorie here or there will not always kill you! But that is for another day.

So now I get to the point of this epistle. Once or twice a year a very unusual event occurs in Manhattan much as it does at Stonehenge in England. The alignment of the setting sun with the skyscrapers on the Manhattan Grid occurs in a surreal way. Now my silly little iPhone camera does not do it justice, but the setting sun in the west fits perfectly between the buildings on certain streets such as 57th Street viewed from the far eastern portion of the City. It was quite funny as we and many others tried to get in the middle of 57th Street at 3rd Avenue, dodging cars and people, to get a picture looking to the West. Horns would honk and some pedestrians would say nasty things, but our conflagration of people ran out onto the street at every light change to snap pictures of the event. Back and forth. Snap. Back and forth. Snap. You could envision what Stonehenge is like and wonder similar thoughts of its builders. And to top it off, when you looked to the East, there was a super full moon. It was just such a unique thing to see and I enjoyed it tremendously. Why I was not struck by a car I do not know, but all was good. And the fellow photogs were chatty and friendly in all ways. We were sharing a special NYC moment.

And in a minute or two it all ended. Nature inexorably continued its movement forward as it has always done and will do in the future. I on the other hand began to feel my sore hamstrings, sore left foot and tiredness. Oh the humanity of looking at the closeness of the view in the rear view mirror. It is so much closer than we think and as we age it gets even closer. So today will be interesting and I must now try to jog now while I am able. I will try to ignore what seems to be America's decline and hope she is able to survive at least a little while longer. I like having the right to live off of the fruits of my labor even though some say I did not deserve whatever was accomplished. Nature and hence science are really so very strong and our human abilities so weak and insignificant. My family knows all about that.

El fin

Was all this just for me?
July 16, 2014 at 8:47:05 PM

I decided to go into the City today, July 15th, just a few nights ago when my new friend "Barbara the Author" invited me to her dinner party at Ruth's Chris on 51st, Midtown Thursday the 16th of July at 7:00PM. This is to celebrate her new how-to -cook book entitled "Musical Pairing: The Art of Harmonizing Music to Your Meal", her web site, and her mobile APP. It is amazing who you meet on the bus to and from Clinton and my new friend will teach this country bumpkin a few things or two. She is one bright person. Everything sounds so exciting from our chats and e-mails. Her book is even for sale on Amazon.com! That is extra sweet. I have never been to anything like this but it should be very exciting and educational.

My run today in Clinton was difficult as the hamstrings, knees, and left foot are having issues. Oh the humanity of the long distance runner. Arriving in the City after my run with Beth (who as an aside is improving beautifully) and a nice breakfast, I noticed immediately that a group of saxophonists were playing in the small park at the 66 Street train stop called Richard Tucker Park for the "Lunchtime Concerts" events which are held every Wednesday at noon. The place was packed and the music great. It was thereafter I noticed that barricades were being placed from Fifth Avenue to Riverside along 66th Street where my apartment is located. The barriers continued to up all the way to 72nd Street and went down to West End Avenue as well. Something big was happening. Dogs were sniffing along with their police handlers handling, everyone looked serious, man hole covers were being welded to the streets, helicopters were flying high in the sky all over the place, and in general it looked like something important was going to happen soon. It turned out that tomorrow between 3:30pm and 8:00pm something big was going to happen.

At first I said to myself that this was a strange way to greet me back home to NYC particularly since I had only been gone a few days. Then I realized this preparation was not for me, but rather President Obama. Was he coming to visit me? Had my letters brought him here for my advice? I think not, particularly as I have written him a few scathing letters from time to time about his policies. Odds are he will visit Whoopi Goldberg at the View which is right down a block from my place or attend some fund raisers. I realized the preparations that go into having the President here are off the charts difficult and expensive and I hope this visit is really important and necessary and not just a photo op. The President probably needs a rest from the pressures of golf and of not making decisions in Washington, DC. But I digress.

Anyway, I spent most of my afternoon feeding my melanomas along Riverside Park at Pier 1. I had luckily found a free Wednesday NY Times crossword puzzle in the dear sweet compactor room which was completed by me in record time due to the fact that it was so easy it belonged in the NY Post. I then took my trusty new 5s iPhone and took videos of many of the helicopters flying overhead for my grandchildren to view. Benjamin particularly likes helicopters and seeing them high in the sky going whoosh whoosh whoosh. Arriving back at my apartment I ate my mandatory sushi from the Gourmet Garage along with other things that tickled my fancy. Having just finished a walk to and about Central Park, I am ready to have a glass of wine or a beer and prepare to watch some TV and then watch the twinkling lights as they put me to sleep. Tomorrow my free Tai Chi class takes place at 7:30am in Bryant Park and I need and want to go. I am a regular there. Since it will be difficult to navigate around my apartment from 3:30pm until 8:00pm tomorrow, I look forward to one great thing and that involves Barbara and her dinner party.

This trip into the City was different than others. I was not going to go and get away or to find something to do. I was actually going into the City to do prearranged things like sitting along the Hudson River, Tai Chi, and the dinner party tomorrow evening. That is a subtle different mindset from prior trips and I am pleased about this newly found attitude. Color that good. My recovery from grief is strikingly on a good course, and although there are setbacks, the good days markedly outweigh the bad days.

Welcome to NYC Mr. President.

Albert D.

New York is changing.
August 21, 2014 at 8:05 PM

I sit on the bouncing Trans-Bridge Lines bus typing this note having just left my Tai Chi class in Bryant Park a bit early.

When I arrived in the City yesterday, I'd did my usual thing including getting food and running along the Hudson River in Riverside Park South. All was good. I even finished the NY Times crossword puzzle. I relished my apartment. It is a haven unto itself but also a point of departure to my experiences.

My dinner with Barbara was at 5:30pm at a Japanese restaurant called Guzan on Third Avenue between 86th and 87th. Just another word or two about Barbara. In a prior note I mentioned her new book and the magical tasting party she had invited me to, showing me and forty other people how music can affect the taste of food. I had a wonderful time employing the concept of her algorithm to assist one in the pairing of food and music. She may get rich on this concept as it works! Yes it does! Anyway, we set up last night's dinner last week. Then it dawned on me that Guzan was just a few blocks from the Metropolitan Museum of Art.

And so Albert, not Beckett, arrived about 1:00pm at the Met and enjoyed the art museum for about three hours. I first went to the roof top garden which has a wonderful view of the City from on high. It really is a sight worth seeing. Since we would be eating sushi for dinner I spent the rest of my time mostly at the Asian section of the museum on the second floor. I wanted to be in the mood. And I was. So, anyway, on my way out of the museum about 4:15pm, I stopped at the Greek section and looked at steles or tombstones from 600 BC. Wow. That is old!

I walked over to find the Guzan restaurant and afterward went to an Irish Pub to rest a bit before dinner. More about that in a minute. 1040 Park Avenue had to be seen. Yes, that is where Jackie Kennedy lived with her family prior to her death.

Dinner with Barbara was delightful. She is lovely and intelligent and caring. She has been through a lot and is a new friend for me in the City. We chatted for a long time about many things including writing as she does that in her spare time. I had shown Barbara my cell phone music list which included Patsy Cline just before we ordered. As we began to check out the menu I kept hearing "I Fall to Pieces" coming aloud from my left front pocket. Somewhat embarrassing to put it mildly. So I turned the stupid iPhone off and I was forgiven for my technological indiscretion. No one should use their cell phone while in a restaurant unless you are President of the United States and I am not even sure of that. The meal was great as I asked Barbara to do the ordering. Her choices were quite good and I moved a little higher on the anti-rube scale. Maybe lower? We conversed about many topics and had a great evening. Then I walked her home to her Upper East Side apartment noticing how beautiful the area was and made mental comparisons to the Upper West Side where I live. The 86 cross town bus took me to

Columbus Avenue where I transferred to the 7 Bus to 66th and from there walked home to my apartment. Sounds like I know what I am doing, yet that would be untrue as I had to ask the bus driver for help!

Now back to the Irish Pub. Things indeed may be changing in the City. The Pub was typically Irish and even the bartender had a brogue. I really wanted a glass of water and after entering said to give me a glass of cold water and I would be happy to pay as if it were a glass of Guinness. I then went to the Gentlemen's Room. So he brought me a Guinness. Such is life. As the place had just opened and only had a few people in it, the bartender and I had a chance to talk as I sipped my unwanted drink.

The bartender lived in Queens. No way could he afford to live in the City. Although from Ireland, he had been in the States and at this bar for seven years and loved his job. He then said some interesting things about the happenings around the pub. The pub will close in six years. Its lease will not be renewed. A developer had bought the building and many adjoining properties so as to construct expensive high rise condos. Many of the condos already were under contract for sale many years in the future. There used to be two other bars around the block, but they had been forced to close. All the little stores in the area were inexorably closing and would be gone soon.

If this is true, NYC will change. Of course land values will continue to skyrocket. That is still an economic issue of supply and demand. But could NYC become just a barren land of condominiums? Of the super or uber rich? The character of many of the neighborhoods without the small business establishments will be sterile and unappealing. I like my barber Michaele and like my Chinese launderer. It is fun to go to an inexpensive bar for a drink or a pizza shop for another inexpensive meal. In short, things will change.

In a sense therefore, I may be living in the last vestige of what makes New York City the City that I truly enjoy. I may be at the tail end of all the wonderful things I have previously written about. I hope not.

David, Mark, Lena, Ang, Amelia, Benjamin, and Daniel have given me a very special gift for my soon to arrive 70th birthday. Yes, a wine tasting sail for two on the Hudson River on a vintage 82-foot, 1929 sailboat. It is scheduled for September 2014 and will be exciting as I continue my new life. Thank you kids and grandkids for such a wonderful gift.

And now I return to Clinton and eventually Harvey Cedars. I clearly note the changes in my life which are all for the good. There is much more to life than mere existence.

Albert D.

70th Birthday Weekend.
August 29, 2014

Getting old is just that. Getting old. Yet, I had a magical birthday weekend as I now write a first draft of the final chapter of The Beginning portion of my book. Yup, I have made it to 70 years of age. Quite unusual for a Rylak to get much beyond that. Has something to do with the Polish and German genetic structure and too much fat in many of my culinary delights. And so Amelia, Benjamin, and Daniel, you dear sweet little grandchildren, here is a long weekend which you might try to emulate. Catch me if you can.

My 70th birthday was wonderful. Ironically I felt no different than before. So to the extent that age is in your head, there is no difference. But, age is not just in your head. There are certain physical or scientific things that happen as you age.....like feeling tired after you complete a task that at one time would be a snap.....like being a tad forgetful in almost forgetting to send Benjamin an e-mail of Happy Birthday Wishes to supplement the card you did remember to send.....like running half the distance in twice the time! Anyway, I have started modifying my runs as promised to shorter times right now. I will also do some yoga, stretching, and cross training.

I awakened early on August 29, 2014 to a beautiful day. I was indeed above ground, had a pulse, and spoke to a few friends without dribbling from the side of my mouth. I had received wonderful gifts from everything to a wine tasting boat ride to chocolate cupcakes and many things in between such as a very fine vintage cognac. My sons called and many cards, well wishes and e-mails appeared. How sweet is that? About a quarter of my friends have already died or are incapacitated so I am quite special now in many ways! In the morning I ran with a beautiful young woman named Beth and it was a good and longer run. I felt good. Still do.

And then Liz took me to dinner as promised to a secret location. It was The Golden Pheasant in Erwina, PA about ten miles north of New Hope, PA. It is a lovely very old and very romantic place. Salmon and halibut were the fish de jure for us and when coupled with the coconut milk sauce on the accompanying rice, heaven appeared. The atmosphere was charming happy and totally enjoyable.

And so then Saturday appeared and after a last minute change of plans, Liz decided to accompany me to the City after I finished my shortened run of 50 minutes. I think most people had left the City as one saw mostly tourists. After collecting some food we arrived at the apartment and decided to just hang out in Central Park. Firstly however, I went to get my hair cut or better put, have some of my gray hair cut off. I always leave the blond in place. And yes, the sun does brighten up the blond measurably. And so off to Le Pain at Central Park where we "people watched" as we drank an Arnold Palmer and a watermelon juice and lemonade iced drink. The raspberry scone was great. To spend a day in NYC intending to do nothing is a good thing. And we pretty much did nothing. Walking around the Park in the lovely weather was pleasant and relaxing. There were many artisans of some sort or another plying their wares and assorted people playing instruments for whatever pittance you might toss into their open instrument cases. Tourists were all over the place taking selfies in front of structures and in general having a good time.

And so later we headed back to the apartment. Upon reaching 65th and Central Park West there was a small crowd. Apparently it was the 30th Anniversary since the movie Ghostbusters was first shown and the "new" Ghostbusters were at a building which was a scene in the film, dressed in full regalia. It was quite adorable and appealing. Liz even had a photograph taken by me with one of the so-called new Ghostbusters. There is always something going on in Manhattan.

Continuing the resting mode, we relaxed at the apartment and then went off for an early dinner at an Indian restaurant named Mughlai on 71st and Columbus Avenue. Good food what with chicken Tikka Masala and some kabobs. Lamb is not my thing but all else was quite good. The owners were quite accommodating. And we had to walk off some of the meal. During our walk we saw the prices of some condos posted on the windows of nearby real estate sales offices. Amazing. That fellow I met at the Irish Pub while waiting for Barbara last week was right. Manhattan has priced most people into beyond Brooklyn and into Queens and

Harlem. What a shame. It was fun to also see another location in the movie "You've got mail" called La Mode Cleaners. All of this just ties together so wonderfully.

And then Sunday came. I still felt in my 60s but a tad tired. After breakfast in my apartment I took a nice jog up into the Riverside Drive area. In the park there was a touch of reality as a dead large rat, covered with flies, lay bottoms up in the walkway. Yuck. So there are rats in the City. Who knew!? Animal and human I guess.

For no apparent religious reason I felt it appropriate to go to church. So Liz and I walked up to a beautiful old Catholic Church called the Church of the Blessed Sacrament on 71st between Amsterdam and Columbus Avenues. It was built in 1917, the same year my late father was born, and I really liked it. We got there early and sat through the tail end of the first service in Spanish. I liked that mis amigos. Esta muy bien. The priest must have been bi-lingual as he later did the service in English. For the English service, the place was packed and the homily quite good. Believe it or not, I enjoyed my sojourn into the beyond. During the service two babies were baptized which was beautiful. Dressed all in white they looked like porcelain dolls; they did not mind the splash of water upon their foreheads but just slept as some babies do. Not Rylak babies. The priest was indeed good and I would love to chat with him someday. He just had it all together. Bottom line is that my intention is to go to many churches and synagogues and even mosques to learn. Who knows? Perhaps I will learn something. I will do this even though as mentioned some time ago in another note, I have been excommunicated both from the Catholic Church and Lutheran Church. I think they would gladly take me back if I asked however.

After another walk we decided to go to Isabella's on 77th and Columbus for a late brunch or early "linner". Yes, "linner". Great place. I guess it truly is the place to see and be seen as they say. Everything was special and the food delicious. The cost? Not half bad. And then we walked around the neighborhood at a location where there were many tents with farmers selling their produce. Hot as heck but still fun. You see, the farm does come to the City. This is so typically Manhattan.

As an aside, I have to tell you that New Yorkers and their dogs are interesting. It seems as if the dogs rule the roost more often than not. Yesterday was quite hot. So, many dogs were carried around in their owner's arms. Many dogs were in little doggie carriages being pushed around and fed and watered. And so it is. God bless Fido!

After returning to my apartment the deluge came and the skies opened up. I still think it rains to clean the sidewalks of dog urine as well as to water plants and the like. When we later took a walk that fact became quite evident. Some of the more odiferous scents had disappeared and all were good with my nasal cavities.

After a very light dinner in my apartment we took yet another walk. Manhattan is a walking City. You do not need a car. If the distance is too great, take the bus or a subway. I love Lincoln Center at night. It is beautiful. Yesterday there was the sixth consecutive outdoor opera via film, "Werther" by Massenet. We saw some of it and moved on. It was A typical opera. Marriage....love....suicide....big finale. We also went to Columbus Circle to see the lights and the hordes of people. All so very great to just watch. Even saw a skyscraper that colored its top red, white, and blue. Frenetic and wonderful are good definitional words. How to feel alive at age 70!

Soon Morpheus called again and I awoke while the sun was rising. Such a wonderful sight. After a great run south at Riverside Park, we had breakfast and now sit on the bus back to Clinton this actual year 2014 Labor Day. Why don't we work on Labor Day? Beats me. Interesting to note while the news was on the television this morning, Central Park was shown to be alive with noted singers singing, runners running, and happy people being happy. Did not have time to stop and see all this excitement. After all, you have to draw lines somewhere?!

One problem with living in three different locations, often in the same week, is that you tend to forget what food you have where. So I take a photograph of my kitchen refrigerator as I leave. It helps. I clearly had a very nice 70th birthday long weekend which although not over yet, is soon to pass into the history books. As you can tell, I am adapting well to my new life style, at least as best as I am able. So Amelia, Benjamin, and Daniel, come to the City and do what I just did, all at your leisurely pace. You will love it. Beats retiring to Florida. No worry, this is all in my book for you to enjoy.

Love and hugs,

Grandpa

I speak the truth. It just seems some times that I do not.

September 6, 2014

Today I decided to run in Central Park even though the humidity was in the upper 80 percent range. So when I arrived at the Park from my apartment, I continued jogging and then realized that I was in a group of people that had just started a four mile run in support of a cure for autism. So I ran with them. What a hoot. There would be other runs today by other groups I am sure, but these people we all happy and jovial and just having a great time. Since I felt good after the run, I decided to run around the Park again, but this time the entire Park, a distance beyond the four mile route. Dumb move which violated my 70th birthday promise to go easier. Actually, I followed that promise for many days by running a shorter time. Today was an exception. I simply felt good as I slept well last night. The promise continues tomorrow.

And so I continued running, sweating like a baked stuck pig. During the run many unusual things happened. Since I usually run alone and do many things alone, my sense of hearing seems to have gotten better, particularly when I run. This happens to any person who is alone often. And so I listened a lot. Many of the young men running discussed their work in a very analytical way. Their jobs, their income, and how important they were. Their expected bonuses. The women were so different. They discussed feelings or how someone hurt them or how someone lost her job and cried, or how someone had an attitude. They also discussed many non-work things like kids and hopes and aspirations. I know this sounds so chauvinistic but it is true. This is what I heard. Perhaps I was delusional but I do not this so. When I liked a conversation I kept running with the runners speaking and listened. When I did not, I either pulled ahead or fell back to the next group and listened there. It helps pass the time and makes the running mentally easier. So I conclude from this small sampling that there are fundamental differences between men and women. Of course there were couples that ran together but their conversations were very difficult for me to listen in on. As it should be!!!

After another three miles I met a fellow who was training a high school woman to jog and fast walk. He and I struck up a conversation which was great. He was a former marathon runner who gave up those types of activities when he turned 79!! Holy crap. His fast walk was faster than my jog. He told me to join him at 9:30am on Saturday mornings at a large building in the Park on 92nd Street. I will go to his fast walking class there someday. He also gave me some advice concerning running. This is cool stuff. When running up hill and it is getting to you and seems difficult, close your right eye. Then your left brain takes over and you will feel better. Sounds like BS, no? It is true. I tried it. So David, when you do that DC Half Marathon next week, try it on the hills. He also said to lower your arms when running downhill. It helps you recover. Works. Interestingly enough he also pointed out to me that in Central Park the street light polls have the nearest street number painted on them with the letters E and W for East and West. So simple and so true and so easy to orient myself now.

Anyway, after two hours and 15 minutes of this effort, I was quite tired. I stopped and walked from the Park to my apartment hoping to cool off. I did not want to walk into my air-conditioned building and have a heart attack from the temperature change. And I did cool off and I am still alive. Drinking water during the run would have been a good idea. Anyway, it was my longest run in a couple of years, so I am pleased.

So my dear grandchildren who someday read this, learning can take place anywhere at any time. Now off to have breakfast and then to decide what else to do today.

Albert D. from NYC

It Just Gets Better Every Time
September 30, 2014

The NYC experiences just get better every time I go into the City. Hard to believe. Jude is a friend of mine and he is referred to as the Silver Fox. He is so full of knowledge of the City and is my sitting buddy often at Pier 1 along the Hudson River. He has current information on anything New York from sail boating to restaurants to where to meet women of my age. I love it.

This now really is my last note for my book and I want to give a summary of a few of the exciting things I have done of late. Like my wine tasting trip on the Hudson on a large 1920s sailboat with Liz which was a gift from my family. Going to Roosevelt Island via the tram and seeing the magnificent park representing the Four Freedoms mentioned by President Franklin D. Roosevelt. Like jogging 2.5 hours around the entire upper part of Manhattan with my running buddy Beth last week and both of us feeling exhilarated. Eating the finest sushi in the world at Amber on 70th at Columbus Avenue. Touring lower Manhattan and being awed by the Financial District. Tearing up at the Freedom Tower. Like taking my brother Frank and his wife Julie to everything imaginable between Bryant Park and my apartment just last week to include the Met where we saw Islamic Art and even to American Girl. Going to Cafe Lalo with Liz for a dinner consisting of desert only and a glass of milk. Noting how my barber' place of business had raised the cost of my haircut by $3.00 which irritated me to no end. Like being in the City at Central Park for the Global Citizens' Festival 2014 and lawn bowling on the grass fields designated for that purpose with Jeff who invited the experience. Everyday a new and different adventure appears. I have truly become a broken record and a great advertisement for the City. I do not know how long I will continue this adventure, but I now know the City and it is good.

THE END OF THE BEGINNING

And so, The Beginning portion of my part-time life in Manhattan (and a couple of other places) for more than a year has come to an end and it will no longer appear in this writing. I have no idea what the future will bring or how much time I have left on this earth as I just plod along accepting what life has to offer. Becket no longer exists as an alter ego or otherwise. Many times in the future I will feel melancholy, a sense of loss, regret, lonely, and sad as the slightest thing can set off those types of feeling. These things will never heal. Nonetheless, I have come a long way since our losing fight against cancer and my sojourn into New York City. Running away is not an option. On the contrary, the car is in drive and I move ahead, but always checking the rear-view mirror for whatever emotion may appear. Al Rylak is a totally different person. Bitterness has dissipated but not the sense of unfairness. Neither I nor my family will be defined by the tragedy that befell my dear Ginny and the resulting harm and loss to us all. We simply will not let it happen. My dear sweet grandchildren will live lives that are diminished but not because of us the living. Somehow, someway, Ginny is making sure we are all okay. I am doing my part. My "Added Thoughts" which follow reflect my thoughts before May 16, 2011 as well as a few afterward and show a different person. I suspect that I was feisty, happy, self-confident and opinionated. I also have added some more recent notes to show how life can go on even in the midst of tragedy and afterward. My hope is to continue thinking in the same manner now that I have been through the course life has set for me and those I love. Overall I am okay. I have a feeling that my life will take me to many places, all of which is good.

Thank you for taking the time to read this writing. Perhaps it will be of help to some. Perhaps it will help you help others.   You may be in my position someday.

Albert D. Rylak, formerly known as Beckett

Added Thoughts:

Many politicians are asses
January 31, 2009 at 10:53pm

Well people, another politician has proven that he is an ass. It was easy. Vice President Joe Biden was swearing in some high cabinet officials and snidely joked that he would not error in the oath of office as had Chief Justice Roberts at the inauguration of President Obama. Obama correctly grabbed Joe Biden by the arm and essentially made the small-minded fellow stop that type of talk. I give the President credit for this action. Biden on the other hand showed how the idiocy of the past 16 years continues. Let us hope that the President continues taking a new higher ground. The petty bickering has got to stop. We need Abraham Lincolns and all we get are partisan Joe Bidens who as a Blue Hen has done a disservice to his university. This type of silliness is not confined to the Democrats but is rampant in both parties. Of course, the media just loves this lack of civility and feeds on it whether it is Rush Limbaugh or Chris Matthews. Ever wonder when and why the news became a 24 hour a day show? It needs "news" and hence takes any event and dwells on it. We have irresponsible politicians and similar media. Enough said. I ramble and I am tired.

NJ struggles
February 6, 2009 at 7:11pm

New Jersey is struggling now to maintain its leadership role as the most corrupt state in the Union. Blago has propelled Illinois into first or second place what with more politicians in jail or about to be in jail than NJ. Drat. We will keep trying. Having placed a Mayor of Chicago under the frozen turf of the Meadowlands we clearly exceed Illinois and every other state for brazenness. Now, if we can just keep raising taxes and promising the electorate everything, NJ will return or retain its rightful place in infamy. As Mayor James of Newark said at his trial for assorted wrongdoings in public office, including malfeasance in office, "a sucker is born every day or bought every day in this State". A chicken in every pot and a 3.8% raise for everyone. Raise taxes and keep spending. As President Obama said, we will spend our way out of these trying times. See you in Florida.

Welcome to socialism
February 7, 2009 at 4:10pm

Oh my God. Socialism has arrived in America. What with wage caps, Tarp, and the government involving itself in private enterprises, it is over. Dies irae, dies ilia in sanctum fabulos et termini. In a word, SOCIALISM. I quit. The majority of Americans asked for it and they got what they asked for in spades. So, let us raise estate taxes so we are sure that we double tax and keep everyone at the lowest social stratum possible. When I was in the army I noticed the lowest common denominator theory. Given a chance, we all sink as low as we are able. Now we really have done it. I respect President Obama for his victory over Hillary Clinton and I will wish him well, but my God, what are you doing sir????? You are going to spend more money than then Bush did for the entire Iraq and Afghanistan Wars--all in one stroke of the pen. Good luck. God bless America. Got to run or I would go on and on. Nancy Pelosi--quit or something. You are not even capable of putting on your brassiere in the proper fashion!!

Instant gratification
February 9, 2009 at 2:31pm

Today I wonder about instant gratification. Ginny and I are shopping for a new TV. In P.C. Richards are a variety of folks and I noticed a young couple buying a 50 plus inch HD TV with all the bells and whistles; we are talking big bucks here. They had to get on a special payment plan to buy the darn thing--$39 a month with no interest for the first year. They never asked about the second and subsequent years. They have a right to do what they did but why do it in the first place? This is the stuff that has been going on for years and I guess the depression we are in has not changed everyone's' views.

The same point re using the equity in your home for renovations, toys, etc. When did we change our view that you bought a house with 20% down, got a fixed rate 25-30 year mortgage, paid it off and had your house equity for retirement and safety? Somehow we determined that we should borrow on the equity at higher short term rates to buy a second home (and other things)--ergo, drive up the prices of real estate, get ourselves in hock, pretend we had the American Dream when all we had was a nightmare. What with all the economic problems hanging around now, we have had a revolution without a single shot being fired. Our greed has enabled an agenda that requires the government be the do-all-and-end-all for remediating all of our woes. Ask not what you can do for your country; ask what your country can do for you. He that controls the purse strings controls us.

On a lighter note, I had a client thank me for winning her case, saying, "what can I do to thank you for this?". As Clarence Darrow said, "ever since the Phoenicians invented money, there has only been one answer to that question.". Have a great day and thank God for our lovely Amelia who gives me a great big smile!!!!!!!

It's not easy being gray.
February 10, 2009 at 7:43pm

It's not easy being gray to steal a phrase from Kermit the Frog. It seems like I see gray all the time. Some people see in black and/or white. I

298

guess as a result of my training I can see both sides of almost everything. When I was living in Pennington, in high school and college, a dear friend (who has since died) and I would sit down with a bottle of Cutty Sark and begin arguing. We would take the polar opposite sides of an issue, such as the Vietnam War, religion, whatever. We would become quite vocal and the veins in our necks would seem to almost explode. My dear then girlfriend Ginny Campbell, often thought we were going to come to blows. By the end of the evening we more often than not had reversed positions, arguing with equal vigor for the opposite position. I guess that is why I just cannot deal with Limbaugh, Pelosi, Reed, Schumer and the like. They just see in black and white. Gray is a pretty nice color you know. Wasn't there a story about a man in a gray flannel suit? One of my favorite birds, the titmouse, looks just like a a gray cardinal. Gray can even be spelled gray or grey. One of my favorite cars was gray and I have had Grey Goose Vodka on one occasion. So, while it's not easy being gray, it ain't too bad either.

Greed
February 12, 2009 at 12:17pm

When I was growing up in the '50s and '60s, it was not uncommon to strive for success and actually get to that point. Even the lowliest of us could work hard, save and attain the American Dream. At some point selfishness took over our routines and the American People as a whole, became greedy. As to the current economic crisis, you can blame corporate greed, governmental excess or whatever, but the focus really should be on individual greed. Corporations do not exist except as the alter ego of individuals. So, blame the banks, profiteers or whomever for the current situation; but do not forget to blame yourself. At times I think there is an inconsistency in hating greed and accepting capitalism. It is inherent in the capitalist system that some greed is a good thing--the profit motive etc. At some point however, greed permeates your character and when that happens greed becomes institutionalized. That is what has happened in America and throughout the world today. It is the reason we have the current economic crisis. Our greed has led to dependence on the government which may lead us into a form of government which we can no longer accept; totalitarianism. Got to run off to court. Al

Strange
February 13, 2009 at 8:27pm

It is really strange as you age, that when you have contact with kids from high school it is as if there has not been a passage of time. There must be something about those formative teenage years that binds. You pick up discontinued conversations and end them!! You seem to forget all the water that has gone over the dam and just revert back to the time of the golden earlier years. Weird. Is it because you did all sorts of things, legal and illegal, together for the first time? Or, is it just nostalgia revisited? Beats me. As I make this journey through Facebook, memories wash over me and all of them are good. I remember not just old friends but their parents, where they lived, and events. Strange. Is it because we forget that we are old and life's journey is ending when we contact our past? For one shining moment Camelot reappears. How morbid! How great! How true!!

Power of the media
February 17, 2009 at 5:26pm

The power of the media is overwhelming and quite frightening. Our Founding Fathers never could envision the current television influence and twenty-four hour a day propaganda on Fox, CNN, MSNBC etc. which claim to be news. I have always felt that the media is prejudiced and that is to be expected. We all have our biases and prejudices. Nonetheless, the media has taken this silliness to a new low. Just today I learned again that the American public still supports the economic stimulus package. They have not read the 787 billion dollar Economic Recovery Bill, have not gotten their information but through the media which has adopted President Obama as its current super star and finally, are so desperate for change at any cost, that they simply mimic the media. I tried to read the main bill--it is impossible to understand. Our leaders voted on the bill without reading it!!!! My God...what are we doing? Change for the sake of change is silly. Are we in such dire shape that we cannot think things through? Candidly, the Fifth Estate needs to regulate itself and try to stop making policy. It helped to destroy the Bush Presidency; it helped to create the vitriolic conflict in Washington DC today; Nancy Pelosi and Harry Reed to name two culprits. I do not want to regulate the press, but it needs to regulate itself. When examining a witness, you always need to understand their motives and their agenda. Ergo, when we watch TV or read a newspaper, do the same thing. I wish the President well. I pray that he does not take us to a place from whence we cannot return after he is gone. As an aside, I thought it was interesting at Rutgers when I was a student, that when issues were to be placed on TV or in the newspapers, those in interest came out of the woodwork. When the cameras stopped rolling, there was a dearth of "interested parties". Had I only known that this concept would be taken to the current extreme. God bless America. Let us really start to think and appreciate the blessings of the freedom we have here. I fear that we will lose it.

Harvey Cedars
February 17, 2009 at 7:34pm

Long Beach Island; the Whytes; 80th Street; Captain Gus and May; The Neptune Market(per Mike); Noonie burger; Foodies; The Oasis; The Owl Tree; Neptune Liquor Store; The Plantation; Barnegat Light House;

Loveladies; the Rylaks; Harvey Cedars Shellfish Company; Will; Poochy; Albert D. Rylak Annual Quadrathlon; shack; The Boat Yard; Fire Company; Ship's Wheel; the Causeway; the Boulevard; the Krug family; the Houghtons; the Halperns; Zeke; the Hedges; "Down the Shore"; Barnegat Bay; the ocean; the bay beach; sea glass; The Harvey Cedars Ice Cream Parlor; Boat House-Garrets; the water tower; Kinsey Cove; sunsets; dolphins; cedar trees; outdoor showers; crabs; the "Virginia" Sea Ray; big red; surfing; wet suits; kayaks; jet ski; water skiing; tubing; body boarding; body surfing; horseshoe crabs; running of the blues; Karyn M; Captain's Inn; Fantasy Island; skee ball; cochinas; starfish; jelly fish; grilling; the boathouse; the island house; Hoagers; Freddy; the Misterioso; noodles; "Amelia Ann Boston Whaler; Gary; Quarterdeck Inn; Seann and Carolyn; Andy's; Ginny's meals and hospitality; Jersey corn and tomatoes; Kelly's; Viking Village; Kubel's; Loveladies; North Beach; Surf City; sea gulls; white ducks; Manahawkin; Maiden Lane; bicycles; Dog Day Race; Chowderfest; Haymarket; Widas; Viking Motel; Walter the giant crab; Gunning River; Bible Conference; Sandy Island; Houghton's Rowboats; H.C. Dredging Company; Whitehouse House; family and friends; balloon slingshot; sea horses; clams; shells; barnacles; jetties; moss; salt water; sunburn; sunscreen; Susan and Linda; funny hats; Sunfish sailboats; rowboat; skim boarding; beach badges; beach chairs; miniature golf; trampolines; Surf City 5 and 10; sand; dunes; west wind; green heads; flies; high tide; hurricane; fireworks; paddleball; horseshoes'; basketball; jellyfish; sharks; snow fence; Penny; Mallard Lane; Sparky; Merchants; Mr. Baum; bikinis; Kinsey Creek; Liz and Ben; memories; minnows; Pilsner; bunker; sandbar; pilings; dock; bulkhead; Swedish fish; broken tail lights at the Neptune Liquor Store telephone poll; and this is just a start!!!!!

Albert D. Annual Quadrathlon
March 15, 2009 at 8:38pm

The history of the Albert D. Rylak Annual Quadrathlon will be presented at a later date. Four significant events are required to receive recognition for completion of the Quadrathlon; a five mile run from the Rylak home in Harvey Cedars to Holly Avenue in Loveladies and back; a nine mile bicycle ride from the Rylak home in Harvey Cedars to Kelly's Restaurant in Barnegat Light and back; a half mile swim around Kinsey Cove commencing and ending at the Rylak bulkhead in Harvey Cedars; a three plus mile ocean kayak paddle from the Rylak bulkhead to a specific mustard colored house in Loveladies, and back. The said Quadrathlon takes places over the summer each year in accordance with the recommendation of the Rules Committee. The Rules Committee consists of the following: Albert D. Rylak. Each event must be sanctioned by the Sanctioning Committee which consists of the following: Albert D. Rylak. There is no time limit for completion of the Quadrathlon except that it must be commenced and finished while the sun is shining; in short, it is a Zen-like event. Furthermore, the Quadrathlon flag (an old triangular orange lumber flag found along Long Beach Boulevard, improved by Gra Campbell and finalized by Ginny Whyte) must be flying during the event. In the event of small craft warnings on Barnegat Bay and if you run eight miles rather than five miles, you will receive credit for an Ultra-Quadrathlon; if you complete the Quadrathlon twice in one sunlit day, you receive the honor of being a Dual-Quadrathlete. All persons who complete the Albert D. Rylak Annual Quadrathlon have their names placed upon the Quadrathlon Plaque and the year(s) of completion. Jordan Muller has the distinction of having created the aforesaid Plaque in the shape of a surfboard and the art work has been presented by Pendergast Signs Hunterdon County, NJ.

The following persons are credited with finishing the event at least one time:

Albert D. "Mr." Rylak
Lena "the Leenster" Fairless
David "Daf" Rylak
Mark "Binky" Rylak
Scott "Gitti" Smallwood
Jordan "Duod" Muller
Rob "Tuna" Caughey
Sandra "the Love" Love
Michael "M-Dub" Whyte
Karyn "Whytedog" Whyte
Seann "Clydesdale" O'Mara

The following persons have expressed an interest in competing in the event for the calendar year 2009:

Albert D. Rylak
David Rylak
Lena Fairless
Don Mulligan-first timer, in training
Carolyn O'Mara-first timer
Ron Koby-first timer
Dana Mathews Mulligan-first timer newly added
Michael Whyte

This note will be continued in the near future but due to time constraints, it is hereby and herewith ended forthwith.

A thought re cell phones and our children
April 12, 2009 at 6:19pm

Today I happened to notice again a parent at the supermarket on the cell
phone with a young child in the appropriate front seat just sitting there.
Another at her car unloading groceries while her daughter just sat in the
car-- the mom was on the cell phone. Another driving his SUV with three
kids in the back seats--the dad was on the cell phone. My gosh; do we
ever speak to our kids anymore? I imagine that world peace and the
economy were being discussed but I doubt it. Seems to me we make
choices all the time and too often we choose the cell phone over time with
our kids. Children are a special blessing; they spend so little time with us
and then they are gone. So, perhaps, when you are with your kids, put
away the cell phone and speak to your kids; they will learn so much from
you.

Fish
May 6, 2009 at 8:22pm

Well, as promised I want to talk about fishing. Had a crappy day today
dealing with the government agencies. I am beat. Now to fish. In the Bible
or some other book it is said that you can feed the masses by giving them
fish. Or, you can teach a person to fish so that he/she can feed his or
herself. He who controls the fish controls all. Republicans and Democrats
are both into giving the masses fish. The quantity and type of fish is
controlled by the feds. Today there will be one trillion fish given;
tomorrow more. Also, perhaps we will give bass to one group, trout to
another, and Mahi-Mahi to our favorites. Perhaps sushi to those that are
really extra good. Good is defined by the government. Irritate the
government and you get moss bunker.

God forbid if you teach the people to fish for themselves. If that were done you would not have government as it currently exists. People would take care of themselves and the government need only provide assurance that the body of water in which we fish is safe in the event of a disaster. So it is with true conservatives. Let the people do what has to be done. Let us fish for our own food. If you choose not to fish, feel free to starve. If you are disabled and cannot fish, the people will take care of you; not the government. Government not only provides the fish today but taxes the rods, reels, bait, and charges you a fee for a license. We have too much government. It is time to have less government, not more.

October 14, 2009 at 8:11am

I got up early this morning and was off on a jog about 5:30 AM. As the sun had not yet risen, I kept running on the roads. The temperature was about 38 degrees and it was really dark. I was wearing my shorts, long sleeved tee-shirt, gloves and a ski-cap, and proceeded to run up along Spruce Run Reservoir. It was invigorating. The fingertip moon and a number of unknown planets and stars shone brightly in the sky. As I ran along Spruce Run Reservoir I could see the mist over the waters looking as if a huge cloud had descended from the sky. For some unknown reason my left foot and right hip did not ache too much and I picked up the pace. Now the sun began rising and to my left I saw a large herd of deer. An immense proud buck deer appeared closest to me and you could see his breath as he stood there in defiance protecting the herd. Then, he and the herd scampered into the woods with their white tails held high. Fascinating. Surreal. I wondered what I would do if the buck deer and his huge rack of antlers had decided to attack me!! In any event I continued my run home and when I arrived I saw my dear wife sitting at the breakfast table having a cup of coffee and reading the newspaper. Life is good.

9/11 trial

January 8, 2010 at 3:50pm

I tried to send this earlier but it is lost in cyberspace, maybe. I had a thought. If we "have" to try the 9/11 terrorists in the US, why does it have to be in Manhattan? Of course we want to give the bastards a fair trial, and I suggest that they cannot get a fair trial in Manhattan; far too much prejudice. Further, the safety of millions of people will be jeopardized. A change of venue is necessary. No law requires that defendants be tried where the alleged crime was committed if they cannot get a fair trial in that location. Albert D. must insist that the trial be fair, so let us change the venue to the Grand Canyon. I recognize that the TV and radio broadcasting may be impeded a bit due to terrain features, but no defendant has the right to a Bully Pulpit at a trial. Let them orate and pontificate all they wish as they will only be heard by the jury and court personnel. We give the defendants a fair trial, we protect millions of people, we lessen the exorbitant cost of the trial, and we allow the defendants free speech but not a microphone. On the other hand, perhaps President Obama will change his mind and allow an enemy combatant to be summarily tried at Guantanamo and dealt with accordingly.

Education

January 10, 2010 at 3:12pm

Might it be nice if all the schools in America made sure they taught each student at minimum the following:
Typing, history, writing, current events, and at least one year of a foreign language. We have a great educational system and my respect for teachers is boundless. Spoke to some kids today at the gym. They did not seem to know the name of the President before Obama. Shocked me. Then, when I reminded them that Bush might be the name to recall, they really did not know why they disliked him so much. Pity; I would

have liked to hear their argument and position. And, their vote is equal to anyone else's. Perhaps there should be a poll tax again (just kidding) or at least a basic citizenship requirement to vote. Of course in days of old when knights were bold, you had to own property to exercise your franchise. In economic terms that is extreme, but it is frustrating to acknowledge that the right to vote, so very important, is treated sans respect. The less knowledge you have the more apt you are to follow the demagoguery of the demagogues. Democracy and demagoguery cannot coexist. Typing is important because if your brain is going a mile a minute and your fingers cannot keep up, you lose important thoughts and concepts. Writing is essential as it is so easy to simply spout off like I am doing now; yet more difficult to "put pen to paper". History taught fairly without bias will give you the background to understand the present. A foreign language just broadens your horizons as you realize that the world is far broader than the USA although one can pick up a multitude of languages almost anywhere in our country. It is the study of current events that enable us to make intelligent decisions that have a direct impact on our future. Yes, watch Fox News and CNN and read!!! Then you may become a good American Citizen irrespective of your positions.

Footprints in the Snow
February 10, 2010 at 9:23am

I guess we all want to be remembered for something at different times in our lives. It is hard to believe that someday we will never be here and life will go on. Perhaps that is why if religion did not exist, it would have to be invented. Perhaps that is why we have tombstones. People will know we were here. In another note I wrote about a trip my son David and I took to Rochester, NY when he was applying to medical school. While he was being interviewed for hours, I jogged all over the city and came upon two cemeteries. Although both cemeteries had tombstones, the Jewish cemetery had stones placed on many of tombstones. That was a sign that someone had been there. Poor Christians would never know if they had visitors!! But I digress.

I was jogging up by the Spruce Run Reservoir today in the snow. As I entered the roadway up toward the water, I noticed footprints in the snow; human and animal. I jogged for a mile or two along the footprints and it eerily felt as if a person and a dog were running with along with me. However, I could see no one else. After a few miles I caught up with Kim and her dog Butch and we chatted. I continued on as she reversed her direction and headed home. A snow plow went by and erased all the footprints behind us. There was no proof that we had been there. After a bit, I decided to change direction and run home. As the snow kept falling I came upon more footprints and dog prints in the snow, and knew that Kim and Butch were ahead but not in view. Again I felt as if the three of us were jogging the roadway together. As I stared at the footprints, I became enraptured in what I was doing--much like a beagle on a scent. Beagles never look up but just follow their noses even past a rabbit standing right next to them! Anyway, I practically bumped into Kim and Butch after a bit!!

The footprints I left at the reservoir are all gone now, whether covered by snow or removed by a snow plow. No one will know that I jogged up there today except Kim and Butch. Ironically, no one will really care and that is not a bad thing. All that matters is that I had a great run.

I am off to work. God bless America for the opportunities she gives us!!!! Must in my small way try to keep the economy going.

ADR

Hysteria
February 25, 2010 at 12:01pm

The media does it again. I know there is a snow storm coming to NJ today. I am turning off the radio now. Too much information about weather patterns, accidents and other wonderful facts. As with politics, the mass media devours every event and makes it a crisis. The media love to create hysteria so as to keep our interest and financial support. It gets all the listeners/subscribers/watchers needed to pay for commercials and continue its self-importance. The media systematically ruined the Presidency of the second George Bush and now a different facet of the media is trying to destroy the Presidency of Barack Obama. I miss the old days when we were told a snow storm was coming and every hour there would be a little forecast or current report; not sixty minutes an hour of insanity-go get salt and a snow shovel-go get a week's supply of food-call all your relatives to make sure they are safe-gloat if you live in Florida-stay home from work-if at work, check the snow fall in anticipation of an early departure-watch watch watch-read read read-listen listen listen-there is nothing going on in the world except the weather although C-Span has some interesting stuff on it re national health insurance. We really need to control the media and we all know how to do that; simply ignore the media for a good long time. Perhaps then it will stop over-medicating us on the weather issues and the news issues as well. Perhaps it will finally stop taking positions on issues and simply report the news as news whether it suits their political philosophy or not!! Enough said. Time to shovel the walkway sans trepidation and with a little skip in my step.

Albert D. Rylak Biathlon a/k/a/ the Blizzard Run
February 26, 2010 at 7:46am

Team Rylak is proud to announce the creation of a new event which may be used for training for the Albert D. Rylak Annual Quadrathlon. The event will be known as the Albert D. Rylak Periodic Extreme Biathlon shortened to the "Blizzard Run". The Blizzard Run consists of two events under extreme conditions. Firstly, there must be a blizzard-at least a foot of snow on the ground and continuous winds of at least 40 mph. One cannot commence the event until after the first snow plows have created a path in the roadway and loaded your sidewalks with snow. The event must be completed as the sun rises for to do otherwise would be too dangerous what with all the SVU nuts on the road. Secondly, the event begins by having each entrant shovel his/her walkway. Then, immediately thereafter, each entrant must commence a five mile run, all along the streets of Clinton, NJ. The most difficult part of the Biathlon is running into the wind. The least fun moment is constantly looking backward to be sure you are not run over by snow plowing trucks or idiot drivers. You must have a tough skin to compete in this event as you will periodically hear someone yell "jackass" or "you idiot" and worse. After the running portion of the event has been completed, you must reshovel the walkway as it has been covered with snow whether from the sky or from the plows. Since the Albert D. Rylak Biathlon is not timed, it is a relaxing way to start your day; you have to budget at least two hours however. Having just completed the event, it would be nice to have a partner or two for fellowship and competition. This statement has been authorized by the executive committee of the aforementioned Quadrathlon.

Summer reading at the beach.
April 8, 2010 at 2:17pm

Summer reading at the beach to try to understand what is going on in Washington, particularly with reference to health care reform, income taxes, and class struggle: Atlas Shrugged by Ayn Rand, Animal Farm by George Orwell, and Catch 22 by Joseph Heller. Most important is the first listed. Productive citizens will indeed disappear, the pigs will rewrite history every day, and the ante will be raised as it is approached. This is scary stuff. I feel as if I am living in a dream that has become a nightmare. I am not making this up. Stop looking to the government for solutions; look to yourself. God bless America.

Curmudgeon
July 22, 2010 at 4:54pm

This has been a particularly bad day for me. I have been a divorce/trial attorney for 41 years. In 38 days I retire. Divorce is a fact of life and I understand and accept that. It is necessary and liberating. What I do not understand is the "juvenilization" of a large number of people today in the divorce context. I will discuss this below, but I want it understood that the purpose of all my Notes on Facebook has been to enable my dear grand-daughter Amelia (and any other grandchildren that may appear) to understand her grandfather. I do not just want to discuss simple issues about friends, outings, and meals, etc., but important matters of all natures. I mentioned in a prior Note that when I was a high school and college student, my dear friend Jack Meyers and I used to argue all the time about political and social issues. It was exhausting and fun. It sharpened one's mind and brought gray to issues which were otherwise black or white. People do not do that anymore. We just let the Left and Right pundits speak to us. But I digress.

Too many of my friends are acting like teenagers in high school. A middle aged couple I know just split up. The wife moved in with her boyfriend. Okay, no big deal. Her boyfriend has a wife. Okay. He also has three children. She has four children. He is unemployed. She is unemployed. They need to be happy. They divide a family for their happiness. There are many cases just like this that I encounter. People are stressed. The economy has smashed their dreams. Both parties are looking for Mr. or Mrs. Goodbar. The anchor of the family seems to have been set free and it bob about the waters. Just like in high school. One "significant other" this month--another later on. Why is there so much unhappiness? I think that people got stuck on themselves and thought they were just wonderful-entitled-perfect-----and the booming economy of yesteryear allowed this to happen. Now we swim in "crap" with an economy that has brought us to reality. We realize that we are just not so special; so, we flee on situation and look elsewhere.

What I have mentioned above does not involve cases of domestic abuse or other nastiness. It is not just "falling out of love" which is okay. It is taking the easy way out just like we did in high school and "moving on". I believe in divorce in the correct context. Margaret Mead understood that for many marriages, divorce does not end a marriage. It is already over. The divorce simply finalizes the dissolution. That is okay with me and accepted. People are allowed to divorce.

This Note may irritate some of my friends. That is okay. Perhaps I am an irascible churlish person. A curmudgeon. Nonetheless, I am sad today from what I learned. The events I have mentioned are happening in droves. Do what you must, but do not be afraid to hug the one you love and accept the frailties that we all exhibit. Try hard to keep the family unit in tact if possible. If not, exit with dignity and the children in the forefront.

I am done. There will be many more Notes by me in the future. Amelia--I hope you understand me and accept me for what I am. I mean no harm and only ask that we try to do what is right.

The Brood Mare and the ATM
July 28, 2010 at 8:37pm

Well, here goes. As a divorce attorney for 41 years, I note that the male element of society often feels predisposed to defeat in divorce courts. Here in Hunterdon County, the group that dealt with domestic violence cases was called the Women's Crisis Center. Believe it or not, this sends a message to men and it is not a good message. Even though most domestic violence is committed against women, men are victims too. Usually in more subtle ways. After fifteen years of trying, my lobbying to change the name of the group was successful. The name was changed to Safe in Hunterdon a year or so ago. This was a fair thing to do. It reflected reality.

In divorce cases, the courts are more often than not predisposed against men qua men and in favor of women. The adversarial system promotes this and we must change the system to reflect mediation and compromise. Unfortunately the previous and current system promotes a battle in which sides are taken and positions, even silly ones, are reinforced. Too many people regress to their high school days and act that age--not as mature adults. As an explanation, consider the following. A divorce is filed and the Husband and Wife separate. There is no way in heaven that their current level of income can support two separate households. Nonetheless, Judges act with impunity in forcing the primary wage earners, which yes, are the males usually, to pay all the carrying costs of the marital life style even though it no longer exists. The Husband becomes embittered and as the system inexorably moves along at a snail's pace, the vitriol and anger of the Husband increases. He feels as if his only role is that of an ATM. A role of providing exorbitant sums of money to the Wife and children. This attitude very often exacerbates the anger and any hope of settling the divorce case is decreased. Of course, legal fees rise and as the battle proceeds both parties are trapped in their divorce proceeding because of finances-MONEY. The lawyers have two different ATMs from one family unit to assist them in putting their new BMW in a heated garage. Why not sit people down in the early stages of a divorce and counsel the parties on maturity and anger management training? In other words, do not wait for a crisis before you counsel people; take proactive steps early on.

Another way the ATM syndrome is exhibited in a divorce context relates to the issues of alimony and equitable distribution. In New Jersey, there is no fixed formula for alimony and a Wife or Husband can be ordered to pay alimony. There are thirteen assorted factors that are considered. With two wage earners or even one, alimony can be settled with ease if the parties are amenable to that. Problems ensue where equitable distribution enters into the picture. Equitable distribution is basically the fair division of all assets and debts acquired during the marriage. So far so good. The real problem is exhibited when you take a case with a business owned by the parties or one of the parties. Assume the business is worth $1,000,000.00. Clearly the Wife is entitled to a portion of the business. Let us say 50%. Hence, the parties should each walk away with $500,000.00 from the business. Sounds easy. Yet, judges uniformly force the defeated Husband to get a loan to pay the $500,000 to the Wife (yes, he usually keeps and gets the business!) and impose alimony as if the $500,000.00 loan did not exist. The ATM machine Husband has no hope of ever recovering from this scenario. Contempt is rears its ugly head. Then the next phase enters the picture and it is not pretty.

Often I see the embattled Husband in these circumstances lash out against his Wife and sometimes his entire family. Yes, that includes kids. He views his Wife as being treated as a brood mare by the courts. She has done her job in producing and caring for the kids. The ATM machine must now pay and pay and pay for an eternity. I do not agree with this feeling, but it exists. As the economy has weakened under Clinton/Bush/Obama economics, we realize that too many families are not based on love and respect, but on things and money. Families are damaged forever by their inability to sustain their life style. When I meet with a Wife I first find out whether she has children. If she does, I then ask her what she does for a living and invariably she says "nothing". Can you believe it? Me thinketh she feels she is a brood mare! Children and family care are the noblest of jobs/professions. When the Husband demeans himself and fatherhood with such silliness in lashing out at his spouse, no useful purpose is served. When a Wife thinks she does not do anything "other than care for the kids and the family", she demeans herself and motherhood.

Before you criticize this Note, try walking in my shoes for a while. As an aside, the case I have set forth above was not one of mine, but heard in open court; I listened in. And, change the word "Wife" to "Husband" and "Husband" to "Wife" (gotcha!) and you will see that silliness in the Court system is just not the province of male hood. Women are capable of being as stupid and idiotic as men and very often are. Women at least have a variety of support groups to help them through a divorce if they choose to use them. They know how to emote and shed a tear. Men on the other hand have been trained by society to remain stoical. Their tears are internal. We men need to be more like a woman in that regard! Albert tires so the typing stops. Have a great and happy evening. God bless America.

Life is like a moving snowball
August 5, 2010 at 12:13pm

Just was thinking about life and our impending end of like. Seems to me that life is like a moving snowball. When you are born the tiny little snowball starts moving on its journey through life. It seems it takes forever to go a decade. The more the snowball moves, the more snow it accumulates. The larger the snowball, the faster it moves. At about age forty, you realize that the next decade will speed by. The fifties even faster. Now in my sixties, the damn thing is quite large and moves with rapidity as never before seen. If you make it to your seventies and on, I guess a decade will seem like a flash in time. There is no way to slow that damn snowball down as physics and science control. Too bad I did not know this when I was younger; then I might be better prepared for the snowball to stop moving. Not too bad an idea to hug someone you love today; before the thaw!!

The government is not the people
October 27, 2010 at 8:41am

A friend from Chicago suggested that the government was "the people". A very astute observation but not correct. The government is simplistically, a group of people that rule us. They are elected by the people, but since we do not live in a Democracy, our elected officials should rule from their hearts and minds, not necessarily as their constituency demands. It takes courage to do this. To President Obama's credit or discredit, he has ignored the people and proceeded with his social agenda and legacy legislation which he was elected to do. He essentially ignored the concept of jobs for which he will pay a dear price. Nonetheless, he did what he said he was going to do. This was expected and in a way, I admire him for doing what he said he was going to do. I say this action was a disconnect from the people. As Lilly Pupster has said, "show me the facts". Well, come November 2nd we will see if the President and members of his party acted as "the people" or were disconnected from the people. The facts will be known then. The critical issue facing America was and is jobs creation and that has not been the primary concern of the President. On the contrary billions of dollars have been wasted on purposes that were not successful in creating jobs; that had no relation to job creation. Months and months were focused on reforming health care. Tis a pity that C-Span was not used;

that the "same old back room deals" seemed to take place; that the health care issue superseded the jobs issue. I do not give a rat's ass about President Obama's legacy. I care only that we keep this country safe from its enemies and that we pass through this economic downturn quickly. Where have you gone Joe DiMaggio? My view of the role of government has been set forth in another note herein about "fishing" which says it all. Thank you for allowing me to digress. Go Cubs!!!

"November"-with a little license from "Annie" for my liberal Democratic friends. God bless America!!
October 6, 2010 at 9:42am

The sun'll come out in

November

Bet your bottom dollar

That in November

There'll be sun!

Just thinkin' about

November

Clears away the cobwebs,

And the sorrow

'Til there's none!

When I'm stuck with a day

That's gray (blue?),

And lonely,

I just stick out my chin

And Grin,

And Say,

Oh!

The sun'll come out in

November

So ya gotta hang on

'Til November

Come what may

November! November!

I love ya November!

You're always

A day

away!!!

Disturbing article
December 22, 2010 at 8:42am

I read a disturbing article today (12/22/10). The Associated Press reported that almost one quarter of students who try to join the U.S. Army fail its entrance exam. Too many of our high school students graduate not ready to begin college or a career it opines. The Educational Trust found that 23 percent of recent high school graduates did not receive the minimum score needed on the enlistment test to join any branch of the military. One of the test questions is "If 2 plus X equals 4, what is the value of X?". Lastly, further data shows that 75% of those aged 17 to 24 don't even qualify to take the test because they are physically unfit, have a criminal record or didn't graduate from high school. My experience also shows that many who graduate high school need remedial work in writing and reading when they get to college. It is time to worry. I know that a goodly percentage of people do not know who the President is now or who was the previous President; they do not even know their Senators or members of Congress from their district. Candidly, you have got to earn the privilege/right to be an American citizen in my opinion and once you earn that privilege/right you have a duty to constantly protect it. Being a citizen of course involves among other things simply being born here or fitting one of the other requirements set forth in law. Being a good citizen requires so much more. Sometimes I think that too many of us do not deserve to be citizens of this great country. Now shut up and do a random act of kindness for someone!

Jack W. Rylak
January 8, 2011 at 4:52pm

Jack W. Rylak died on December 22, 2010 at the age of 57; he was cremated on Christmas Eve. He was my younger brother. A graduate of Hopewell Valley Regional High School, he served in the United States Air Force and thereafter worked for numerous employers in the Trenton, NJ area. He was a resident of Independence Manor Assisted Care Facility the past four years and is survived by his mother Lottie, his son Justin, Justin's wife Camille, and three beautiful granddaughters. He is also survived by his brothers Albert and Frank and his sister Autumn and their families. Throughout Jack's life he suffered from many physical maladies as well as many mental problems, including Schizophrenia and Bi-Polar Disorder. Although he is finally rid of his demons, Jack deserves to be known as a basically decent man who suffered tremendously during his life but kept fighting nonetheless to achieve happiness. His death is sad not just because of his passing, but also because the world lost a fundamentally good man who fought but lost the good fight. Perhaps his death will bring a realization to us all that mental illness is just as serious and important as medical conditions such as heart disease and the like. Every life has value and we as a society will be judged by how we treat the most vulnerable of our citizens. So Jack, the world was indeed a better place because you were here and you are missed.

Attitude
January 19, 2011 at 4:47pm

I am trying to think who the Republican's will put up for their nominee in the next Presidential election. Does not seem to be anyone worthy of the honor. Sad. Also, at the gym today a woman came up to me with her friend and with condescension said this is "that conservative". What brazenness. I told her to go and F herself and that I was tired of this type of holier-than-thou attitude. She did not have the market captured in intelligence and rightfulness. I am glad I did what I did and would do it again under the same circumstances. I believe in America and the American dream. Period. If you don't, tough. And I thought that we were going to now be more civil in the future. What a joke. All the current politicians have to be kicked out of office. Conservatives cannot be intimidated by anyone and must push their positions. No one has all the answers and if you think you do, you are an idiot. Enough said for now.

Egypt
January 31, 2011 at 4:32pm

What a crazy world. Jordan, Egypt, and Yemen have had or are having riots. More will follow. Okay. Take Egypt-many of the rioters are apparently against Hosni Mubarak and want democracy. Okay. There have to be a few bad guys in there as well that want Jihad and do not give a rat's ass about democracy. Okay again. Some of these same people are looting Egypt's treasures. Whatever the connection. Okay and again. US policy in the region is to support Mubarak even though he is a dictator and has harmed his people. Why? Human rights are less important that the right and stability to use the Suez Canal to transport oil and also to protect Israel. How would you like to be the President today? Things are not "okay". Now some protestors are even shouting anti-American slogans. Everything is seemingly America's fault. This is an opportunity to really screw things up and we have to really pray that the President and his advisors know what they are doing. Any good ideas? God bless America.

To my physician friends
February 11, 2011 at 12:53pm

I am in day two of this seminar on Health Care at the Ritz in Naples, FL and I wanted to share a little knowledge with all my physician friends. Go the "concierge medicine" route!! It will make you much happier in the long run. Now for a few random thoughts. Obama Care resulted from two separate statutes. The Patient Protection and Affordable Care Act (33/10) and The Health Care and Education Reconciliation Act (3/30/10). These two acts really should be entitled The Attorney Full Employment Act!!! (Joke). They are really a clusterfuck of insanity and have so little to with real patient care but politics.

The concept is that under the new health care laws, providers will be paid less (cutback in Medicare payments) and hence money will be saved-- even though millions of more citizens will be provided services. Congress cannot seem to go outside the box in its analysis. It really makes sense in my humble uneducated opinion to ask Doctors what to do to achieve financial savings and to provide a certain level of care. That was not really done. On the other hand, there is no financial incentive for the Doctors to tell the government how to save money now as under current law they will suffer the burden of loss of income!!!

The federal agencies dealing with Obama Care are well intentioned at times but have to deal with broad based regulations and rules of a national nature. Hence there are so many exceptions. Nonetheless, it seems that the government has decided to make the Doctors the enemy and not part of the solution. I suspect this has to do with the redistribution of wealth. Let the Doctors participate in providing the guidelines to benefit patients. Do not make this a class struggle.

You must know the following terms and understand them in relation to your practices, or you essentially risk civil and criminal prosecution:

Safe Harbor
Stark Law
Anti-Kickback Law
Accountable Care Organization
Form 990 disclosure
Gain sharing
Capitation
The feared "whistleblower" who could be your colleague
Civil Monetary payments
False Claims Act
Anti-Trust lawsuits Qui Tam law suits
False Claims Act
Fraud and Abuse Act
Jail
Joint Ventures
Direct compensation and indirect compensation (e.g. lower rent)

and so much more.

All of these things will be in your future vocabulary if they are not already. The government wants savings at your expense. And, one way to pay for Obama Care is to assert large penalties against hospitals and physicians-under the threat of civil or criminal responsibility. Do you know that scienter (knowledge) is not even an element of a crime under Medicare billing? If you submit a bill and it is rejected, you could be held liable for wrongdoing even though you did not know of the error. I feel the Constitution and Bill of Rights have been thrown out the window.

Can the government pay people to:
Not smoke?
Lose weight?
Eat well?
Distress?
Should insurance companies do this?

To David--ER Doctors have to be careful about two things in general:
1. Is the organization being paid the fair market value for the services it provides? It takes 100s of pages to define FMV and if you are charging too much, you violate the Stark and Anti-Kickback Acts amongst other things. That can create real problems.
2. Make sure that the hospital does not direct your actions as clearly the more tests you do to ascertain a diagnosis, the more money hospitals make--or conversely, their limiting of tests can have the same consequence, or worse, lessen the quality of patient care.

More Obama Care
March 29, 2011 at 9:19pm

Not that anyone gives a rat's ass, but I attended another course on a portion of Obama Care in Princeton today; my third one. I thought I would summarize my notes here because the issue of repeal of Obama Care is going to be quite the topic in the upcoming elections. So, here is a little rambling for your edification or ignoring.

We all have to get used to the phrase Accountable Care Organization. This level of health care is pushed by Obama Care and these organizations may be here to stay. Currently medical services are performed on a fee for service basis. Payment is made as care is delivered. Many argue that such a system encourages unnecessary tasks and is volume driven. The more tasks, the more fees for the providers. This system does not work and needs to be changed. Yes, I love physicians, but useless and unnecessary tests are provided at times because some physicians have given up practicing medicine in some cases and just have tests given to shut up the patient or to cover their asses from malpractice suits. What a horrible way to practice medicine. The best and brightest are unhappy. Many physicians are simply leaving the profession. Medicine is being practiced more and more by non-physicians because of the cost and the work load.

Obama Care in principle seeks value based care delivery. It is value driven. The concept is to reduce costs, improve quality, and advance a population's health. A large Health Information Exchange is needed to connect and analyze all information sources so as to make appropriate decisions re health. The Primary Care Doctors are critical with the hope that there will be more preventive care, fewer ER visits, fewer inpatient visits, and less health care cost. It is alleged that care will be delivered in a high quality patient centered manner. Medicaid for the poor will be expanded and payments may be bundled, capitated, integrated in a delivery system, and received in other manners. As an example, assume a population of 5,000 persons in an Accountable Care Organization and a hospital and 100 care providers. If the population can be cared for the sum of $500,000.00 rather than the usual $700,000.00, the hospitals and care providers would share in the savings--an inducement to render efficient care. If the costs exceed the $700,000.00, the Accountable Care Organization eats the cost. I guess the concept that makes sense is if you detect things early, you can avoid future difficult problems-cardiac risk management, diabetes management etc. I wonder however why so many cardiologists are trying to sell their practices to hospitals now. Could it be because the Medicare fees to the cardiologists are decreasing?

The average cost per capita of health care in America is about $7,200.00. The next highest cost is Norway where the cost is less than $5,000.00 per person. This is amazing. And, Americans are not the healthiest people in the world! Also, 20% of all patients, usually the elderly, consume almost 70% of health care costs. Hence some of the politicians use the phrase "death panels". We use too much money to care for the elderly it is said, particularly in the last few months of life. There is a problem to be fixed and as our politicians discuss this, keep all this in mind.

There was much discussion relating to the legal aspects of ACOs but no one but me cares about that. Some interesting facts or concepts: We Americans are largely morbidly obese. That has to be changed. We go to McDonalds and chug fat by the box full. I passed one on the way home and there we are eating crap galore. Although smoking has decreased, about one-third of Americans still have the vile habit to an extreme. We do not want Big Brother telling us what to do. We resent being told to wear motorcycle or bike helmets, yet when we get in a bad accident and our brain is out of our scull, we expect the best care. Simply put, we are not responsible for our health and only await an event to rush off to the ER. Under EMTALA, the ER Docs must give us care whether we have money or not. Oh how wonderful. Did you walk or jog today? Why not? Did you do some form of exercise? Why not? What did you eat for dinner? Did it include a vegetable and some fruit? We need to take charge of our own health and that will lower health care costs. We are simply too lazy to do this or need education on the topic. Our health care cost crisis will not ameliorate until we grasp the extent of the problem and do what is correct. I do not want the government telling me what to do, but unless we deal with the issue ourselves, Obama Care will do it for us.

Having vented, I am not sure these Accountable Care Organizations will work at all from a financial point of view. They are expensive to set up and I cannot see profitability for years to come. In a previous Note I said that Obama Care is really "The Lawyers Full Time Employment Act". After this course, I am also convinced that ACOs and Obama Care are a gold mine for health information technology. Computers take on an even greater role in the health care industry now. Politicians will draw lines as to how the care will be provided as they control the purse strings based upon the information provided. It is also clear to me that it is a young person's world now. I am old and refuse to crawl into my grave without scratching and clawing a bit. But the old are now second rate and the beautiful generation will deal with this as they see fit. I hope they do a better job than my generation. They can do no worse.

Enough said. I am too tired to proof read this but wanted to give you something to reflect upon. And my dear sweet Amelia, putting aside your Obama debt, at least President Obama tried to solve our health care problem albeit, rather expensively. God bless America.

Kentucky-NCAA-College sports
March 29, 2011 at 5:53pm

A friend sent me a note about college sports prepared by a 93 year old fellow. The oldster by the name of Furman Bisher made some interesting observations. John Calipari of Kentucky makes about $10,000,000.00 a year at Kentucky when you add in all the benefits. A Nobel Prize professor makes $200,000.00 a year. Last year Calipari's team had five members go into the NBA. Four of them were freshman who flew the coop after less than a year. They are called "one-and-done" players. Two of Calipari's previous teams made it to the Final Four, Massachusetts and Memphis. Both have had their titles stripped and their banners removed for recruiting violations. Nonetheless, the University of Kentucky hired him. I see the Kentucky fans cheering and the cheerleaders so happy, yet who is kidding whom? College sports are just one big joke and supposed money raisers for the Universities. Do you really think that the one-and-doners went to class? Do you think Kentucky really benefits by this winning in an esoteric sense? In any sense? College sports seem to be unrelated to college in so many ways; perhaps they should just hire semi-pro teams to wear their uniforms and skip the pretense of education. I will not watch Kentucky in the Final Four or beyond if they are so "lucky".   I could say more but that is enough for now.

First day of volunteering
March 30, 2011 at 6:33pm

I just finished my first volunteer session at our local Hospital. I was at the Information Desk with Mary and Barbara, two wonderful people. They mentored me in greeting people, giving directions, using the phones and computers and many other assorted tasks. I will eventually be good at this. The most fun I had was delivering flowers to two new mothers. Their babies were just perfect and the happiness was palpable. The hospital is so lucky to have people like Mary and Barbara. And yes, it is a lot of work which I look forward to doing. I am going to get quite an education in how a hospital functions and how to interact with people from a non-attorney point of view. So far so good. To the gentleman I cut off on the telephone while trying to connect him to 5 West, it was all my fault; the hospital had nothing to do with it and I will get better.

Second Day of volunteering
April 6, 2011 at 4:53pm

Well, I completed my second day of volunteering. This morning I was the paper boy and delivered newspapers to all sections of the hospital and then worked the Information Desk. Only one floral delivery to an employee. This is a good thing as I get a chance to see the entire hospital and become more familiar with the various departments etc. Hospitals are quite the operations and involve more co-ordination than I ever thought; I even got into the ED to deliver some things and see the old room I had occupied a bit ago when it was suspected that I was ill. So there to my son David!! I am getting quite the education. Also, I have met so many of my clients and friends while at the Information Desk. I continue to get more comfortable at the hospital. Today my training continued with Barb and Tina. Boy, are they super ladies. I cannot believe how lucky we are in Hunterdon County to have such wonderful people doing this volunteering. Tina and Barb are just special and there is no other way to describe them. They are self-assured and have worked so long at the Information Desk that it is all second nature to them. They told me that every day was different and from my short experience, it seems to be the case. I also enjoyed seeing some good friends who work at the hospital and wish I could have spent more time chatting with them. President Obama had better watch out as I am becoming a very educated consumer. I return next Tuesday for my final orientation opportunity before I may be trusted to handle the job properly. I am told that it would not be uncommon to be trained for even a longer time which is alright with me. In this crazy world in which we live right now, I enjoy the nice feeling I get from doing nice things for people. God bless America.

The President and New Jersey Governor Christie
April 13, 2011 at 3:26pm

Well, well, well. I just heard President Obama give a speech on the National Debt. He really is articulate and smart. Too bad he and I have a different vision for America. He is right about some things. Medicare, Medicaid, Social Security, and National Security account for two-thirds of our National Debt. So, I guess if we get rid of our old, our poor and needy, and our military, all will be okay. And yes, the big fight over the Budget we just saw in Congress last week was only about 12% of our National Debt. I felt that debate was a joke and now feel even more so at this time. Both parties have just been pussy-footing around the real decisions which have to be made.

What I loved is when the President said that the rich had not been asked to contribute more in the form of higher taxes and that the rich would gladly do so to help the country and to be patriotic. Governor Christie used the same position and said that the NJEA teacher's union would not consent to pay 1.5% of their health care costs but that the teachers would have gladly done that to avoid the current attack on that profession if their union were out of the way. I have even suggested to some of my wealthier friends, Face Bookers, and clients to voluntarily contribute more in taxes to our government. To my knowledge no one gave one red cent more than the tax code required! Got to love it. Only in America!!!

So, this is what may happen, sans any specifics, just as the President suggested. Taxes will be raised on the wealthy however you define that;

in my opinion, the middle class is now "wealthy". Unlike past precedent, the rise in taxes will somehow generate jobs and reduce the deficit and there will be a tax hike trigger whatever that is. There will no longer be itemized deductions for mortgage interest and other items. The tax code will be simple and fair. Government will keep spending at a lower level in all departments and agencies. We will still have Medicare and Medicaid but it is clear that the $106,000.00 limit on taxpayer payment for Social Security contributions will be raised dramatically.

The most important thing to me was the President's comments on health care. In two prior Notes I talked about the Obama Health Care Plan in the courses I attended. I like the concept that a new paradigm of health care will evolve and I give the President credit for that. As per the Massachusetts s Plan, Doctors and Medical Care Providers will no longer be paid on the basis of the number and types of procedures that are performed. That has led to the health care cost increases. What will happen is that Doctors and the like will be paid for keeping their patients healthy in Bundled payments, Accountable Care Organizations and all the other methods I wrote about in my prior Notes. I like that idea.

All in all, I continue to have respect for the President and his ability to communicate. I like him. On the other hand, all of the platitudes in the word cannot bring us away from the economic facts we now face. Housing prices have not stabilized yet. Can you imagine what will happen when Bank of America and others place those millions of properties on the market that are now in foreclosure and which will be sold? Housing prices will continue to drop. Gasoline may be at $5.00 a gallon or higher. All the community organizing in the world will not get us out of this financial crisis. At least now the battle lines are drawn. It will not be pretty, but very exciting to see how this plays out. I am now tired. God Bless America.

Class war?

April 18, 2011 at 3:18pm

I believe in a flat tax rate. Everyone pays something. Period. What constitutional or moral obligation requires a progressive tax? So about half of the American "taxpayers" pay no income tax? Great. So 10% of the tax payers pay about 50% of the income taxes? Guess what percentage the top 1% pay? You want a class war? Think about it. I think not. Let us get out of that mode of thinking. I also believe that every person owes something to this country albeit public service or something else. Perhaps money. President Kennedy was right.

The art of anger

April 22, 2011 at 5:37am

Yesterday I went to pick up something at the Clinton Pharmacy. In mentioning to the sales clerk behind the counter that it was somewhat scary that the economy was so bad, and that this next election was so important on all levels, a gentleman pointed out that this mess was all George Bush's fault. He was serious. I suggested to him that that was only partially the case and that perhaps President Obama and others might bear some of the responsibility for what was going on. He screamed at me that I must have been a Republican, to which I responded that I was a conservative Republican or as silly as it sounded, an early 1960s Democrat ala JFK. He really seemed to get more and angry. Frankly, I really did not want to speak to him any longer. Then he loaded the bomb shell--the best President was Bill Clinton and that we needed another Bill Clinton in the White House. I started mentioning that the federal non-income verification/pushing of minority ownership of homes started at about that time and this in part played some role in the housing crisis. He fumed at that so I "had" to suggest to him that perhaps we should continue the Clinton moral tradition and send Monica Lewinski to the White House to help in any way she could. It was time to leave at that point. I enjoyed the colloquy but his anger was a little scary. I told him to calm down as his neck arteries were straining and if he continued, he might not have to worry about the economy; he'd be dead! Anger never intimidates me. The loud voice should not always get the worm. The point is, cannot we not just speak and have good debate about issues? Joe Scarborough of Morning Joe said something interesting and that was that self-righteousness was a danger. Arrogance leads to moral blind spots which can lead you to believe you are superior to others. That is a crock. In one of my prior Notes I wrote about how I see the world in the color gray. I still hold that view. I am still victimized by it. Things are rarely black or white. So to the person I met at the Clinton Pharmacy, I suggest he take up debate as an avocation and that he posit both views as a possible resolution of his anger issue. Just because I disagree with you, does not mean that I must hate you. Good people can disagree. I am tired so I will stop now.

God Bless America.

Vel' d'Hiv Roundup
April 26, 2011 at 5:22am

Well, I found my friend Clay's suggestion to read "Sarah's Key" worth the effort. Google the above Title and you will see what I mean as to one of its themes. I am angry with the French. How could this tragedy happen? To destroy your own people is pathetic. To destroy anyone is pathetic.

But that is not why I write today. My concern is that we face now the possible extinction of small town America as we know it. Just looking around Clinton, NJ and Flemington, NJ where I have a home, you can see the impact of the computer on so many of the businesses and in some cases the absence of businesses in the storefronts. Take our local bookstore--can they really compete with Amazon.com? So much can be found on the computer and we are all pseudo-experts re everything from legal matters to medical matters to travel, clothing, and almost every business you can find in small town America. The small shops decline as a result of this. And we used to complain so much re the "big box stores". Seems to me that the computer is just one "big box store". What would American be without viable small towns? The only businesses that seem to do well are coffee houses. Look at our nice little store called CitiSpot Coffee in Clinton. This store is thriving. It is time to invest in coffee beans as a precious commodity!!!! CitiSpot offers more than a product however, but an ambiance you cannot find on the internet. Any jewelry store will face stiff competition on the internet, far greater than just viewing catalogs as in the old days. Even our pharmacy will face difficulty with on-line stores. Just a thought--I do not want to interfere with the capitalistic concept of "only the strong survive". On the other hand, you cannot value things solely based on the "monetary value" concept which the computer can lead you if you are not careful. A strong commercial/ business area in a small town gives the community a value that far exceeds monetary value and involves a sense of community and presence. So, perhaps we should continue to patronize our local businesses so as to avoid a sterile environment even if we have to pay a little bit extra so as to keep them around.

Sorry this is Note is disjointed. I have been up for too many hours and my head is killing me. Nonetheless the point has been made. And yes, I am still very angry with the French. God bless America.

Trouble in the Emergency Department
April 27, 2011 at 8:34pm

I just returned from an all-day seminar in Princeton re Emergency Departments and how they might be improved. This has to be accomplished if Obama Care is ever going to have any chance of working and even if defeated, changes to health care have to be made. These issues are important in the upcoming election two years from now, so here goes. I hope this is interesting to some of you. It is important stuff in the long run. Some of it may not be true for every hospital ED, but it has been documented to be the national norm.

Emergency Departments throughout the United States are becoming increasingly crowded. In the last 10 years ED visits have increased over 25% and the number of hospitals with EDs has decreased in an equally dramatic fashion. Fewer EDs, more patients. Certain groups have higher usage of EDs; African-Americans (don't know why this was mentioned), Medicaid and SCHIP (uninsured) comprise 51% of ED usage-in some hospitals a much greater percentage. At least 33% of ED visits were for non-urgent primary care conditions and another 29% for what are called Triage levels 4 and 5, really non-emergent care. Under Emlata, ER Doctors are required to see any patient who shows up and check them out and stabilize them. In NJ, they must also treat the patient. What is crazy is that there is a greater use of EDs for primary care or simply put, for non-emergent, inappropriate purposes. Why is this the case? Well, there are many reasons, but here are a few: The primary care systems (your family Doc) has severe limitations-limited hours-a desire to not work on the late evening hours-a desire to have weekends off- Doctors want a life like the rest of us, etc.; ED Physicians over-test to compensate for lack of primary care follow-up arrangements; a hospital provides access to specialty care; it is perceived that there is a higher quality of care in a hospital setting; the hospital is closer to a person's home; chronic pain patients use the ER very often as their pain is not time limited; language issues arise; a poor person knows that there is no charge for services at the ER while there might be a charge at a Doctor's office; ERs are open 24/7; patients do not really understand what "emergency" means; a tremendous number of patients who utilize the Ed are suffering from alcohol or drug addiction, mental illness and the like; shall I go on? And you ask why hospital costs are so high? I guess a very crowded situation has gone to an even greater crowding. This insanity has got to be handled effectively.

Emergency Care must be provided in the most cost effective manner or the system will implode. I have posited in another Note that people have to take care of themselves and accept responsibility for their care and health where possible. Of course a safety net is required for the really disabled and infirm, but not everyone. So, exercise more-eat right-stop smoking-lose weight-take steps to better your health. This is particularly true since 20% of all patients consume 80% of all health care costs. We have to educate people re what emergencies are and are not. As an example, if your new baby has a fever, use your primary care doctor--not the ED. I was advised that if you step on a nail, you have 72 hours to get a tetanus shot. No need to rush off to the ED. If you have a migraine headache for two hours, you need not go to the ED. Learn basic First Aid. In other words, educate people re the definition of an emergency-education is a key. Also, we have to make our Primary Care Physicians and their offices even better than they are. Make your family Doctors more available. Pay them more for Medicare reimbursement-this Obama Care will not do. Utilize Nurse Practitioners and the like to do follow up care on people. In other words, make patients think of their Primary Care Providers first, not the ED. There are pilot programs to create FQHCs which are Federally Qualified Health Centers. These have helped in pilot programs to reduce cost and provide better care. You almost have to beg a large number of people to take care of themselves and to do what should be done as crazy as that may seem. Even though this may be politically incorrect, if people have no economic incentive to make decisions, there will be an exponential rise in health care costs. Succinctly put, if it doesn't cost you anything, you have no reason to just keep asking for more and more! Hence, there must be a cost for most health care. We need a system with alternatives geared to different locations and people. As an aside, most ambulance calls are not made by people who feel sick or are injured; the assumption is that when someone calls for an ambulance that the ED will be used--why not a primary care facility? Appropriate triage systems are important as well.

On the other hand, if ED Docs only treated true emergencies, they would probably go broke due to the high cost of maintaining the ED facility! Interesting also is the fact that EDs get crowded with patients because hospitals are over-crowded. Do you know the day the ED is mostly used? Monday. The busiest times in the ED are usually 10 AM until 1 PM. Weekends can be the slowest in most hospitals. Also, as another aside, to lower the ED costs, some say to use the hell out of it!!! Do you know what an ED Doc gets in NJ for a cardiac arrest under Medicaid, Level 5 event? $32.30!!! Nonetheless, ED Docs must practice medicine and not baby sit unnecessarily. There will need to be a partnership with the larger Community.

There is a YouTube Video about Brian Regan, a comedian giving a show at the Improv. It is great and gives a good idea re ED health care. I think you will like it. It shows the ED from a patient's point of view. Maybe we all need to do that once in a while. Sorry I have rambled. This has been a long day and I wanted to point out some of the things that I learned. God bless America again.

Well, I really cannot type anymore and I need a long run to clear my head. I have enough knowledge now to be dangerous to myself and others. I have just finished eight hours of this seminar and have another four to go tomorrow. There is so much to learn and my head is jumbled. Even if Obama Care is declared totally unconstitutional and the two acts are stricken, much of the above will remain for you to deal with as you proceed in your profession. There are claymore mines all over the place. Be careful. You probably know all of the above already, but I wanted to type up my notes from today so I thought I would put them on my Facebook page as a Note for no damn good reason.

Adios.

Happy Mother's Day
May 8, 2011 at 4:44am

To all the Mothers out there, whom we treasure and adore, Happy Mother's Day. Giving birth does not make you a mother; it entails so very much more. So, let your Mother know that you love and appreciate her. Too soon she will be gone and you will only be able to tell her this perhaps in other ways. When the story of humanity is written, the importance of being a Mother, a parent, will be number one on the list of important accomplishments. I do not care how much money you made, your status in life, your fancy title, your personal assets, or your whatever. We all know what is really important. In this crazy world, it increasingly becomes more and more difficult to be a good mother or father as well. Too many factors pull us in too many directions. Nonetheless, the innate bond between a Mother and child is so strong and so beautiful. So, Happy Mother's Day to all of you wonderful Mothers.

I have become Obama; Obama has become Bush.
May 3, 2011 at 5:06pm

Today I am very tired. Who knows why? Perhaps tiredness is affecting my thinking. Anyway, when I heard of the death/killing of Osama bin Laden yesterday, I was very happy and flew my American flag. As I thought more about it today however, I felt saddened by the method of the action ordered of our brave Navy Seals. Our President, just as President Bush, put out a hit on Bin Laden and we became the judge, jury, and executioner all in one at the same time; essentially Obama became Bush. President Obama earlier talked about how horrible Guantanamo was and suggested that the trials of the detainees be in the USA with rights to be afforded to the accused. Even Saddam Hussein had a trial and was eventually hung after a trial. If it turns out that Bin Laden was unarmed and could have been captured and taken as a prisoner as has been suggested by some, we may have done a disservice to our cultural and ethical values by this assassination. I have become an earlier version of President Obama!!! Do not get me wrong. The death of Bin Laden, when found guilty, was a given. He did not give our citizens a chance on 9/11/01. So, in war, we throw away the U.S. Constitution on the battlefield, which is okay if we want that. War differs from peace. But if I ever find out that Bin Laden was killed for the sake of being killed, I will be pained a little. If Bin Laden was not armed and could have been taken as a prisoner, he should have been so taken. If armed, he should have been killed. Revenge is not mine but the province of a higher authority. So do not judge me too cruelly for these comments. I think this had to be said. My flag still flies proudly on my porch and always will. And that is all I have to say about this.

Usama Bin Laden or is it Osama Bin Laden or Osama bin Laden or does anyone give a rat's ass?
May 9, 2011 at 4:43am

Well, the bastard is dead. The circumstances will be discussed for years to come and whether the methodology of his death was appropriate is for others to decide. President Obama took a really big chance here as had the operation failed, he would look totally incompetent in this area. So, I give him and the CIA/Seals a lot of credit. It worked. I also give former President George Bush credit for setting up the process at Guantanamo, and elsewhere, that was used to get Bin Laden. The people of the United States feel generally relieved and vindicated. Since the snake's head has been cut off, it is time to vigorously push on to rid the world and more particularly the United State of its arch-enemy, al-Qaeda. President Obama would be wise to pursue the fight with vigor. And yes, sordid pictures of his dead body were unnecessary.

On the other hand, we must now push with even more vigor on the domestic front. Jobs, jobs, jobs are the mantra. Our children in college or trying to get into the work force need to be given hope that there is a future. It looks bleak right now. Gasoline prices need to fall and some people suggest that that may be the case-let us allow off shore drilling. The federal debt ceiling must be raised but only after there are extremely broad cuts in the federal budget. As a people we must learn to live with less, to save more, to readjust our values and to not just live within our means, but to live below our means. We need to look to ourselves and our families as our first responders, not the government. Those that take a chance in business need to be encouraged and rewarded; capitalism has served this country well in the past. The so-called "Tax the Rich" argument is so much BS that the class war generated by such a phrase has to be stopped now. Most of the so-called rich pay extensive taxes-- Get away from the few that do not such as General Electric and some others. The "rich" pay the vast share of all taxes. Everyone should pay some form of tax or if they are unable, some form of military service or public service to give them a vested interest in our country. Yes, I believe in a flat tax rate for all. Obama Care must be eliminated or at least dramatically modified. Why in the midst of this Great Recession the President saw fit to deal first with a social issue and not JOBS, I do not know and its costs are astronomical. As I have said before, spending money to get out of a recession is like having sex to promote virginity. Roe v. Wade has decided the issue of abortion. That is the law of the land. Done. The right to bear arms is in the Second Amendment. If you want to change that Amendment, do it. On the other hand, an AK-47 is not needed in Manhattan. Inflation is going to come. Many say it is already here. When the Federal Reserve ends QE2, watch out because you are going to need to be strapped onto your horse. We already see inflation in food prices; this is just the beginning. It is the 600 pound gorilla in the room. Perhaps the way to prosperity is in the "restoration" of the housing market which can drive jobs. On the other hand, prices may continue to fall as the foreclosure properties hit the market. We have lived in a false reality for years and years. It is time to pay the piper. Enough said for now. I am off for my run in the wee hours of the morning and it is sure dark out there. Since Morpheus continues to evade me, I decided to vent on a few issues today and I have done so. I do feel better. God Bless America.

The beauty of the American system of government
May 10, 2011 at 8:14am

Reflecting on our system of government, I am impressed. When the Democrats controlled the House, Senate, and the Presidency last year, Nancy Pelosi, the Wicked witch of the West" (sorry, but I could not resist), was able to say something to the effect of, "you'll know what's in it when we pass it' in reference to Obama Care. Transparency became opaque. Then the Tiger came to town at election time!! The Republican Party took over the House!! What with the government looking toward a $1.6 trillion deficit this year (that's $125 billion a month in borrowing says the AP), Speaker Boehner has said that the debt limit will not be raised from its current $14.3 trillion cap unless accompanied by spending cuts larger than the amount of the permitted increase in the debt! Fantastic concept. Yes, we will have to discuss Medicare, Medicaid, and other programs, but the time is now. As President Obama once said, " if not now, when?". God bless America. Now we are dealing with whether Obama Care is constitutional. The issue will eventually reach the Supreme Court which very well will sustain Obama Care. That Court is political, sans doubt. So, the easy answer is to correct this situation, if the citizenry wishes it, is to take over the Senate, enact legislation repealing the flawed Health Care Plan hoisted upon us, and if the public elects enough Senators of the proper persuasion, it will be veto-proof should we have the displeasure of re-electing President Obama. The bottom line is that the system can work. The ease of the solution requires the public to take the requisite action as per the law of the land. On the other hand, should the public decide otherwise, we are in more financial trouble than I care to think. God bless America again, and as an aside, let us read things before we enact them!

Set up for catastrophe
June 19, 2011 at 5:12am

To continue my rant against unions and stupid business decisions I have a few things to say. In 1961 General Motors agreed to pay for full health insurance for all union members as a result of collective bargaining. Fifty years later GM was spending $5.3 billion a year on health care for 1.1 million people, only 140,000 of them still on the job! For every car sold, $1,500 went to cover health care costs. How could we compete in a global society with these expenses? Is there any question but that GM should not have been bailed out but allowed to go into bankruptcy?! Sometimes you can just be so successful and win so much that you set yourself up for catastrophe. And so it was. Apply this to the NJEA, the CWA, and all the public sector jobs, and reality creeps in as would be expected at least with reference to health care costs. The former need for unions no longer exists to the previous extent. "Too big to fail" is a flawed philosophy and if you make stupid decisions you should accept the consequences and not rely upon the Government to bail you out. And, I have not even added pension benefits and obligations into the equation yet!!!! That is for another time.

Truer words were never spoken
July 19, 2011 at 8:34am

"Raising America's debt limit is a sign of leadership failure. It is a sign that the U.S. government can't pay its own bills. It is a sign that we now depend on ongoing financial assistance from foreign countries to finance our government's reckless fiscal policies. ...Washington is shifting the burden of bad choices today onto the backs of our children and grandchildren. America has a debt and a failure of leadership. Americans deserve better."
So said Senator Obama in 2006. I agree.

The Guardian Class
July 27, 2011 at 10:46am

A must read--"The Guardian Class" by Dr. Jonathan D. Heavey. Some time ago Ginny and I were at the University of Virginia for David's graduation from his Emergency Department Residency. We were in the Rotunda at UVA sitting at a table with David and Lena, Jon and Melissa Heavey and Jon's Mom and Dad. We had a wonderful time and noted that Jon Heavey was going into the Army shortly after his residency. Jon's experiences in the Army and in particular in Iraq as a physician are sad, exciting and thrilling. His discussions relating to the innocent children harmed by the war and efforts to get them assistance are maddening. His political comments and humor are outstanding. This book is well worth the read and you will enjoy it immensely. Welcome home soldier. You did a good job on this one!!

Jobs
August 18, 2011 at 5:36am

You see Mr. President, you should have recognized that the real issue in your presidency from day one was creating jobs. You have wasted years dealing with side issues and now blame everyone but yourself for what has not been going on. So now you understand the issue. Good. What is another month in getting your plan into action? Too little too late? Stop blaming George Bush, the Republicans, and the some of the Democrats for your mistake. Say "I screwed up" and now devote the rest of your term to trying to fix this mess. Oh, and by the way, stop the class warfare crap and stop the vitriol. Just lead. That is why you were put where you are now.

Have we learned yet?
September 29, 2011 at 7:05am

This depression/recession has been a great educational experience. I hope we have learned some things from all that has transpired. Like:
You really don't need a 4 bedroom house with three bathrooms.
You do not have to remodel bathrooms and kitchens often; live with what you have.
Your home equity is really just that and should not be used for so-called "necessities".
The old Ford can last a couple more years.
Perhaps we should save more for retirement.
Ditto with our children's education.
You do not have to take a fancy vacation every year.
Family is really what is important.
The deprecation of the stay-at-home mom or dad is misplaced.
Really, all those sports camps are over-rated and unnecessary.
Not every child requires an iPhone.
There is a difference between "needs" and "wants".
It is not good to try to live like a millionaire when indeed, you are not.
Just because someone lives high off the hog does not necessarily mean he/

she can afford it.

Credit card purchases should be paid off monthly; if you can't do that, you don't need them.

A brown bagged lunch is a good lunch.

Eating out for breakfast, lunch, and dinner is extreme for most people.

You do not need a separate media room.

Perhaps the "spoiled generation" now knows they are just like the rest of us; equally special or un-special.

Hard work pays off only if you live within your means.

Should have had a little money in the old savings account!

If you lived from pay check to pay check before 2008, it is impossible now; hence make adjustments.

Stop blaming other people for this mess; we all played a part in creating it.

You can cut your own lawn.

We are not entitled to raises every year or the other perks we receive now.

Perhaps you could walk to a store in some cases rather than driving there.

One can always ask, "Do I really need this" before making a purchase.

Coupon clipping is a good thing.

Keeping the heat a degree or two cooler and the air-conditioned a degree or two higher is okay; you will survive.

Spending more time with your children doing things that do not cost money is good.

Husbands and wives and significant others do not have to spend money to have a good time.

Politics is a dirty business; actions always speak louder than words.

Generosity in difficult times is more rewarding than generosity in good times.

There is nothing wrong with telling people you cannot afford it!

There is a chasm between the "haves" and the "have-nots". So who gives a rat's ass?

Just because you have money does not mean you are bad. It means many different things.

Just because you are poor does not mean you are bad. It too means many different things.

The middle class is alive and well with a big attitude check!

I could go on and on but choose to stop here. As is said in "Annie", "The sun will come out Tomorrow ....". We just don't know when Tomorrow will begin. We have to be optimistic that our leaders will "get it" or else the masses will have to lead the leaders. With this education we have received imparted to our leaders, we will survive. Let us hope for a brighter day and God bless America.

Batten's Disease fundraiser
November 21, 2011 at 6:42pm

A year or so ago I heard the phrase Batten's Disease and had no idea what it meant. I did not seem to care anyway. Then I met a beautiful two year old little girl named Naomi who had Batten's Disease. To understand what it was all about my Google search engine was put to work and I was saddened to put it mildly. I think of her daily now. Everyone should Google Batten's Disease. You might just open up your wallet to help pay for research in this area once your eyes dry up and you have used up a box of Kleenex tissues. My daughter-in-love Lena is trying to put together a 5-mile run to raise money for research in this area. My Ginny pointed out a letter to the editor in last week's Hunterdon County Democrat by Kathleen Morgante that I should read. I did. So I called Ms. Morgante. She told me she had two nephews who had died from the Batten's Disease in their late teens and was trying to raise money for research. In a month and a half she put on an event she called "Gift and Give Fundraiser". She was able to raise almost $1,500.00 in one night. What did she do? She had a party in her home which was attended by about 40 people. Word of the party went out via e-mail and a few prominently placed signs. She wrote to a number of businesses. She was amazed that 11 organizations donated dinners, gifts, and other items which were auctioned off or used to help feed and entertain the attendees; a fifty/fifty raffle was held; candy trays and baskets of assorted items were auctioned off as well. She even had a number of vendors present their inventory such as jewelry and donated 30% of the proceeds of sale to Batten's research. Kathleen has promised to e-mail me what information she has and wants to put on an even better Gift and Give Fundraiser next year. I will be there. She said that the entire event had a very "happy feel" about it. I will be pleased to provide that information to anyone interested when it is received. So if a journey of a thousand miles begins with a single step, Kathleen Morgante has taken that step. I really admire her tremendously. Others are walking arm in arm to deal with the issues. There must be some very famous and hence well-known person to head the movement; perhaps Taylor Swift? I have learned of late that the world does not deal a fair hand to everyone. On the contrary, tragedy can strike at a moment's notice and turn your life around so quickly. Rather than say "why me", say "why not me"? So, when you learn of a Batten's Disease fundraiser, perhaps you will think of this Note and open up your wallet to try to help the little Naomi's of this world. If you can do a fundraiser, do it. If you are from Wissomissing, PA and know Taylor Swift contact her and beg for her help. (Or some other famous and caring person). Clearly our leaders in Washington cannot lead. So, let us lead our leaders to try to deal with this devastating disease. Let us simply say that it is time to do what is right. If we do not do it, who will? Thank you for reading this Note.

A few comments about the Osawatomie, Kansas speech
December 7, 2011 at 12:41pm

I do love the way President Obama speaks. He is a good and articulate salesman, good with words and delivery, and is able to take an issue and spin off of it a point of view that is an anathema to me. The President wrongfully defines the issue, then ignores the real problem, choosing to argue what may get him elected. I am a proud conservative and offer no apologies for my thinking. President Obama tries to make it appear as if the Republicans do not want to help the so-called lower or middle classes. He does this by pushing class warfare as the fuel to his argument. We must have these tax cuts!!! Tax the rich!! I guess he feels that this is the only way he will be able to regain the Presidency. Let me give you some thoughts:

1. When I started practicing law the effective top federal tax rate in America was 70%. That tax rate was cut after President Carter left office to 28%. Did the world fall apart? No. On the contrary, we had decades of prosperity. Interestingly too, depending on whose statistics you use, the top 1% of taxpayers pay about 73% of all federal income taxes. The bottom 40% pays no taxes. So this argument about tax the rich is all specious.

2. EVERYONE should pay some form of income tax or other money to the federal or state government, with limited exceptions. It gives you a stake in the country and seems just right to me. It assists in the development of one's character, that which we seem to have lost in America today. Rather than getting unemployment payments for 90 plus weeks, with no quid pro quo, it is time for payback. We have roads that need to be cleaned up and other similar projects exist if you want "unemployment compensation for life". The ubiquitous nanny state must end.

3. I believe in the tax cuts that are the subject of the discussions in

Washington today. They may help stir the economy and relieve financial stress to our citizens. On the other hand, I disagree with the President as to paying for those tax cuts. His simplistic answer is to simply raise taxes on the rich to pay for the tax cuts for others. That is what he is preaching on his campaign stops. Increase the deficit as well he says. First of all, the deficit has to be reduced. Trillions are numbers I simply cannot understand. The President tries to make the Republicans appear to be anti-lower or anti-middle class and has ingeniously changed the argument from the tax cut issue which really is not disputed by most, to a class warfare issue. He knows that his base will love to have gifts from the government for which others will pay dearly. I am sorry Paul Krugman. You are brilliant but also wrong.

4. On the other hand, I have no problem with the so-called rich paying a little higher rate on their tax bill; provided all Americans pay something.

5. The more power the government has, the more we rely on it to "help us", and the less liberty we have. President Obama's speech in Osawatomie, although well given, (Texas aside), really upset me. He wrongfully redefined the argument and we are letting him get away with this. I truly believe in the American Dream. More importantly we must rekindle the American character where bankruptcy is not a God given right, where doing the right thing is important, where you seek help from family and self rather than constantly looking to the Government. The spectacles in Greece, Italy, and so many other "Euro currency countries" offend me. I believe in Greece when they tried to raise the retirement age from 60 to 62 years, there were riots in the streets. Are they kidding?

6. The American Dream is not dead--yet. We owe it to our children and grandchildren to do all that we are able to keep it alive. I predict that under President Obama's plans, or lack of them if you prefer, we are all doomed to second class status. And yes, I believe in Reaganomics provided no one screws it up.

7. When I was a kid in the late 50s and early 60s, I worked for Sal

Rainieri, who was a house painter, for $0.50 an hour. We would work in some of the fanciest houses in Princeton, including the former President Grover Cleveland house. Not once was I jealous of the "wealthy". On the contrary, I wanted to continue to work as hard as I was able, get as much education as possible, do what I had to do, all to arrive at the status of those "wealthy" in Princeton. The rich inspired me and they were to be emulated. President Obama would have me angry with them; would have them be the enemy; would have them give me more than the 50 cent per hour wage I earned and saved just" because". I disagree totally with him.
8. We need a leader. Come on Joe DiMaggio. We need you now. Our current breed of politicians is unable or unwilling to lead. It is time.
As an aside, it was one of my goals in retirement to have a debate society on Facebook much as Ben Franklin had in Philadelphia at the time of the American Revolution; we could hash out so many important issues. Due to circumstances beyond my control this is the first time I have been able to give some input since May 16, 2011. Perhaps there will be more discussion later; we shall see. God bless America.

The Virtual American
March 22, 2012 at 6:26am

I have noticed in the past few years that our business society has increasingly become "virtual" or to put it another way, "phony". Virtuality is even advertised on the radio now. It bothers me. When I started out in law, you earned the trappings of success by hard work and by paying for it. If you wanted a nice office, you paid for it. You hired secretaries, paralegals, and attorneys to work for or with you. Offices were proud monuments to success and rightfully so. They involved significant costs but were a reality.
Now things have changed. Single practitioners and small businesses rent

a small room in a very large building or mansion and then flash on their fancy webpage a picture of a building showing where they practice. This leads to the impression that they are practicing in the entire structure even though they occupy an insignificant portion of it. An idiot can have a web page designed that makes them look like Jesus Christ reincarnated; so professional and so important. Yet the reality is that the person has only practiced law or been involved in a business for a short time and very well may not have any practical experience. In many offices, to save money on a receptionist/telephone operator, there is no human contact on your call to the firm and you get an answering machine with appropriate prompts. Many work from home yet do not tell you that, rather they know that most people want to use successful people for their services and the trappings of success are required. I could go on but will not. The reason I mention this is that I feel we all know that we want the security and professionalism of days gone by, but do not want to pay for it. So we set up virtual offices that in reality are just web pages and tiny rooms; or perhaps a commonly shared conference room as well. It looks so "un-virtually" wonderful. We have come to accept these "non-edifices" because people operating as such are able to reduce their fees or maybe not, but just pocket a greater sum of "profit". So we want it all without paying for it. In other words, phoniness or unreality rules the day in our virtual society. And it will get worse as time passes.

The bottom line is that all of us have to be aware of what is going on and not hire people just because they have a wonderful looking web page or pretty pictures giving indirect misleading information. The best way to hire someone is to ask others if their experience, and I do not mean necessarily Angie's List. Word of mouth is so important. On the other hand, our "virtual" everything is here to stay and will soon become the new reality. Nonetheless, it will always be the virtual, no matter what you call it.

The Albert D. Rylak Annual Quadrathlon and Penn State
July 16, 2012 at 7:21pm

Most of you know about the Albert D. Rylak Annual Quadrathlon. The event has been in existence since 2005 and entails a 5 mile run, a 3 mile kayak effort, a 9 mile bike ride, and a half mile swim. When I devised the Quad, the concept was to get most people to engage in an event which was done at your leisure. It would be healthy and tiring at the same time. There is no clock and rests are encouraged. Even families are able to participate. Although the event is not timed, it just has to be completed in one day. Every year the participation increases and it is run as often as there is interest. Everyone who competes in the even has their name placed on a plaque made by Jordan. Last year was the only year the event was cancelled for the entire summer. You know why.

So, the Rules Committee, me, allowed the Albert D. Rylak Annual Quadrathlon to be held today. It was just completed and this year will be added to the plaque by my name. Yes, there is a plaque. Actually, I did the kayak portion in the dark before dawn, and the run I extended to 7 miles just for giggles. My body is aching and my time is at hand (James Taylor). It is completed but I realize that I am not as young as I used to be. Crap. So, let the games begin. All requests to participate in the event must be approved by the Sanctioning Committee, me, and all new participants are welcome.

Shawn O'Mara, Carolyn O'Mara, my boys and I have had experience with pancreatic cancer. The Rules Committee has agreed that all future dates of completion will be painted on the plaque in purple. Shawn has also volunteered to provide a purple flag which in the future will be flown when the event is authorized by the Sanctioning Committee and is actually in progress, in honor of Ginny, and Shawn's and Carolyn's mothers. Yes, all three died of pancreatic cancer. There is no charge or event fee for participation but from now on the Sanctioning Committee will request that any participant consider donating any sum of money toward finding a cure for pancreatic cancer. So there you have it. We are back in business. I am also saddened for Penn State due to the Sandusky matter. Louis Freeh is a great Rutgers graduate and I know him as he graduated from Rutgers College and Rutgers Law School. His report about the Sandusky matter was scathing to the Penn State Administration at a minimum. It is a situation where the tail has wagged the dog and is not limited to Penn State but so many athletic colleges and universities. So I be clear, I have always hated Penn State due to the fact that they always have clobbered Rutgers in football. On the other hand, it is an admired academic powerhouse which was better known for football than academics. Those Freeh named made sure that football remained strong and should be embarrassed, fired, and the NCAA should impose the "death sanction". Penn State will survive this mess and I hope other Universities reprioritize their goals. Football is just a sport. It is entertainment. Schools primarily exist to provide education. Let us get that straight. To my many friends whom have graduated from Penn State, I feel your pain and still admire your school tremendously. Do something about this mess because as you fix it, you will also fix what is wrong in college sports throughout the nation.

And to, Ray, I here tried to do a Note again for the first time in a long time. Thank you for the suggestion.

Time to end the Record.
August 29, 2014 at 6:45am

On my 35th birthday, exactly thirty-five years ago, I started a record which continues at least until today. (Yes, I had a very good run this morning). Then I weighed 210 pounds, smoked at least 2 packs of Camel cigarettes a day, worked 60 hours a week, and the most exercise I received was walking to the car. I was heading for a heart attack. It was at that time that my wife and later my doctor suggested that I do something about my health. And so, I began a record of running every day since then, missing only 16 days in that 35 year period. The first couple of months I ran many times a day, always trying to cover a total distance of 5 miles in that time period. After I became somewhat svelte, I ran five miles every day as a minimum. During the rest of that thirty-five year time period I would run anywhere from 5 miles and higher, the Lancaster County Half Marathon, the NYC Marathon, and many other assorted distances with friends. I became known as someone who would take the time to train other runners and still do that today. In a true sense running had become a compulsion and obsession. I can remember almost every day I missed. As an example I was told to rest my legs for two days before the NYC Marathon. I did just that but wish I had not. It did not help one way or another. No matter the pain or malady, I ran. I still remember the last run of my 30s, 40s, 50s, and yesterday completed the final run of my 60s.

So now I hope to tame the savage beast. I will run, and run often. But missing a day will be a good thing not a tragedy. My weary legs will get the rest they deserve. No more running 5 miles in a foot of snow. No more coming home from work at midnight and running then. No more running contrary to doctor's advice after a carotid endarterectomy. In short, I hope to begin a life style of lesser stress and keep no written record of what I do. In a sense, I shall disappear on paper. And it shall be. And it is good. My book explains all of this and why I am able to do it.

***

That is it. I am done. Perhaps I have said too much; certainly not too little. You all know what I tried to do here by opening up my personal life and my personal thoughts so that all could see my bared soul. I hope I did not error by doing this. Albert Rylak, with the help of many friends and Beckett, is a survivor by choice or perhaps by default. Many different paths could have been chosen without criticism or rancor. I could still be sitting only inside my house feeling sorry for myself. Many people I know have chosen that path and I feel so sorry for them. When someone they loved died, in a sense, they died as well even though they still walked this earth. I could have gone off the deep end. I chose life. My dear sweet wife in her final act of love told me what to do and I did it and continue to do it. To her last breath she was the caregiver she was born to be. So I give Ginny this rather lengthy love letter knowing that she smiles as she reads it.

Please live each day like it is your last day. No matter what is going on, try hard to forge ahead and be happy. There is no hurdle steep enough to deter you if you try and keep trying. We and you need it. Of course you have to make plans of a financial nature for the future. Of course you have to make plans as to what you intend to do with your life. But never ever be so naïve or stupid as to assume that just because you have plans they will come to fruition. On the contrary, all too often those plans are mere hopes. Just be aware of that absolute fact.

Although my heart has been totally broken, it is necessary to go through the grief process in order to survive. I have not read any of the literature currently available about such process on purpose. Just seeing how I acted, now act, and how I will act in the future is the path I have chosen. No one has to tell me how to grieve. My emotions do that for me. There is no normal. If you loved the person who is gone, you will continue to love that person. If you are lucky enough to fall in love again, your prior love does not diminish but continues. Indeed, it is possible to love more than once. Perhaps those of you victims who have chosen to or been forced to read this book will be able to see what you can do to help other people facing similar circumstances. Perhaps not.

And Ginny, that is my view from Apartment 15T.

Harvey Cedars, NJ   September 2, 2014

Je t'adore

CPSIA information can be obtained at www.ICGtesting.com
Printed in the USA
BVOW09s1652071014

369719BV00007B/10/P

9 781320 156882